MORO ROGERS'

CITY IN THE DESERT ™

THE MONSTER PROBLEM

WITHDRAWN

ARCHAIA ENTERTAINMENT LLC
WWW.ARCHAIA.COM

ARCHAIA

NEW STORIES. NEW WORLDS.
ARCHAIA ENTERTAINMENT, LLC

PJ BICKETT, CEO
MARK SMYLIE, CCO
MIKE KENNEDY, PUBLISHER
STEPHEN CHRISTY, EDITOR-IN-CHIEF

CITY IN THE DESERT
THE MONSTER PROBLEM

ORIGINAL GRAPHIC NOVEL
HARDCOVER

APRIL 2012 FIRST PRINTING
10 9 8 7 6 5 4 3 2 1
ISBN: 1-936393-55-7
ISBN-13: 978-1-936393-55-8

PRINTED IN CHINA.

WRITTEN AND
ILLUSTRATED BY
MORO
ROGERS

DESIGNER FAWN LAU
LETTERER
DERON BENNETT
PRODUCTION MANAGER
SCOTT NEWMAN
EDITOR
REBECCA TAYLOR

FOR MY DAD, WHO TOLD ME TO

"KEEP WATCHING THIS MOVIE, THERE'S GOING TO BE A MONSTER."

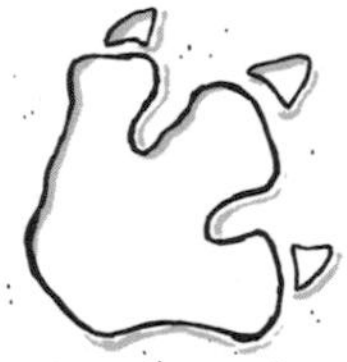

SPECIAL THANKS

TO MY HUSBAND AND PARENTS FOR THEIR LOVE AND SUPPORT, THE FOLKS AT ARCHAIA, AND TO MY FRIEND MINKYU LEE FOR HIS MUCH-NEEDED ADVICE AND CRITS.

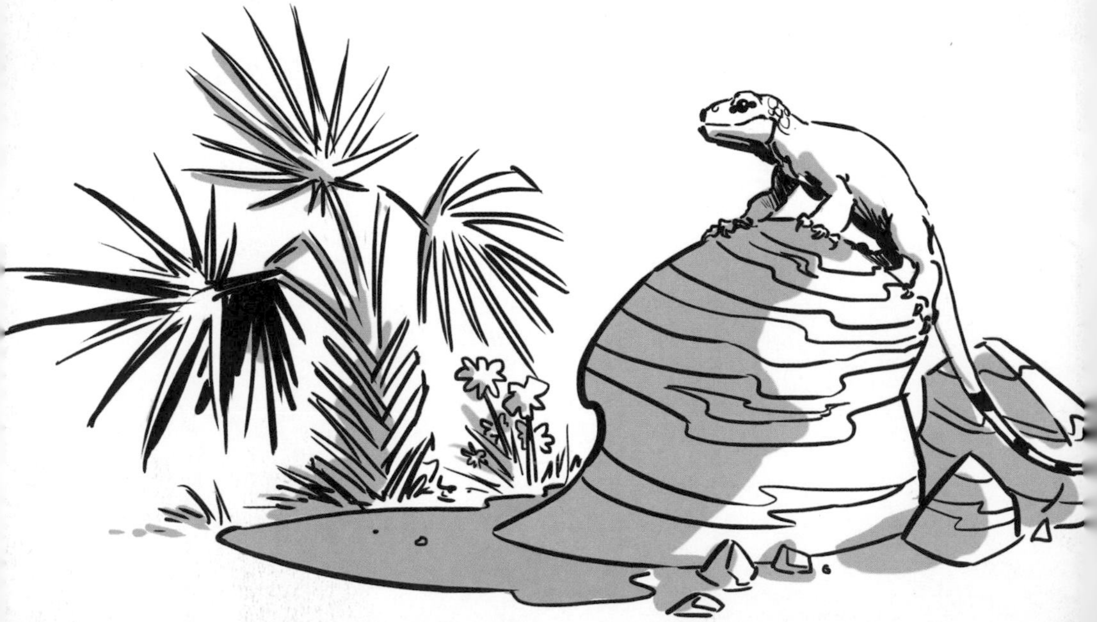

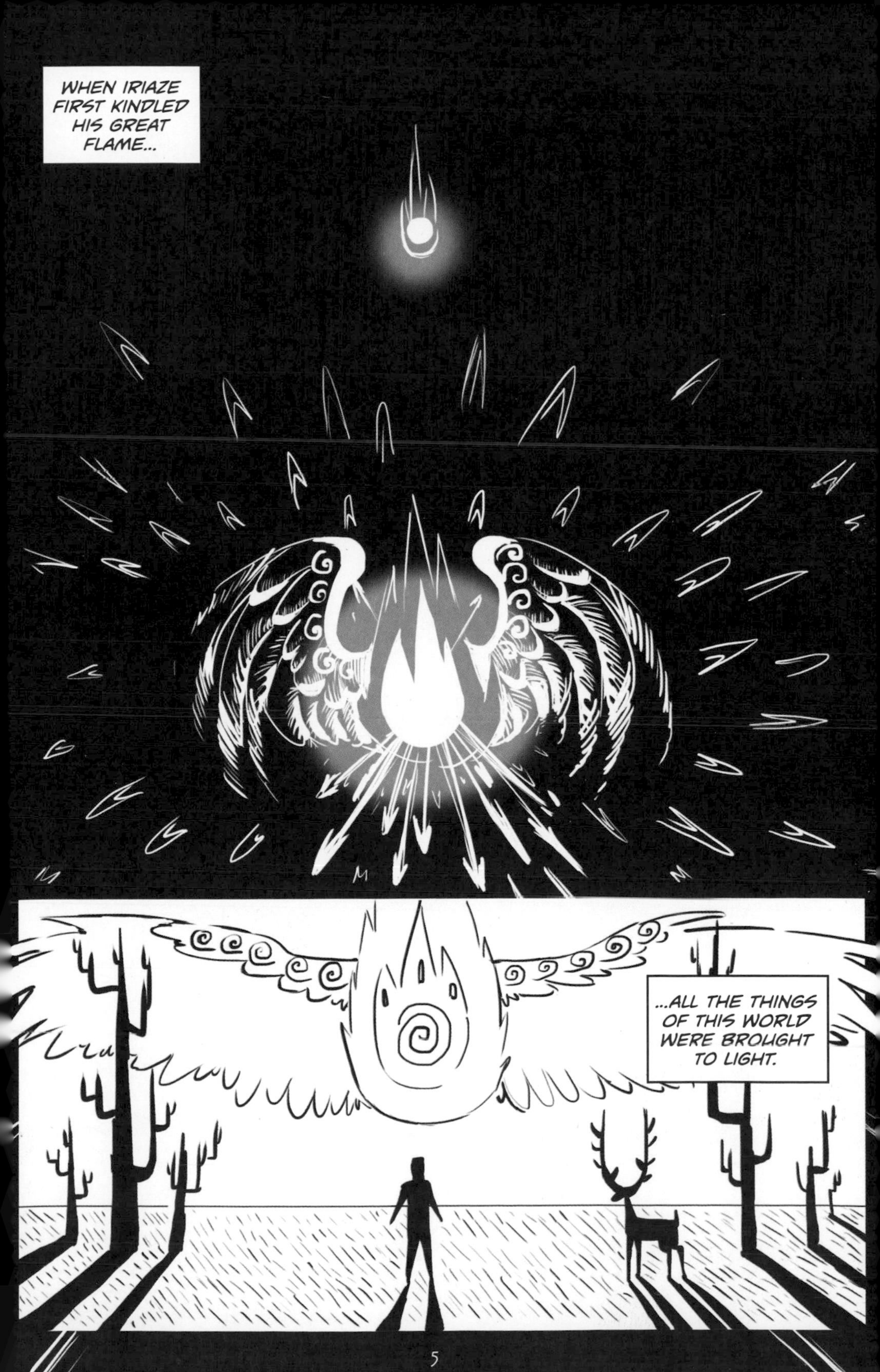
WHEN IRIAZE FIRST KINDLED HIS GREAT FLAME...
...ALL THE THINGS OF THIS WORLD WERE BROUGHT TO LIGHT.

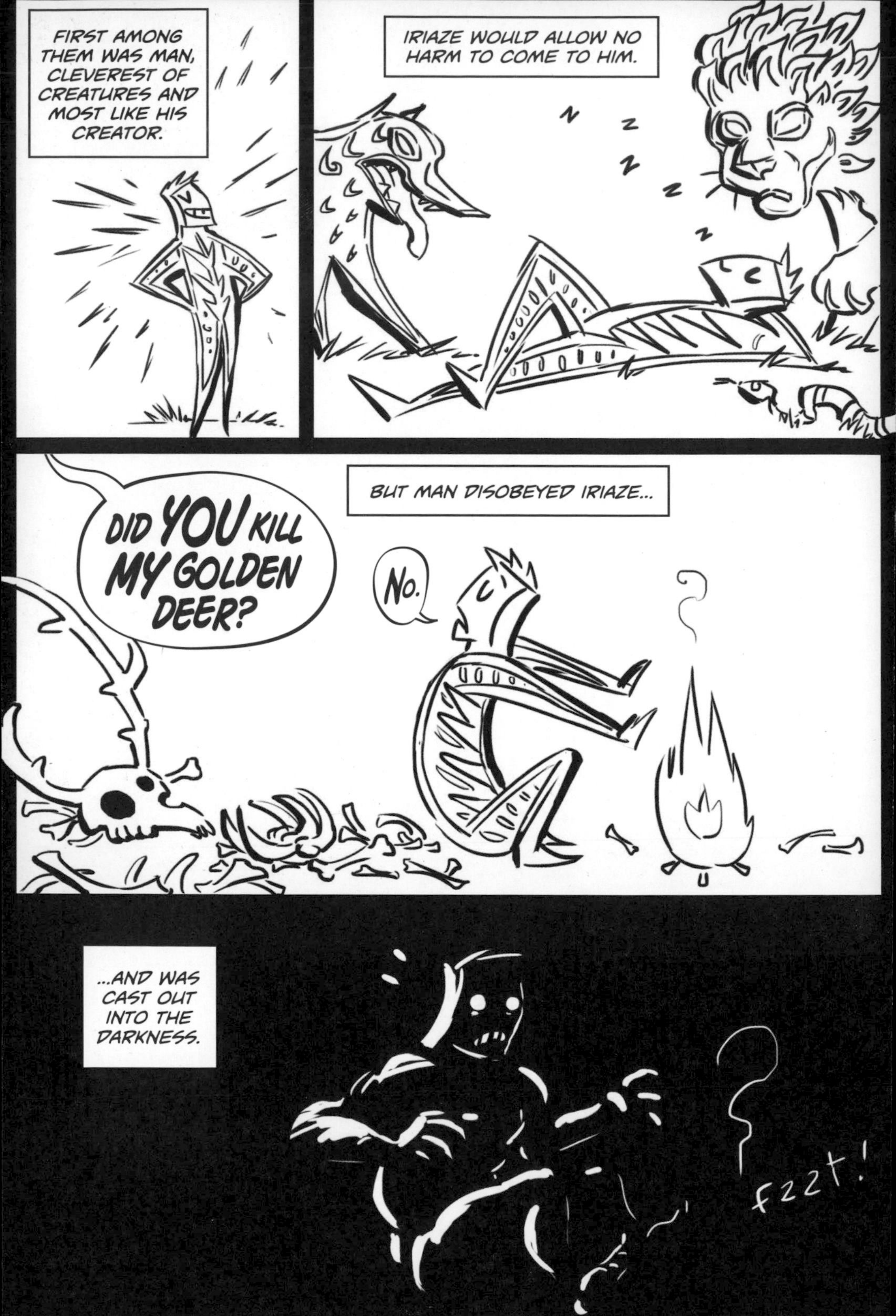
FIRST AMONG THEM WAS MAN, CLEVEREST OF CREATURES AND MOST LIKE HIS CREATOR.
IRIAZE WOULD ALLOW NO HARM TO COME TO HIM.
Z Z Z Z Z
BUT MAN DISOBEYED IRIAZE...
DID YOU KILL MY GOLDEN DEER?
No.
...AND WAS CAST OUT INTO THE DARKNESS.
?
fzzt!

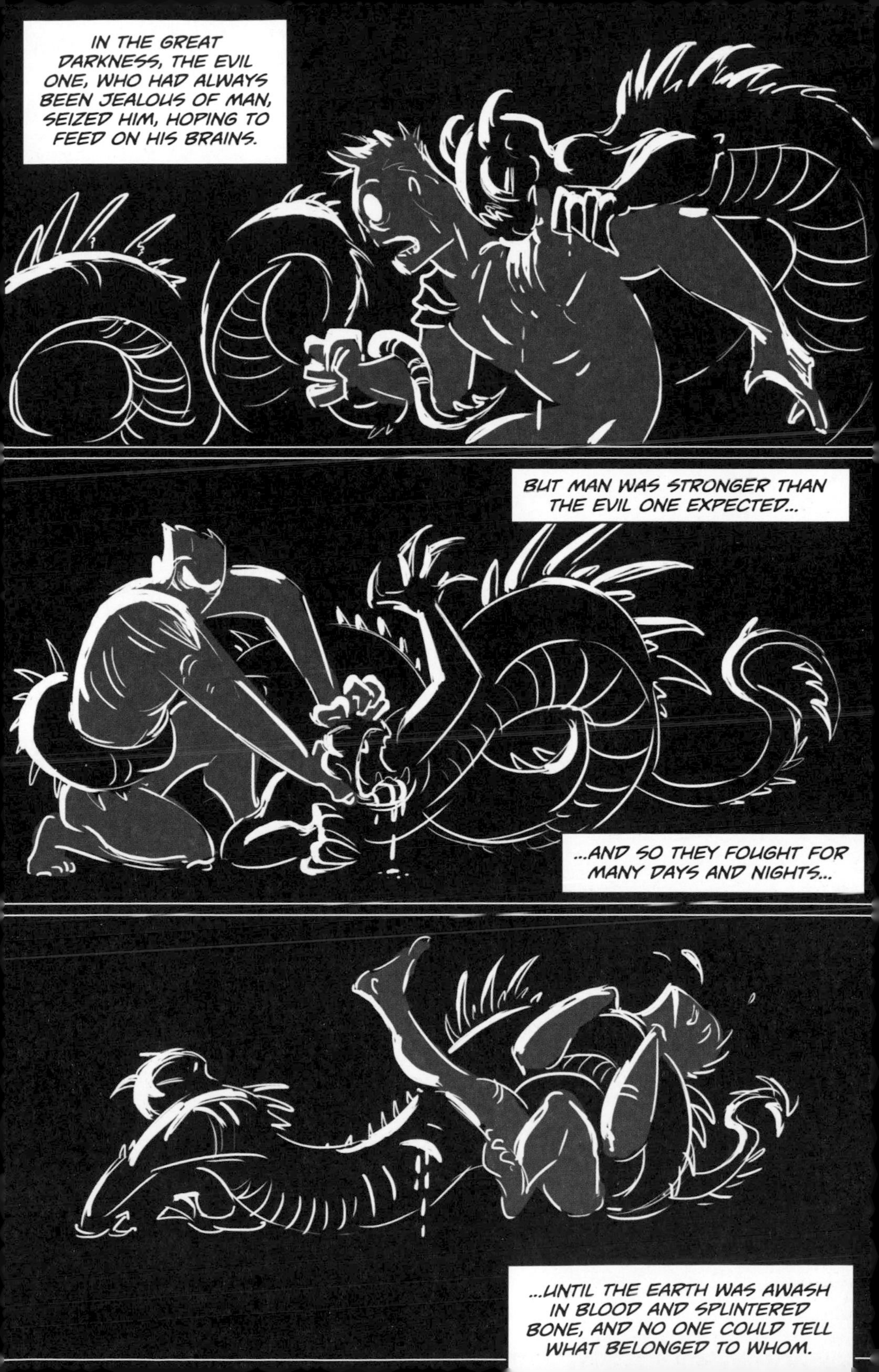
IN THE GREAT DARKNESS, THE EVIL ONE, WHO HAD ALWAYS BEEN JEALOUS OF MAN, SEIZED HIM, HOPING TO FEED ON HIS BRAINS.
BUT MAN WAS STRONGER THAN THE EVIL ONE EXPECTED...
...AND SO THEY FOUGHT FOR MANY DAYS AND NIGHTS...
...UNTIL THE EARTH WAS AWASH IN BLOOD AND SPLINTERED BONE, AND NO ONE COULD TELL WHAT BELONGED TO WHOM.

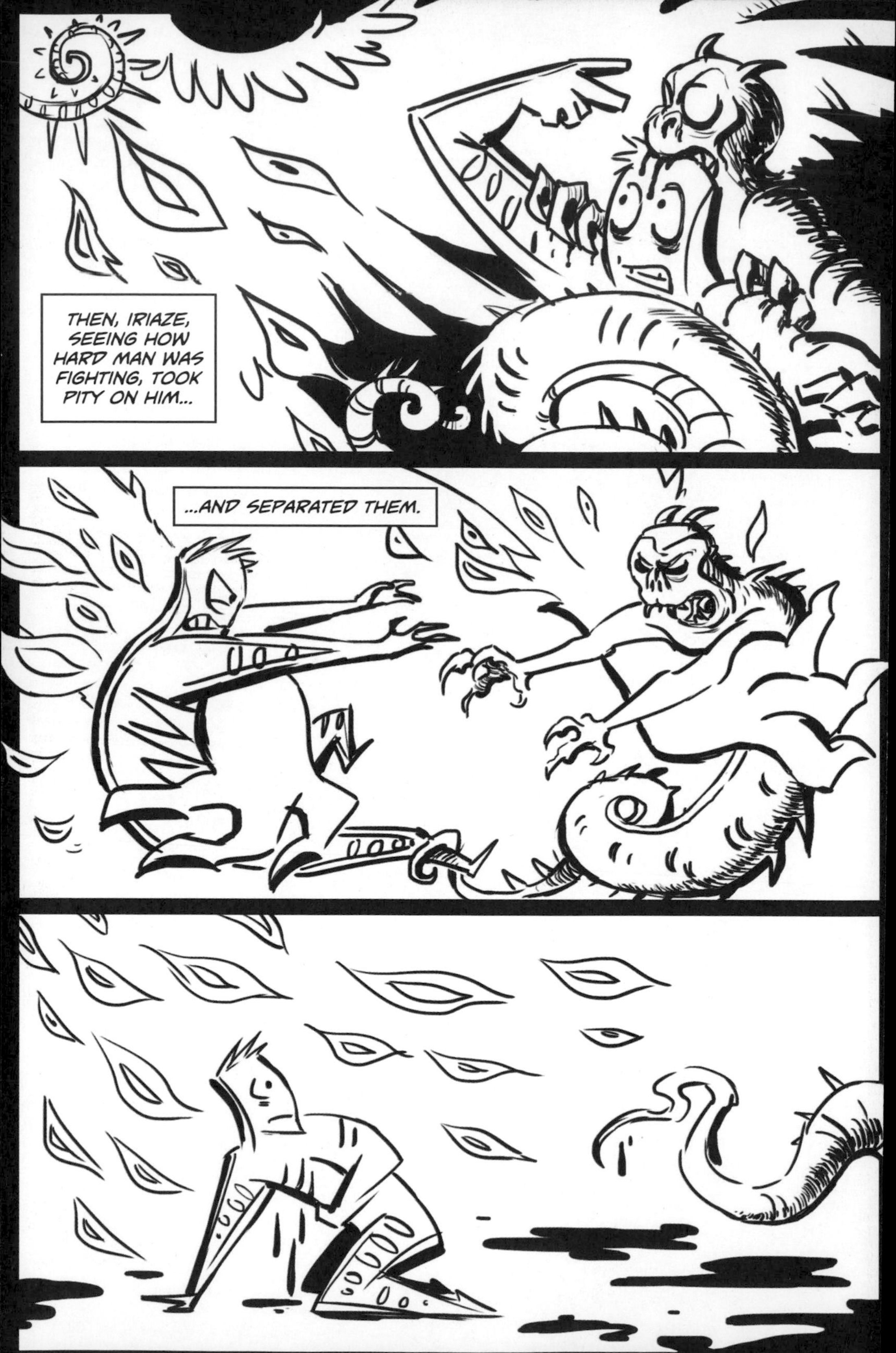
THEN, IRIAZE, SEEING HOW HARD MAN WAS FIGHTING, TOOK PITY ON HIM...
...AND SEPARATED THEM.

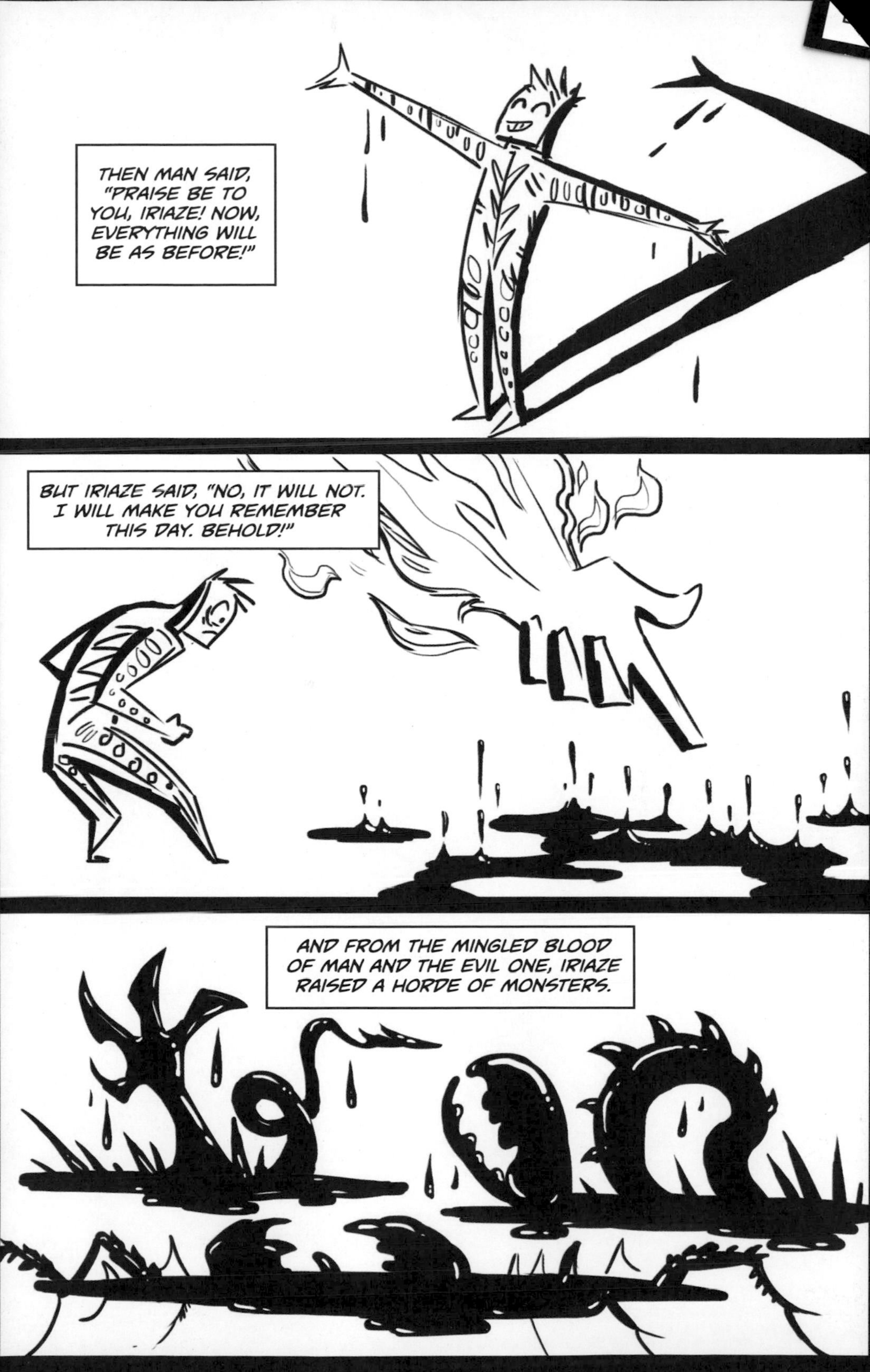
THEN MAN SAID, "PRAISE BE TO YOU, IRIAZE! NOW, EVERYTHING WILL BE AS BEFORE!"
BUT IRIAZE SAID, "NO, IT WILL NOT. I WILL MAKE YOU REMEMBER THIS DAY. BEHOLD!"
AND FROM THE MINGLED BLOOD OF MAN AND THE EVIL ONE, IRIAZE RAISED A HORDE OF MONSTERS.

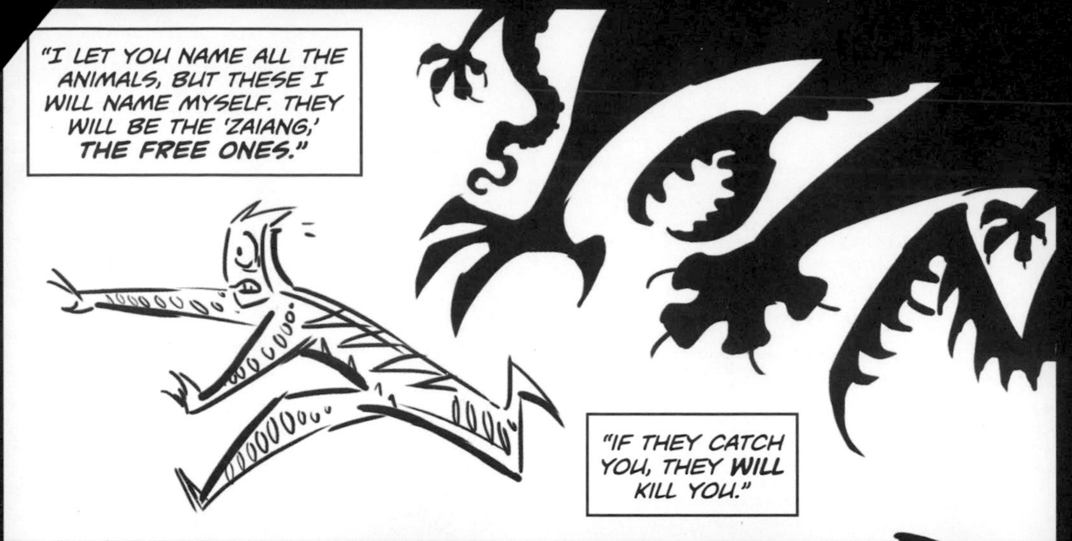
"I LET YOU NAME ALL THE ANIMALS, BUT THESE I WILL NAME MYSELF. THEY WILL BE THE 'ZAIANG,' THE FREE ONES."
"IF THEY CATCH YOU, THEY WILL KILL YOU."

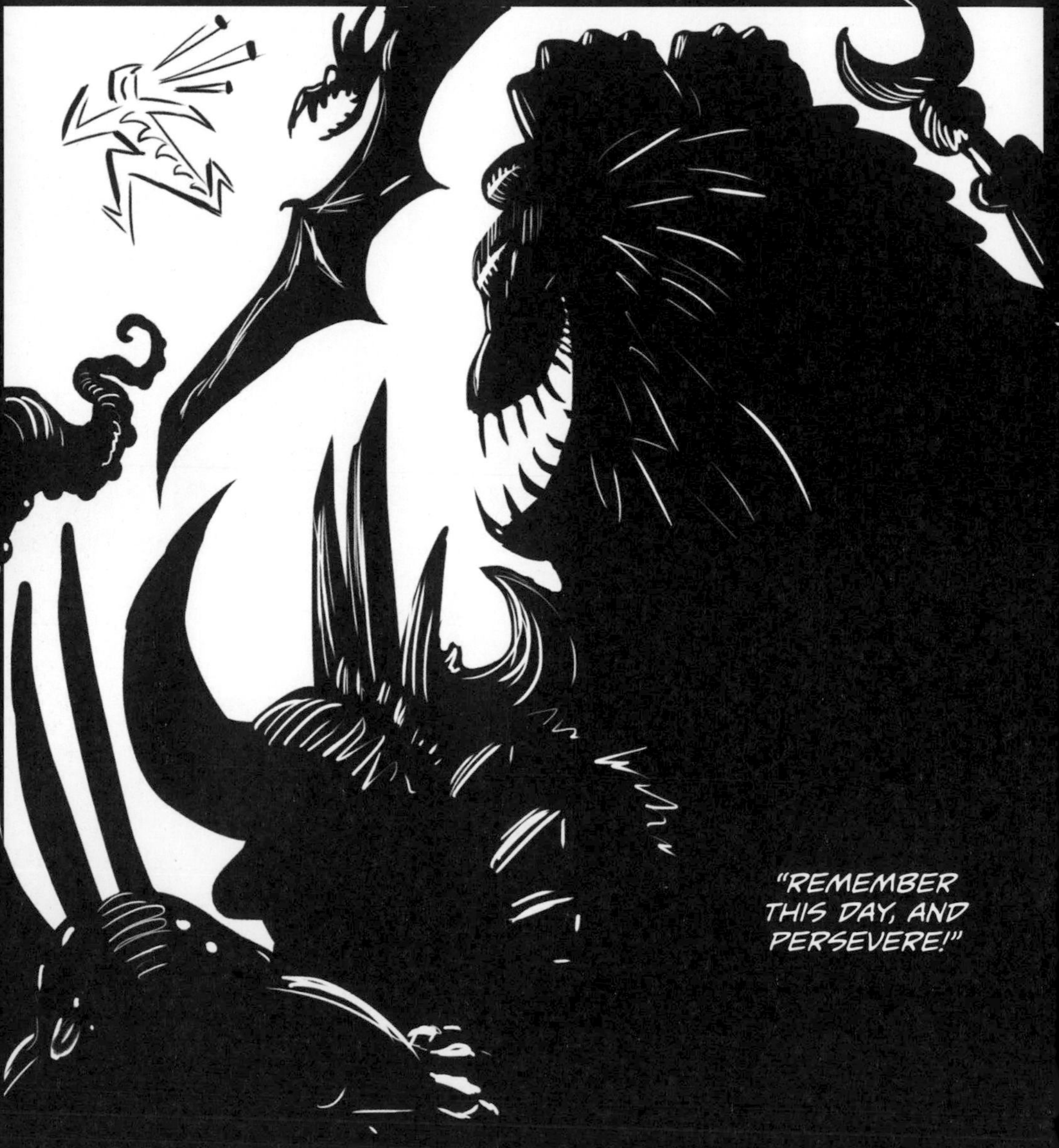
"REMEMBER THIS DAY, AND PERSEVERE!"

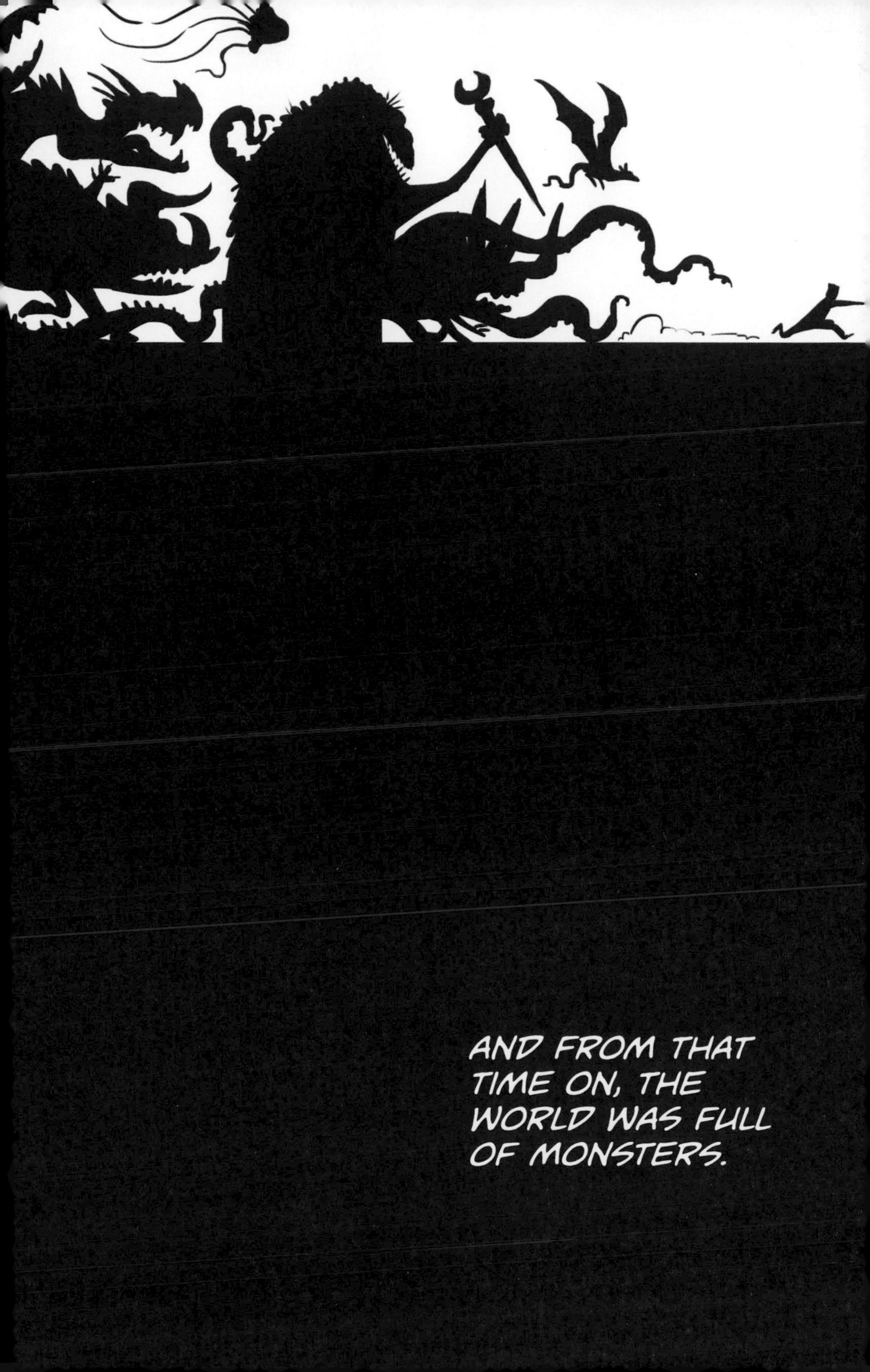
AND FROM THAT TIME ON, THE WORLD WAS FULL OF MONSTERS.

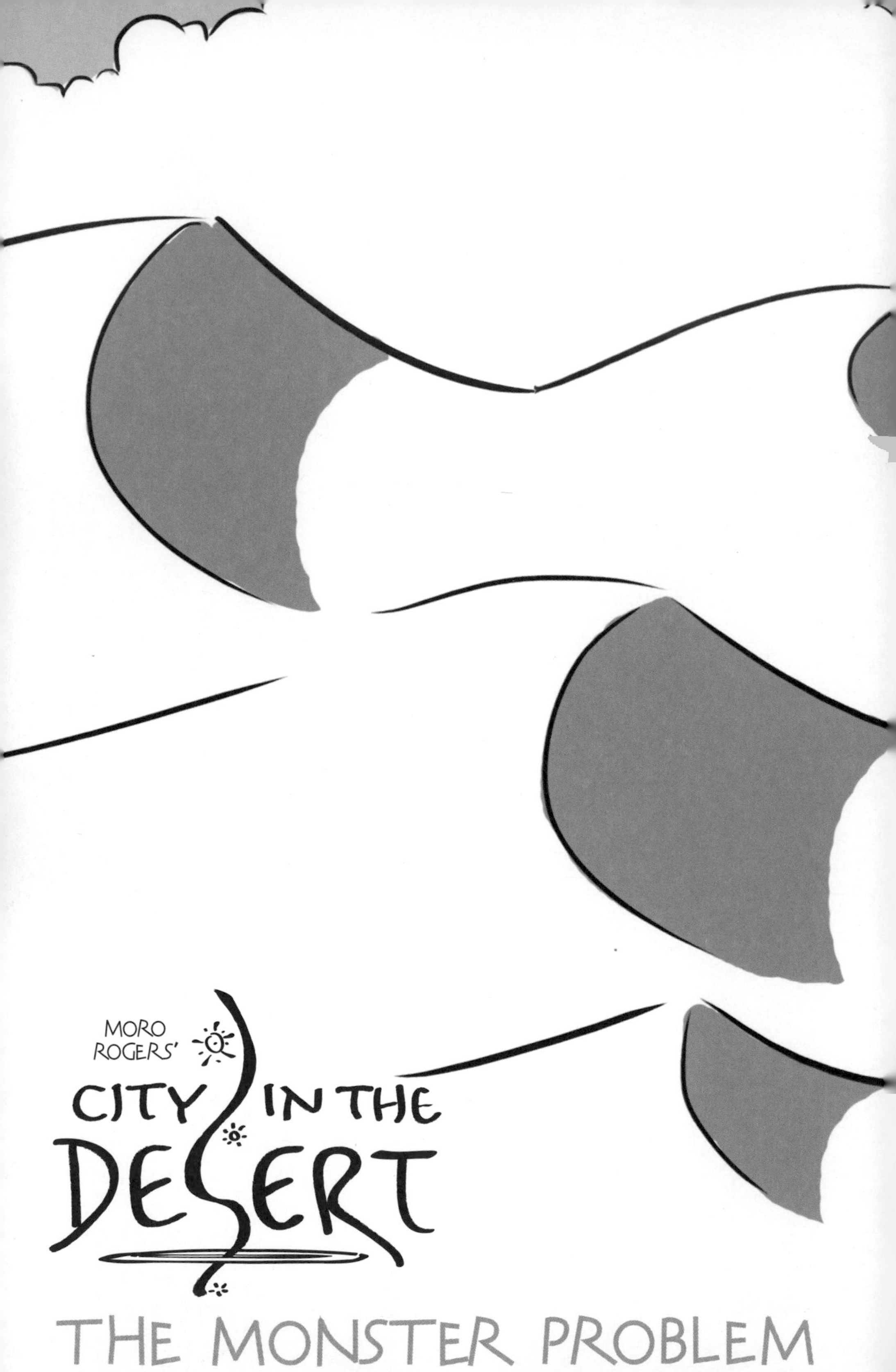

MORO ROGERS'

CITY IN THE DESERT

THE MONSTER PROBLEM

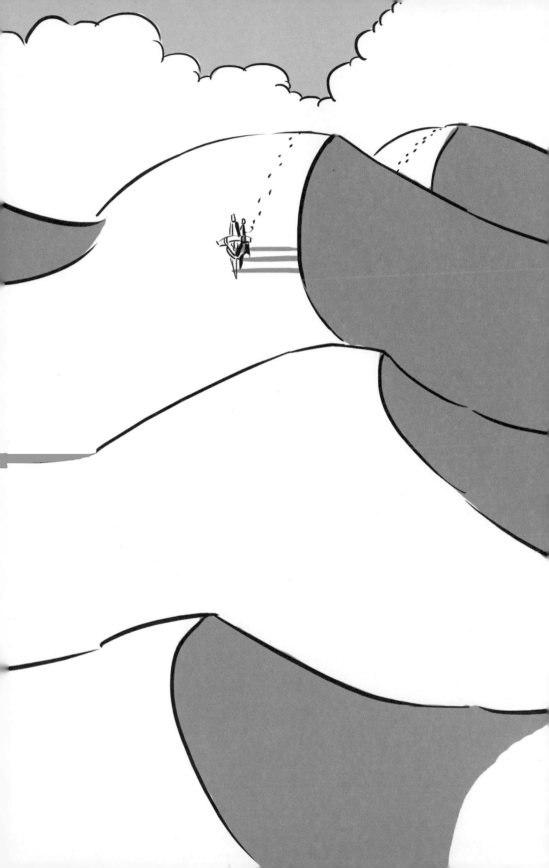

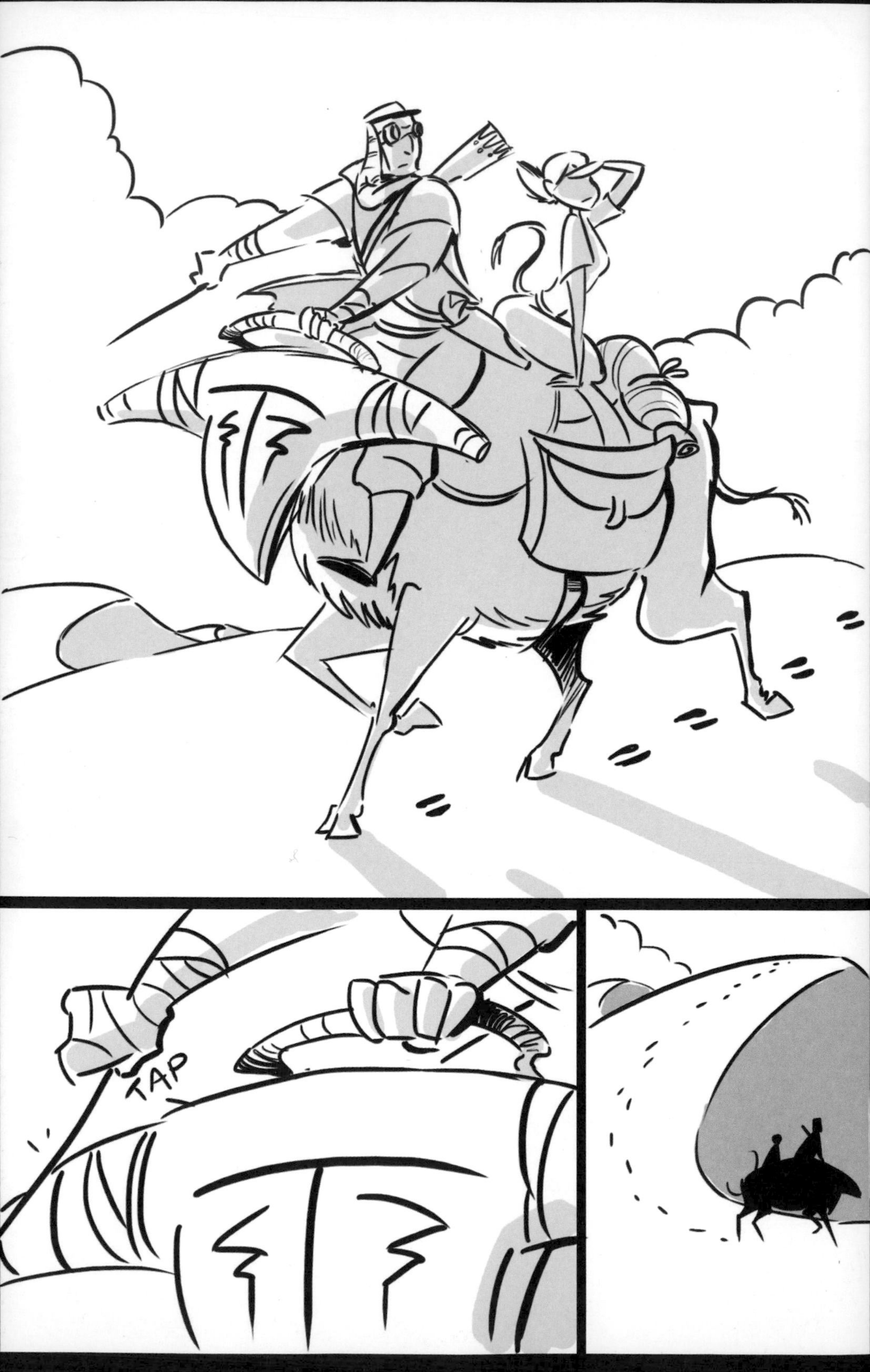
TAP

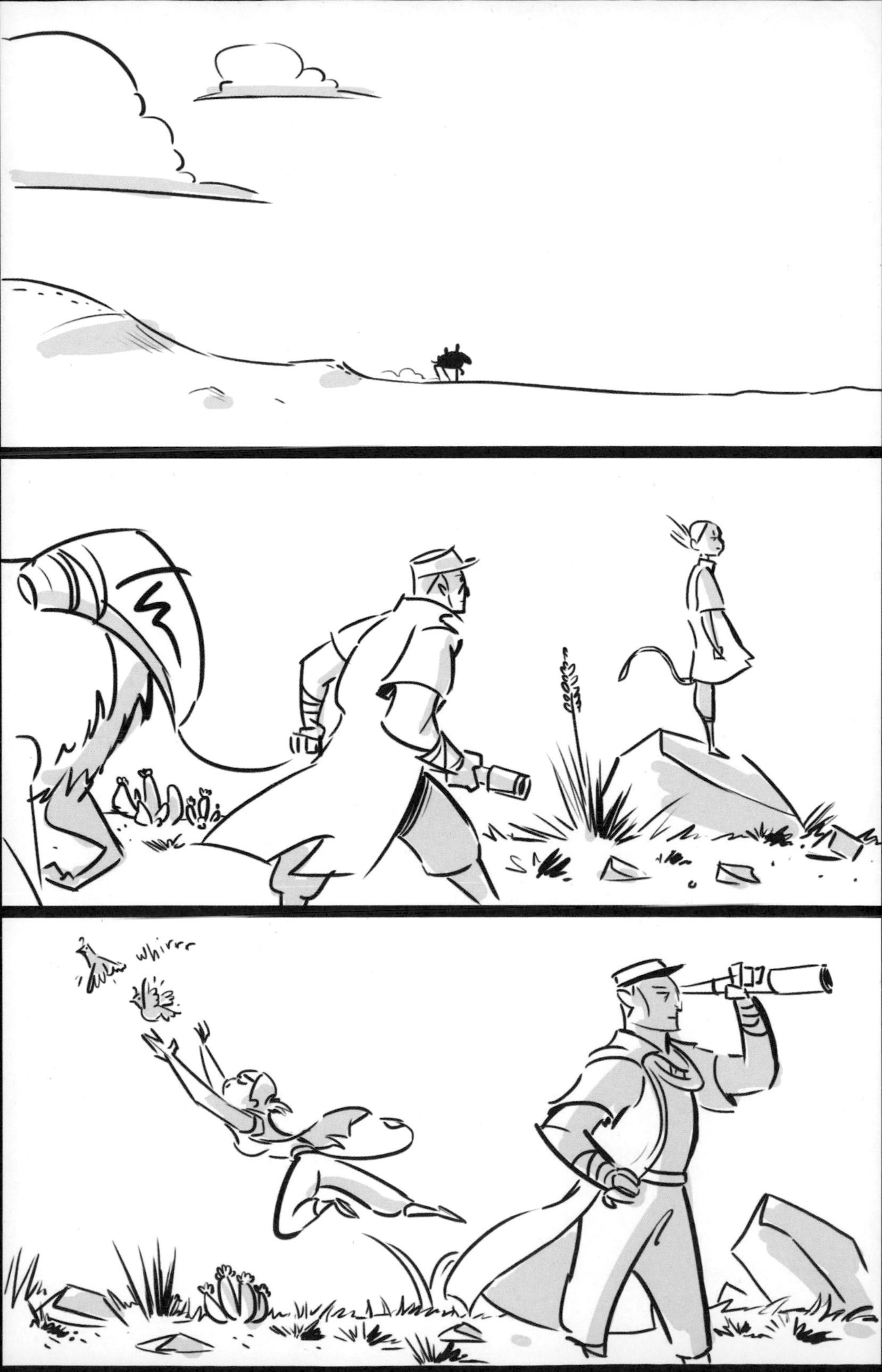
whirrr

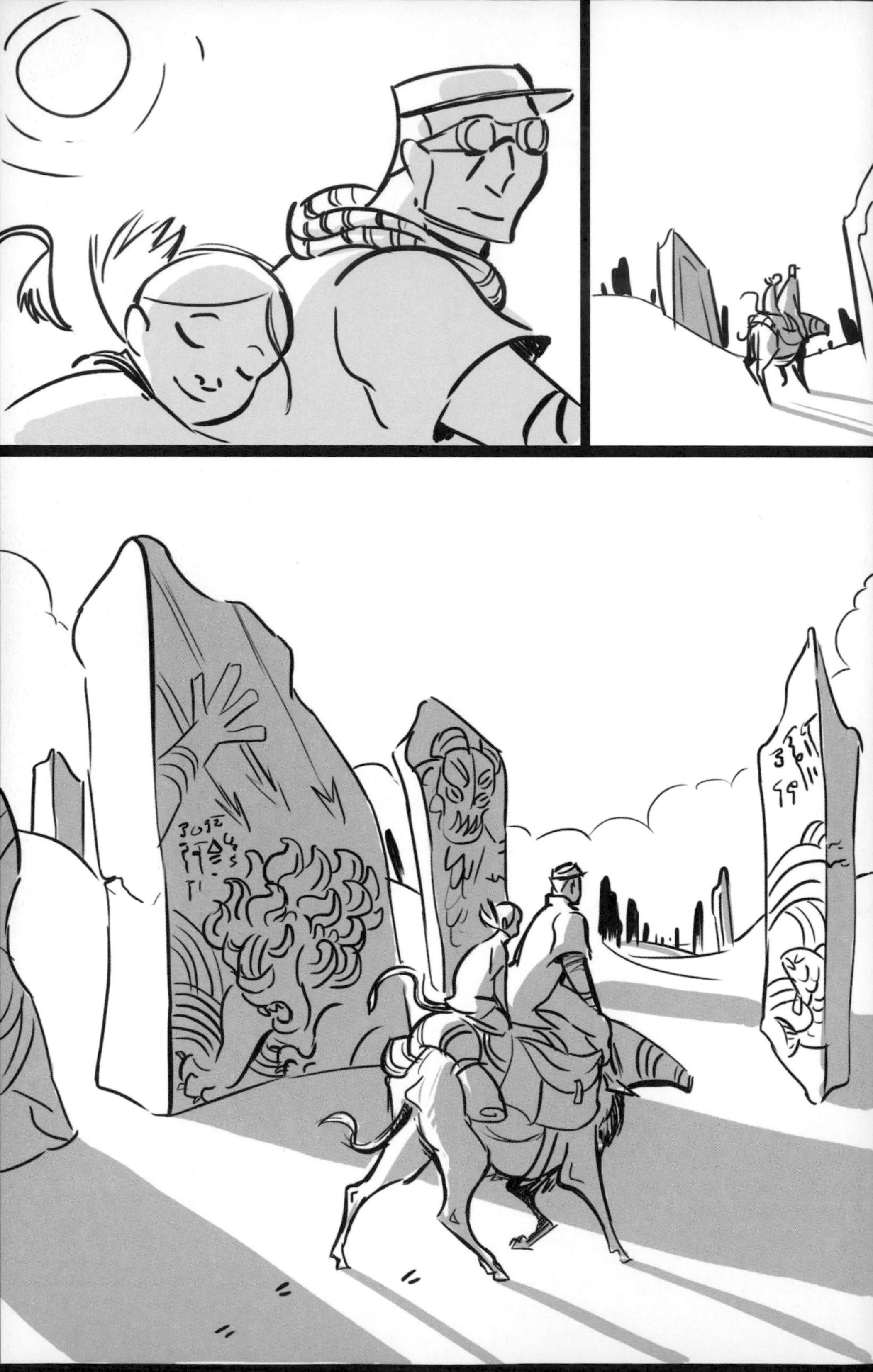

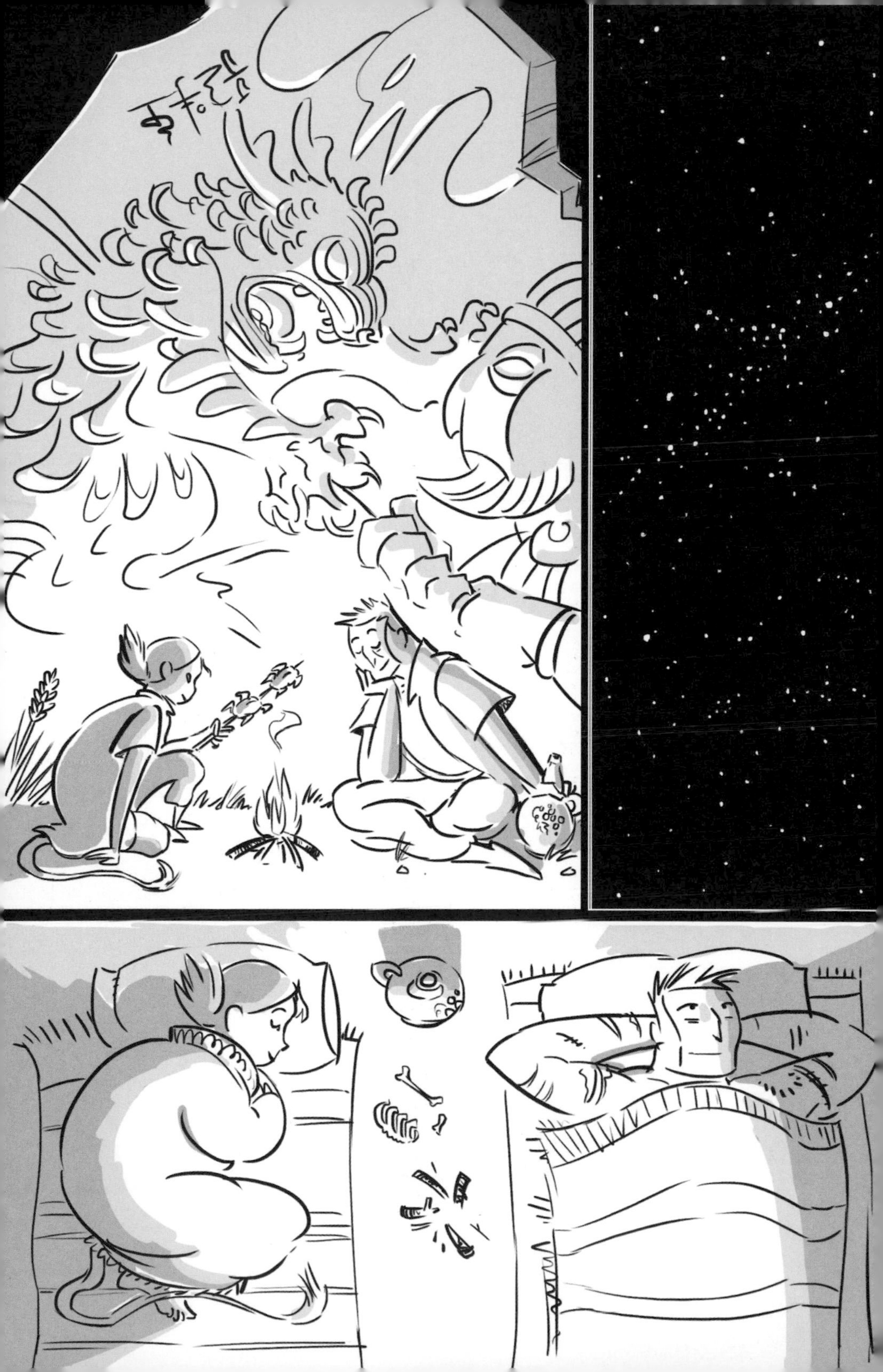

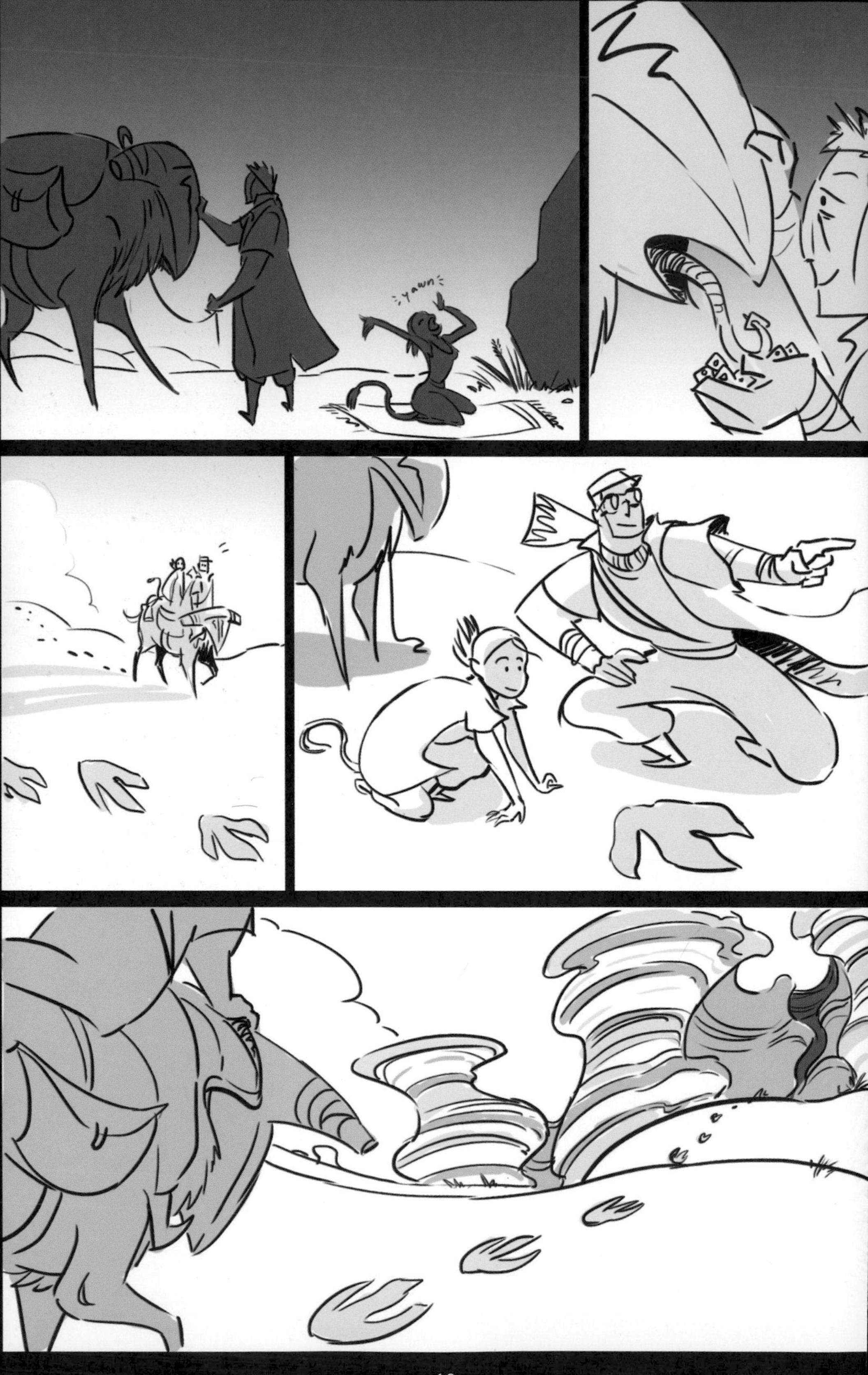
yawn

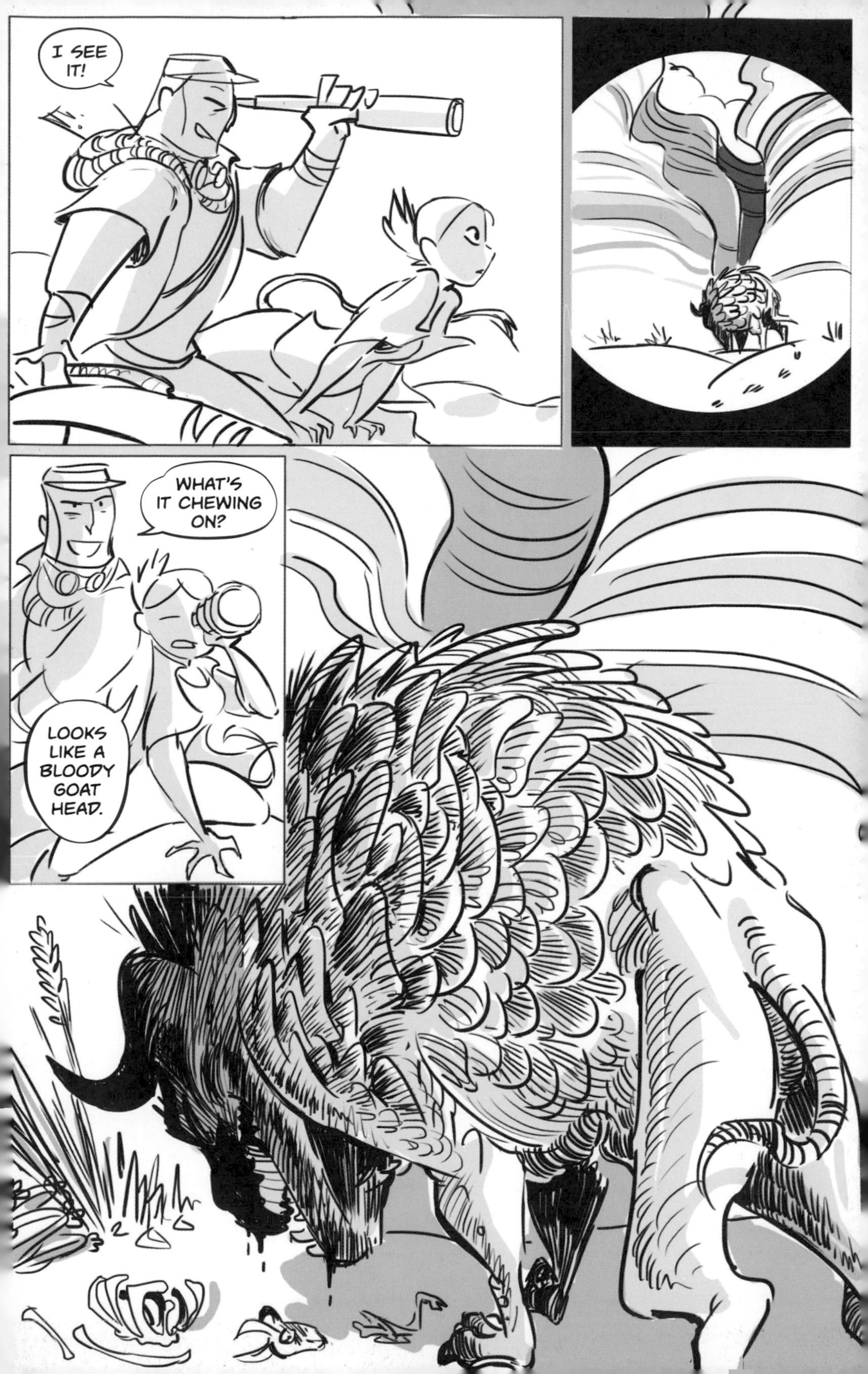
I SEE IT!
WHAT'S IT CHEWING ON?
LOOKS LIKE A BLOODY GOAT HEAD.

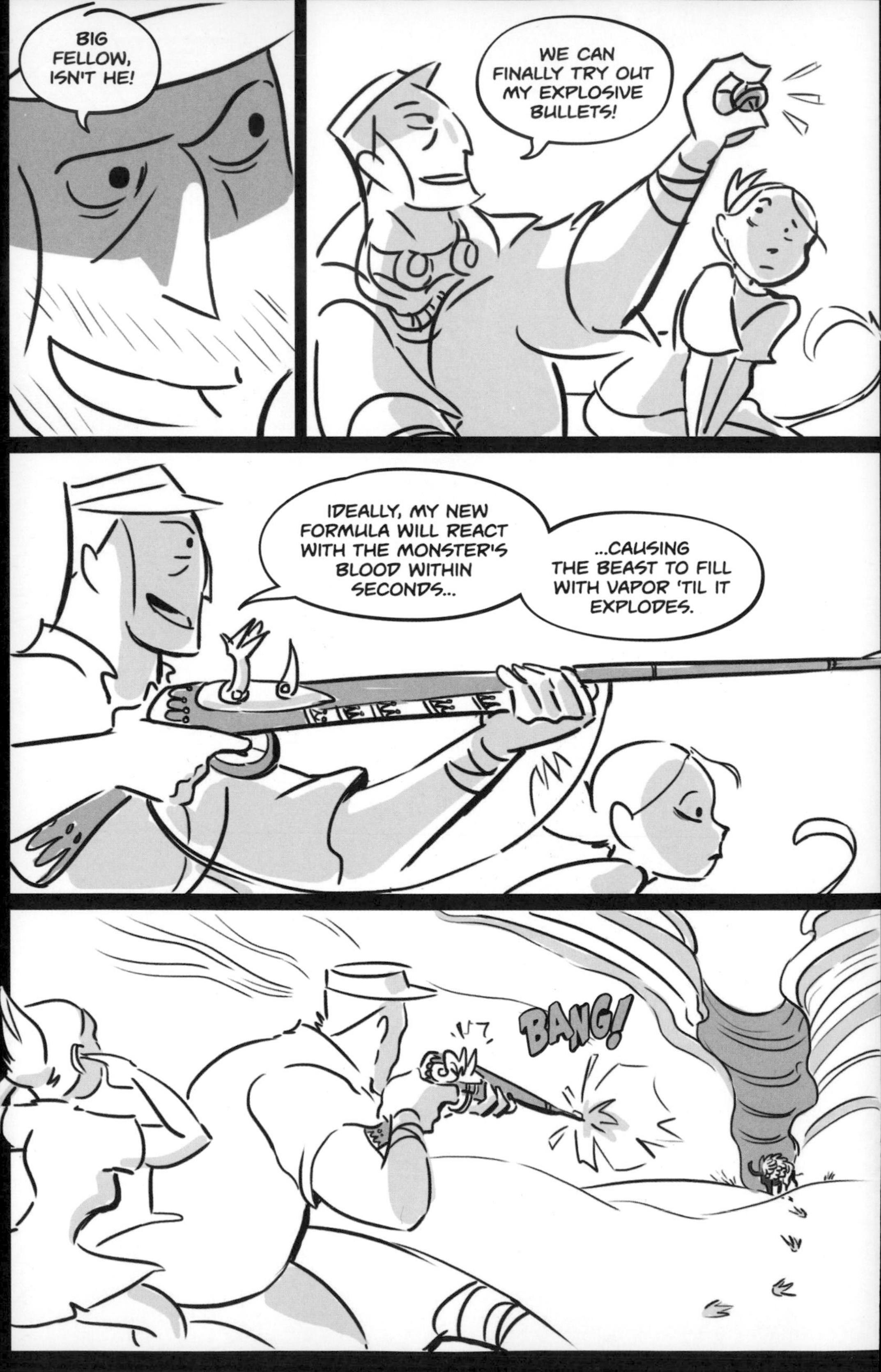
BIG FELLOW, ISN'T HE!
WE CAN FINALLY TRY OUT MY EXPLOSIVE BULLETS!
IDEALLY, MY NEW FORMULA WILL REACT WITH THE MONSTER'S BLOOD WITHIN SECONDS...
...CAUSING THE BEAST TO FILL WITH VAPOR 'TIL IT EXPLODES.
BANG!

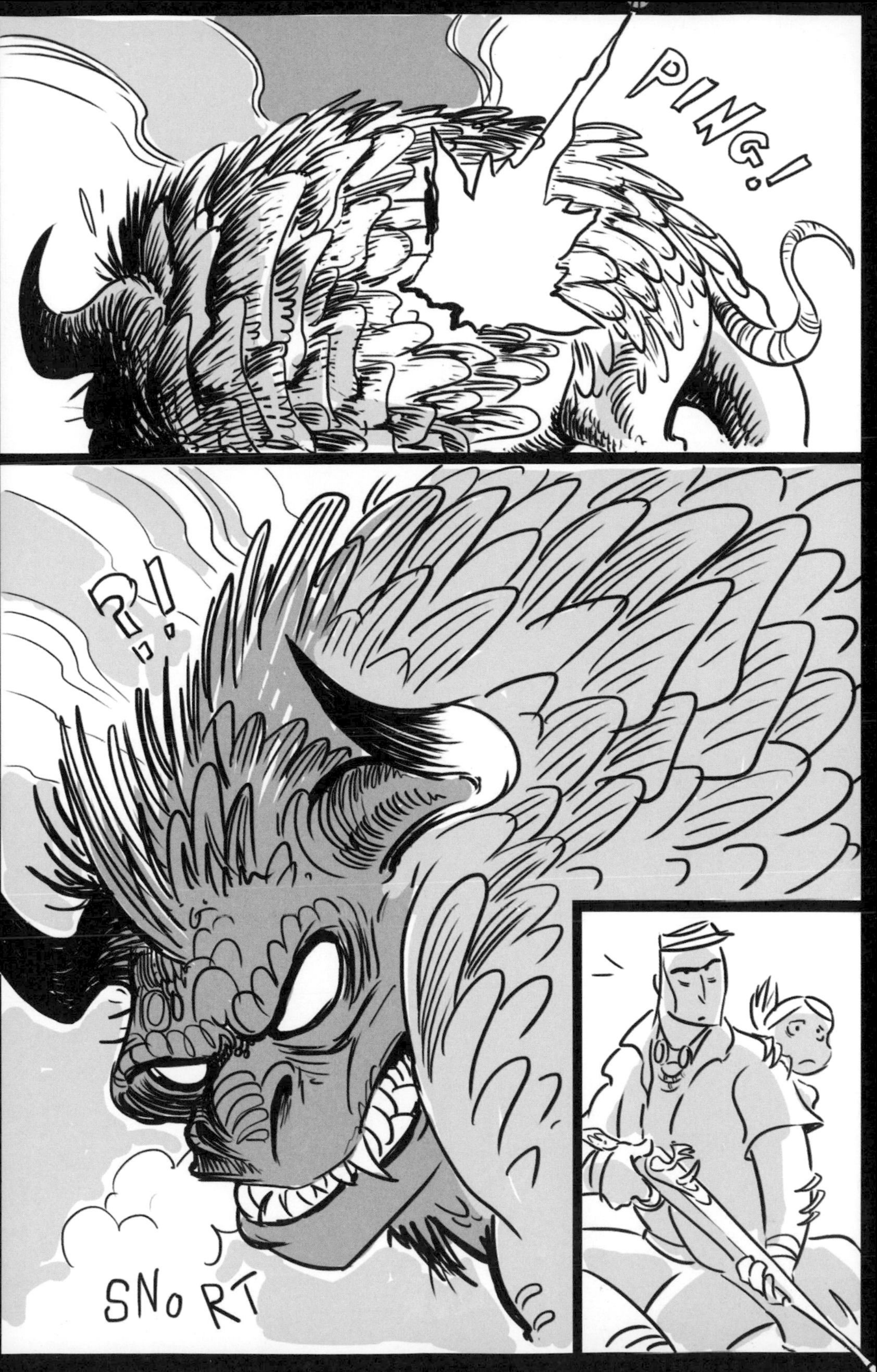
PING!
?!
SNORT

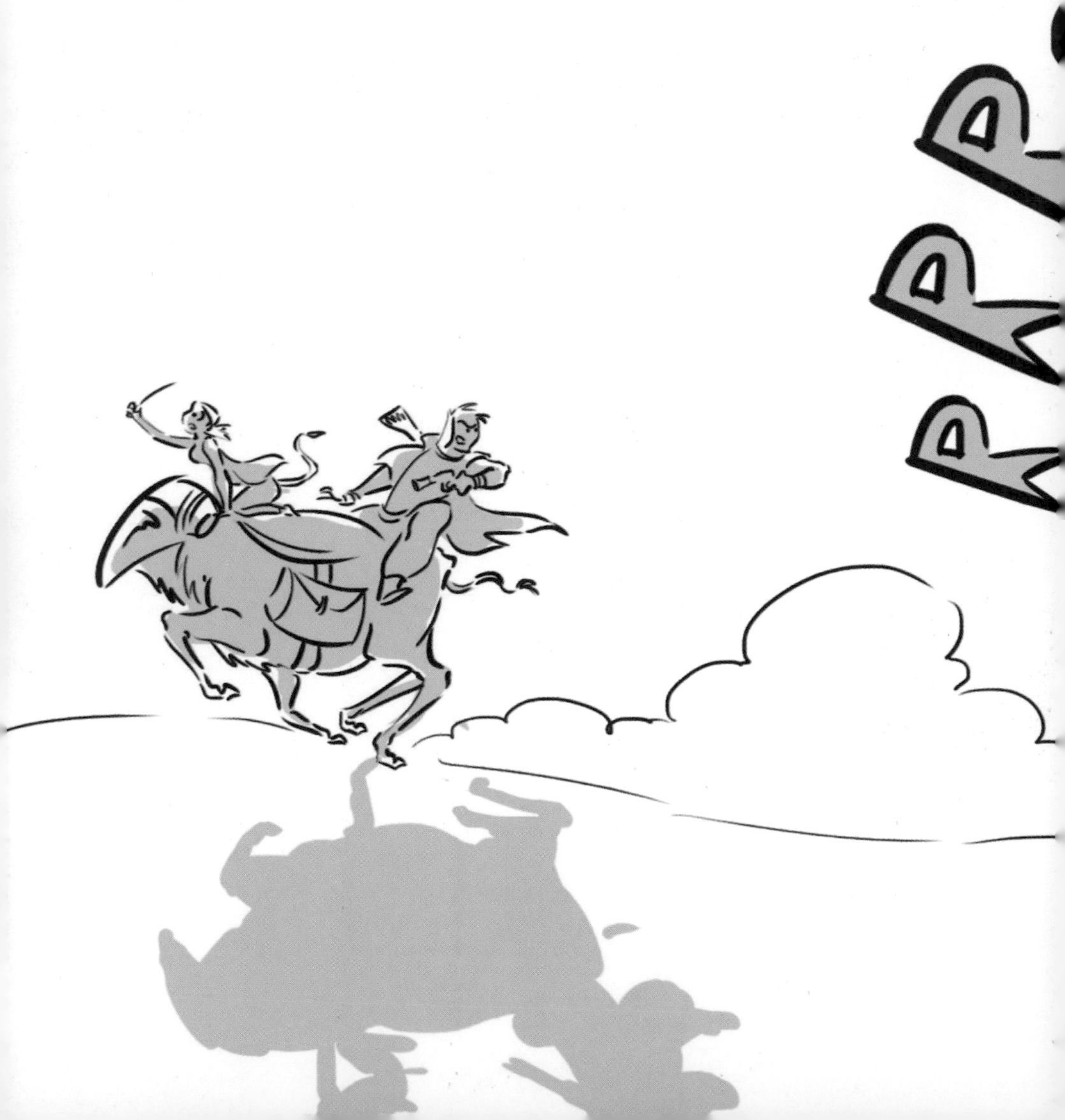

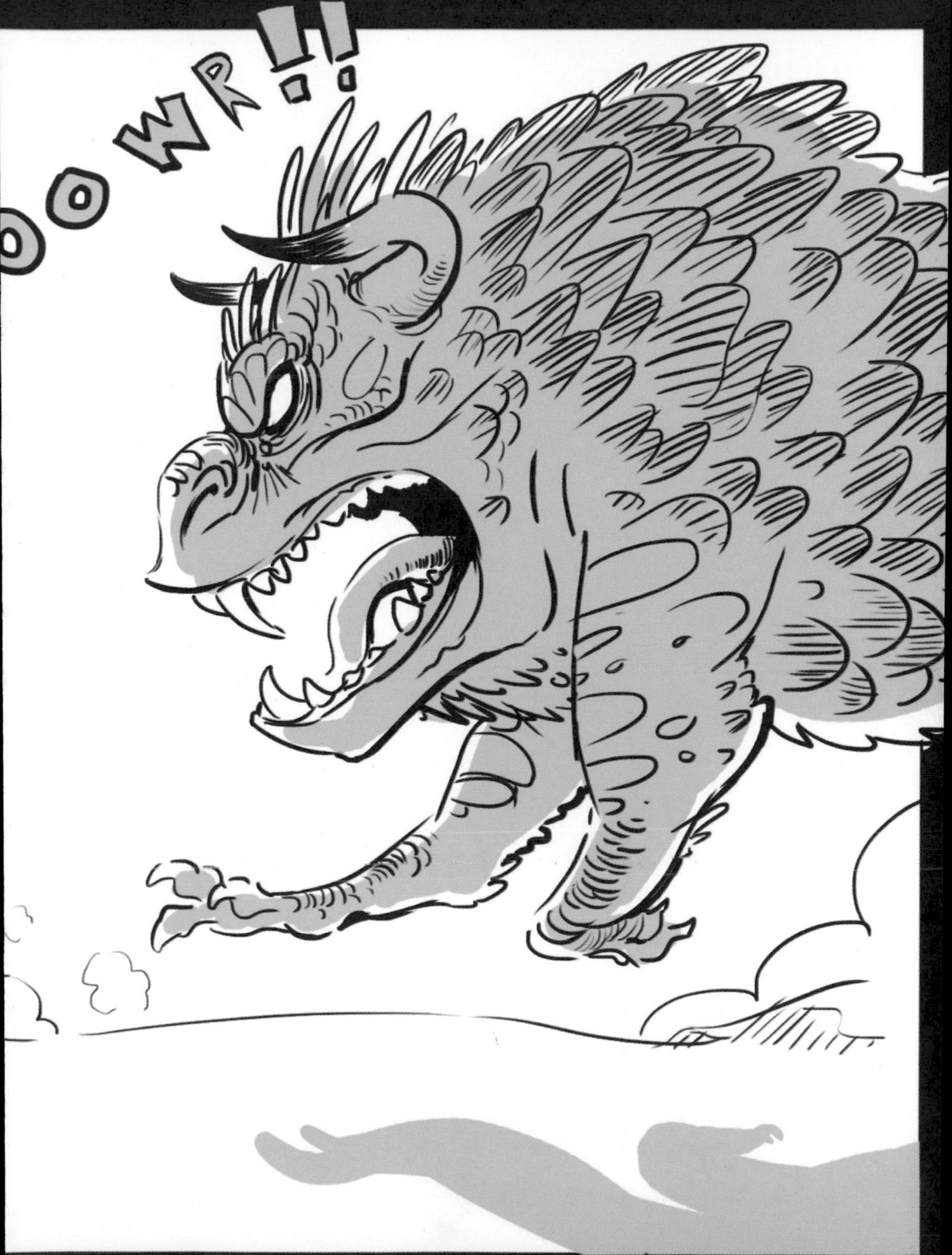
OOOWR!!

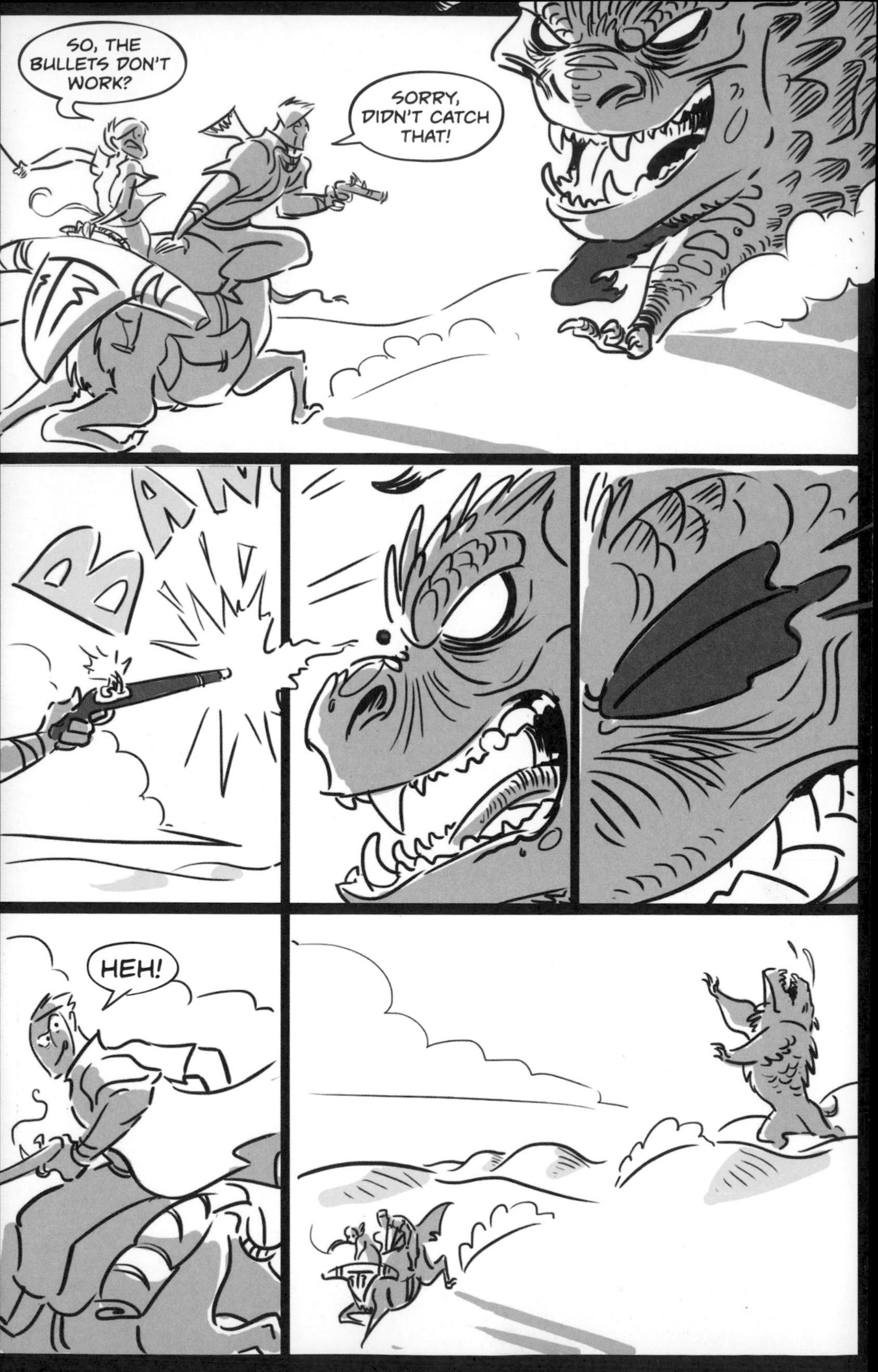
SO, THE BULLETS DON'T WORK?
SORRY, DIDN'T CATCH THAT!
BAM
HEH!

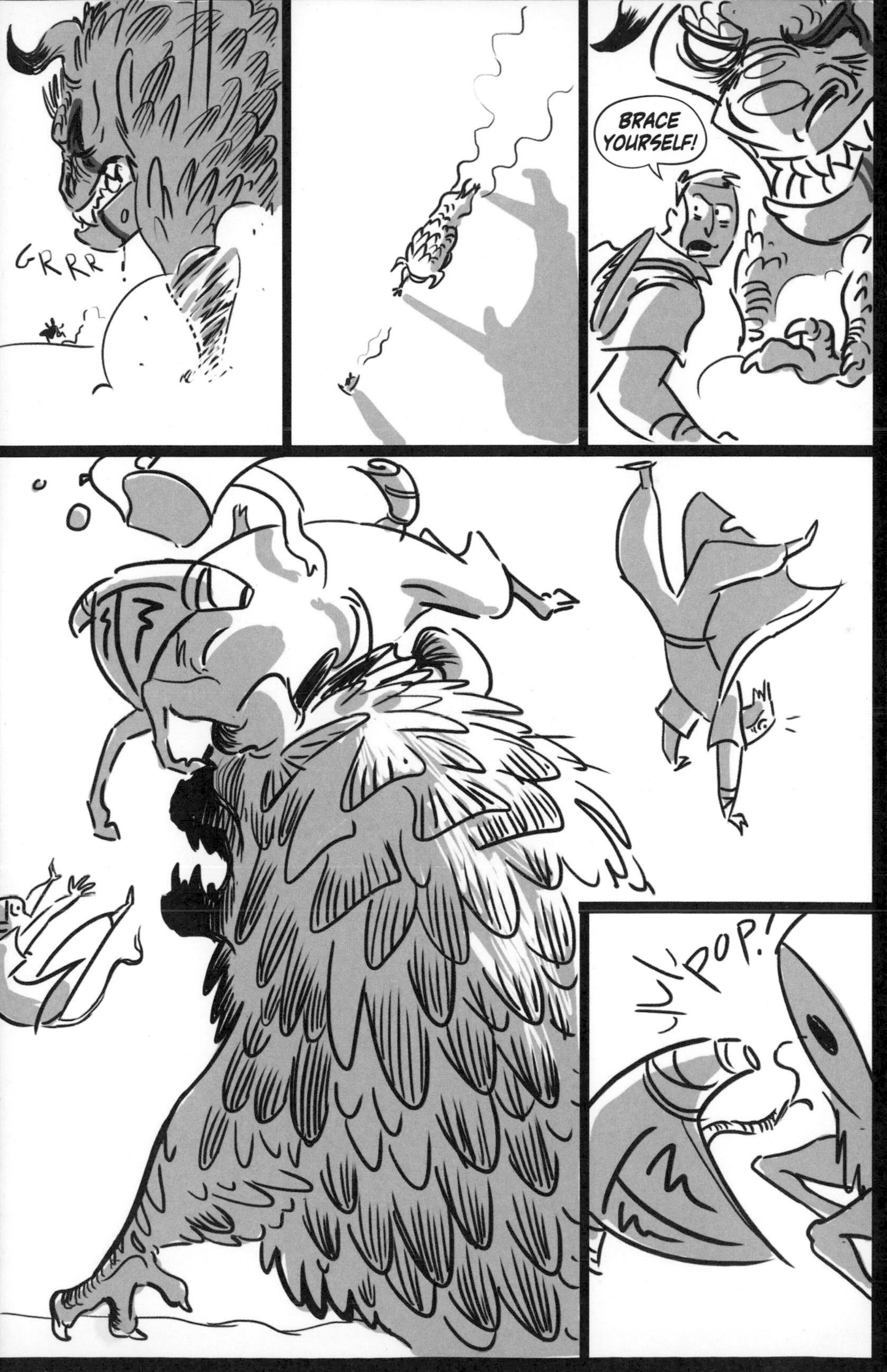
GRRR
BRACE YOURSELF!
POP!

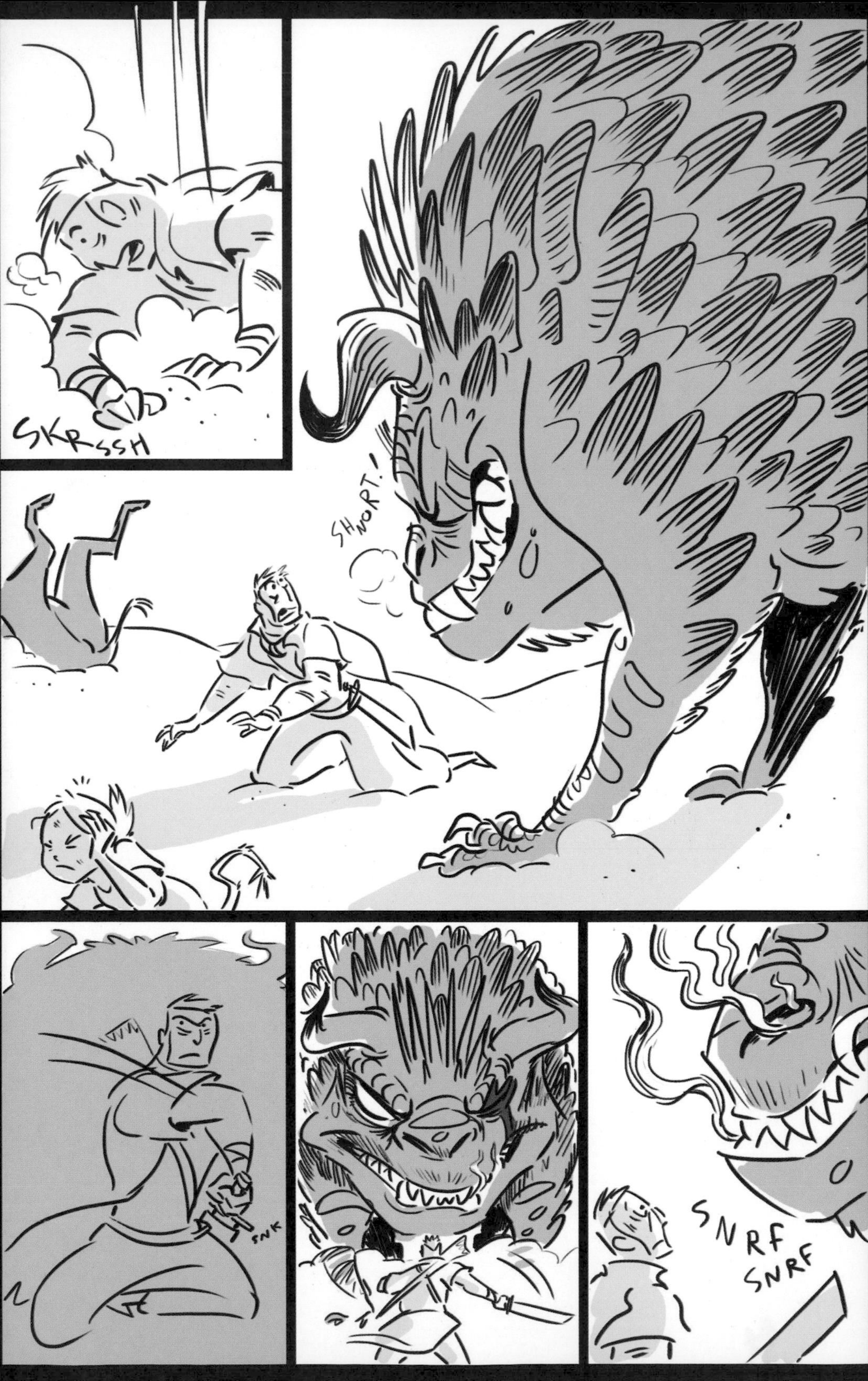
SKRSSH
SHNORT!
SNK
SNRF
SNRF

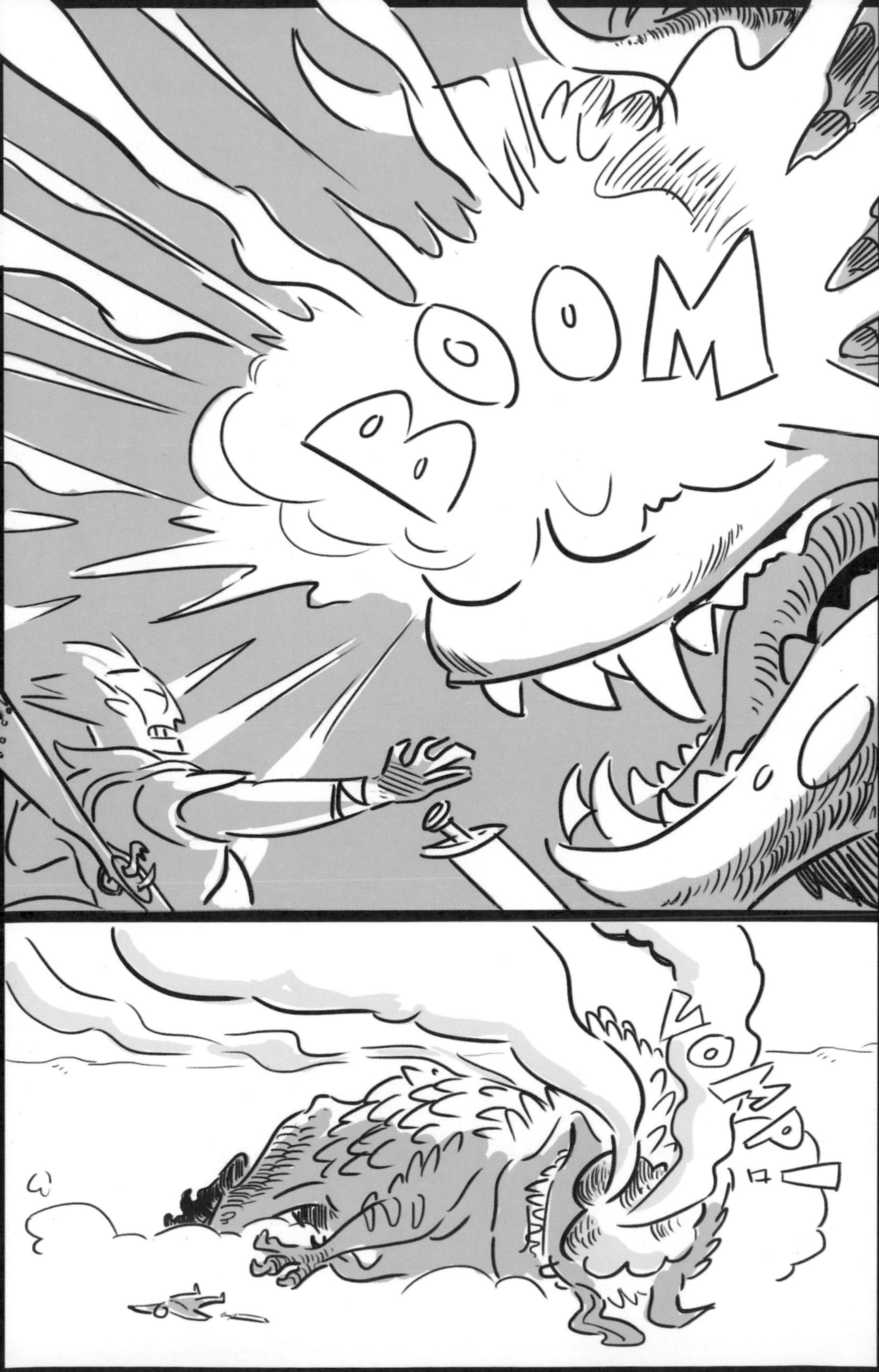
BOOM
WOMP!!

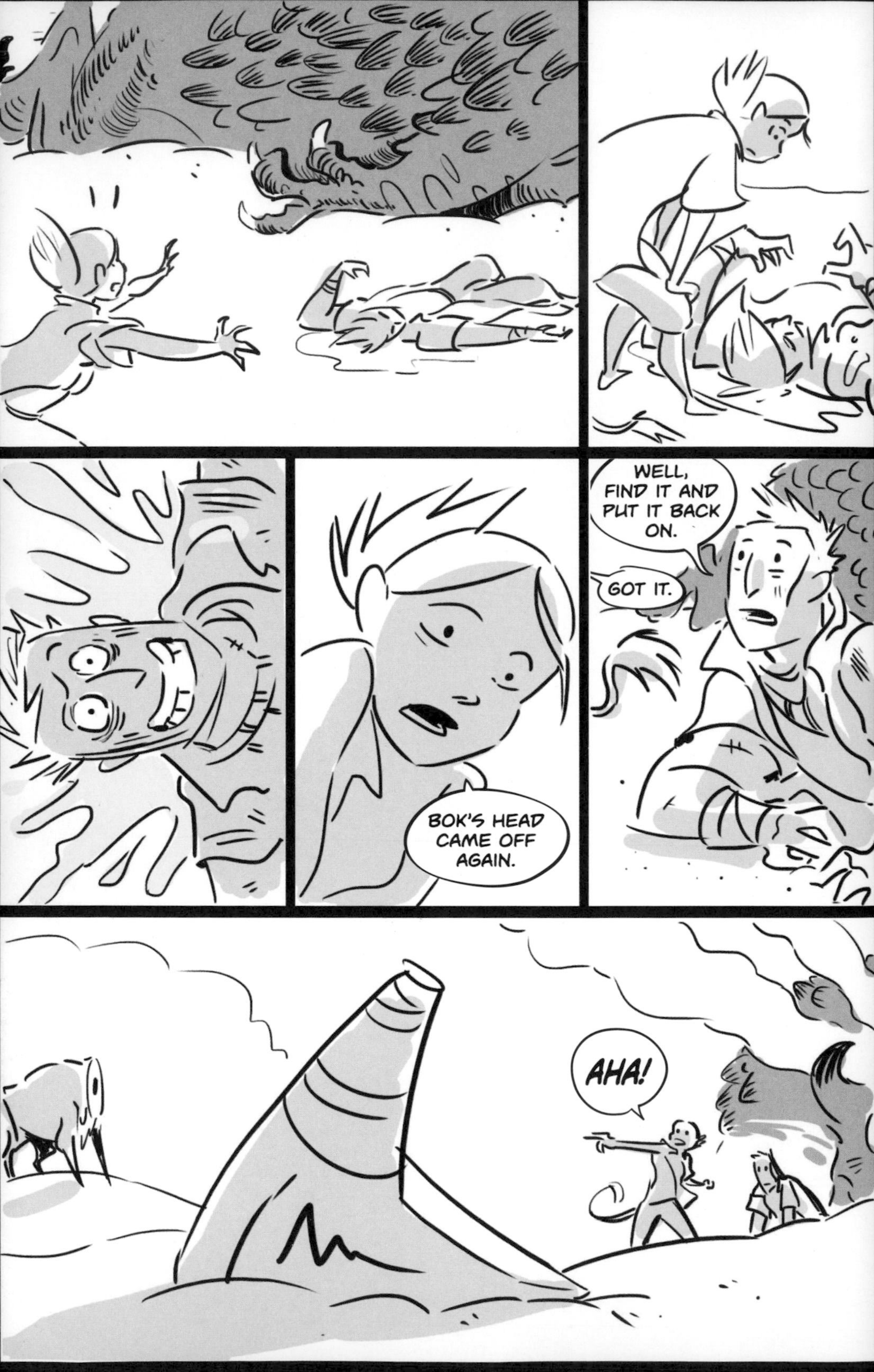
BOK'S HEAD CAME OFF AGAIN.
WELL, FIND IT AND PUT IT BACK ON.
GOT IT.
AHA!

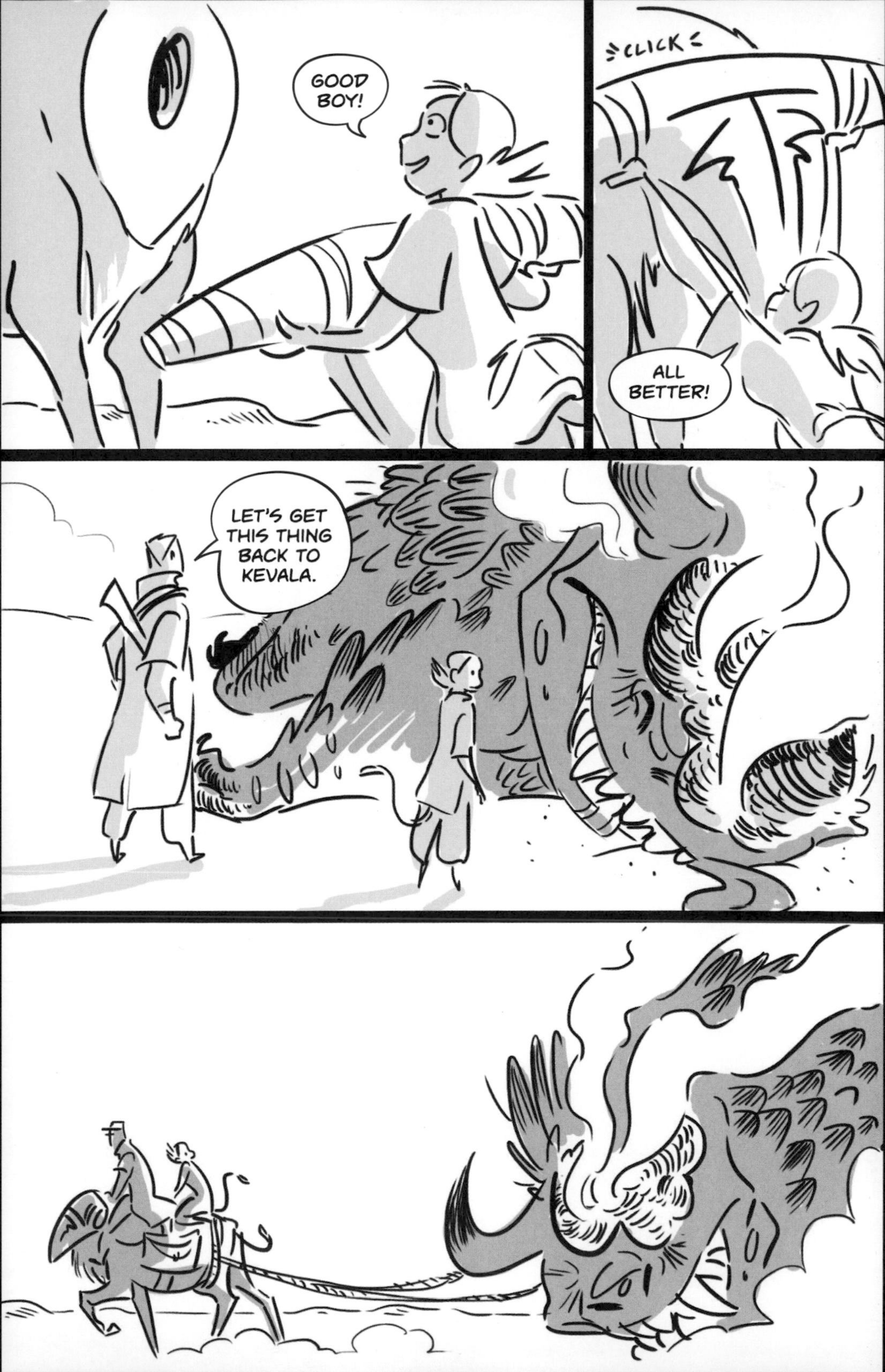
GOOD BOY!
CLICK
ALL BETTER!
LET'S GET THIS THING BACK TO KEVALA.

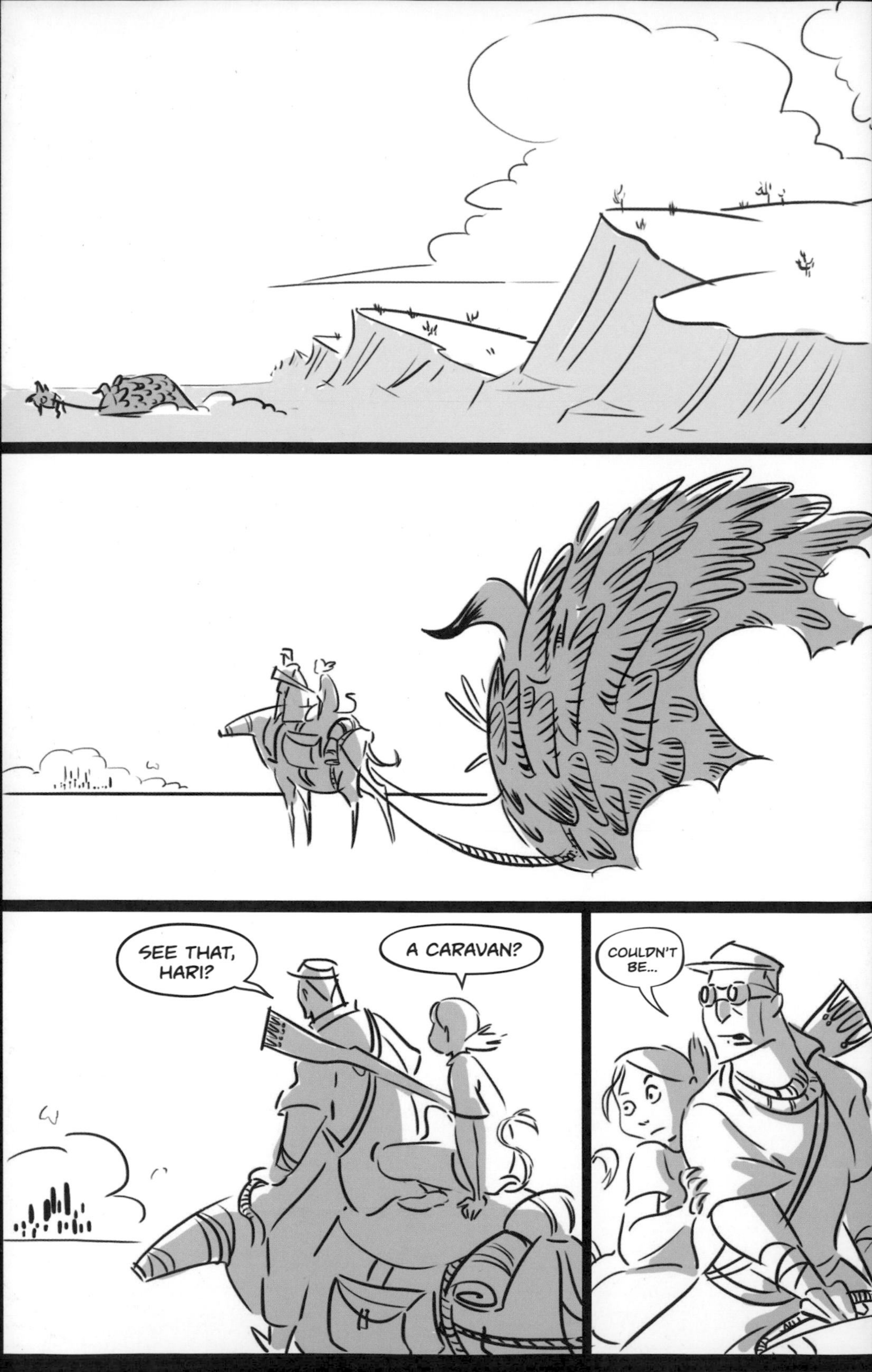
SEE THAT, HARI?
A CARAVAN?
COULDN'T BE...

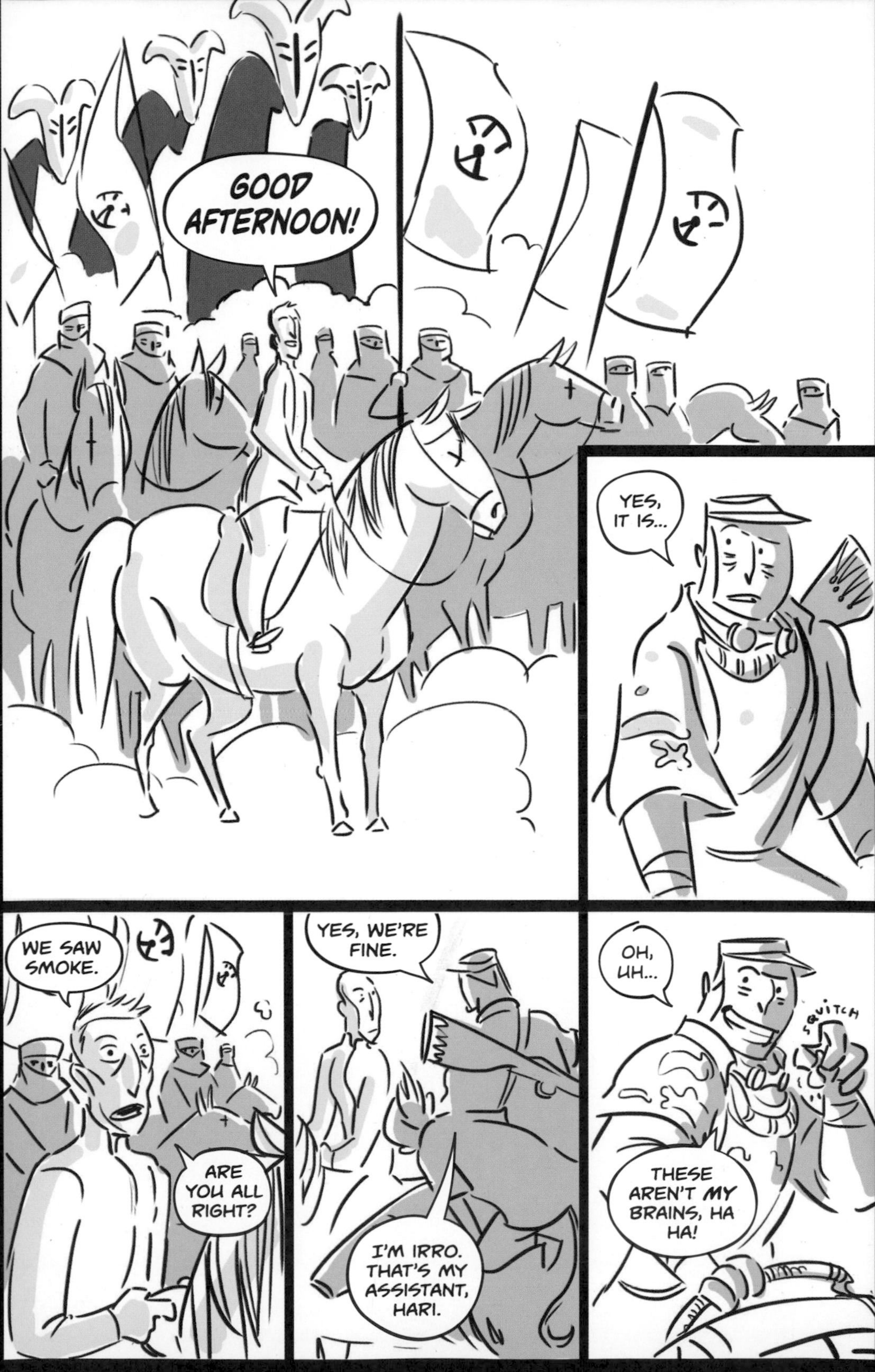
GOOD AFTERNOON!
YES, IT IS...
WE SAW SMOKE.
ARE YOU ALL RIGHT?
YES, WE'RE FINE.
I'M IRRO. THAT'S MY ASSISTANT, HARI.
OH, UH...
SQUITCH
THESE AREN'T MY BRAINS, HA HA!

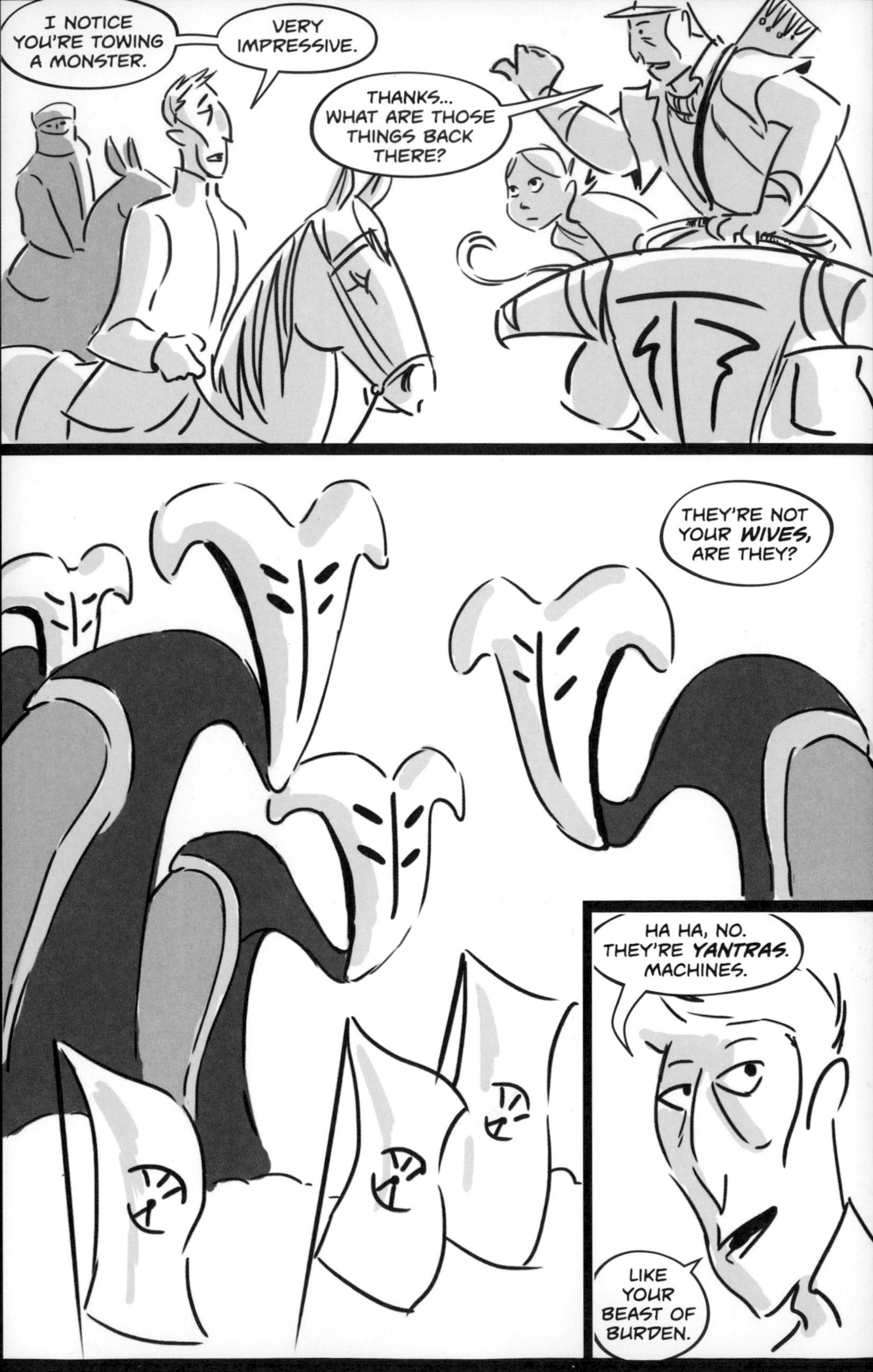
I NOTICE YOU'RE TOWING A MONSTER.
VERY IMPRESSIVE.
THANKS... WHAT ARE THOSE THINGS BACK THERE?
THEY'RE NOT YOUR *WIVES,* ARE THEY?
HA HA, NO. THEY'RE *YANTRAS.* MACHINES.
LIKE YOUR BEAST OF BURDEN.

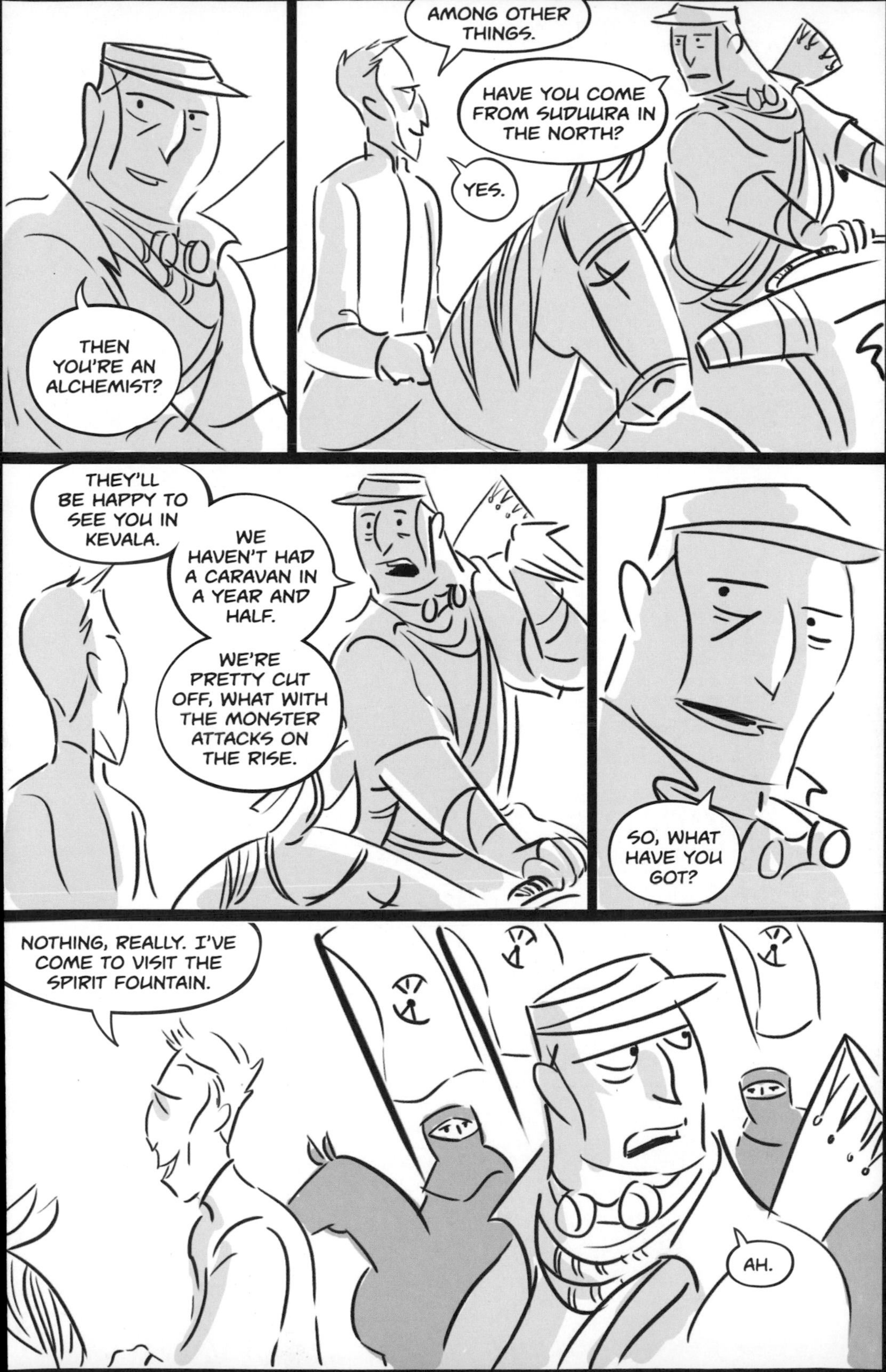
THEN YOU'RE AN ALCHEMIST?
AMONG OTHER THINGS.
HAVE YOU COME FROM SUDUURA IN THE NORTH?
YES.
THEY'LL BE HAPPY TO SEE YOU IN KEVALA.
WE HAVEN'T HAD A CARAVAN IN A YEAR AND HALF.
WE'RE PRETTY CUT OFF, WHAT WITH THE MONSTER ATTACKS ON THE RISE.
SO, WHAT HAVE YOU GOT?
NOTHING, REALLY. I'VE COME TO VISIT THE SPIRIT FOUNTAIN.
AH.

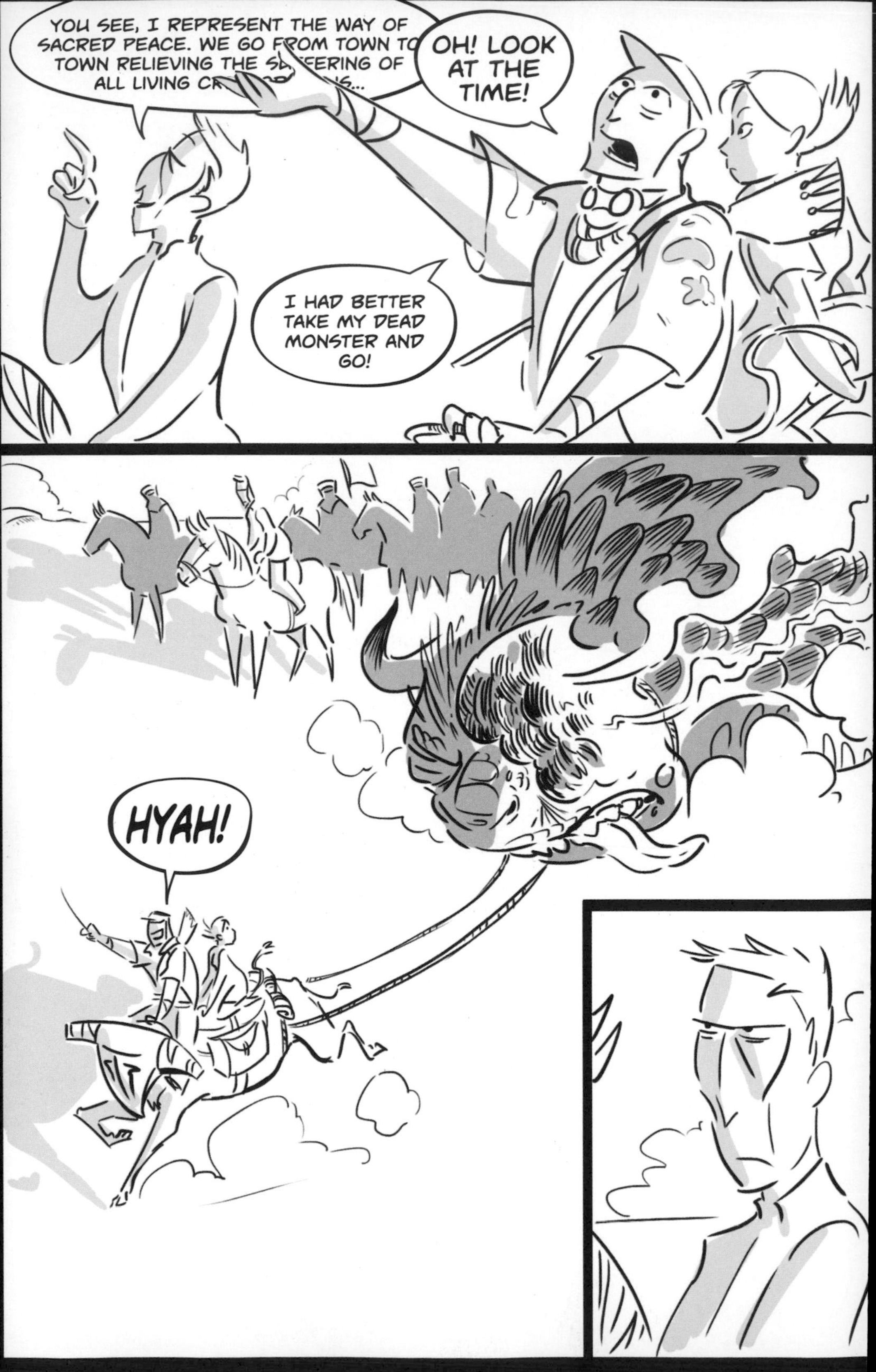
YOU SEE, I REPRESENT THE WAY OF SACRED PEACE. WE GO FROM TOWN TO TOWN RELIEVING THE S FERING OF ALL LIVING CR S...
OH! LOOK AT THE TIME!
I HAD BETTER TAKE MY DEAD MONSTER AND GO!
HYAH!

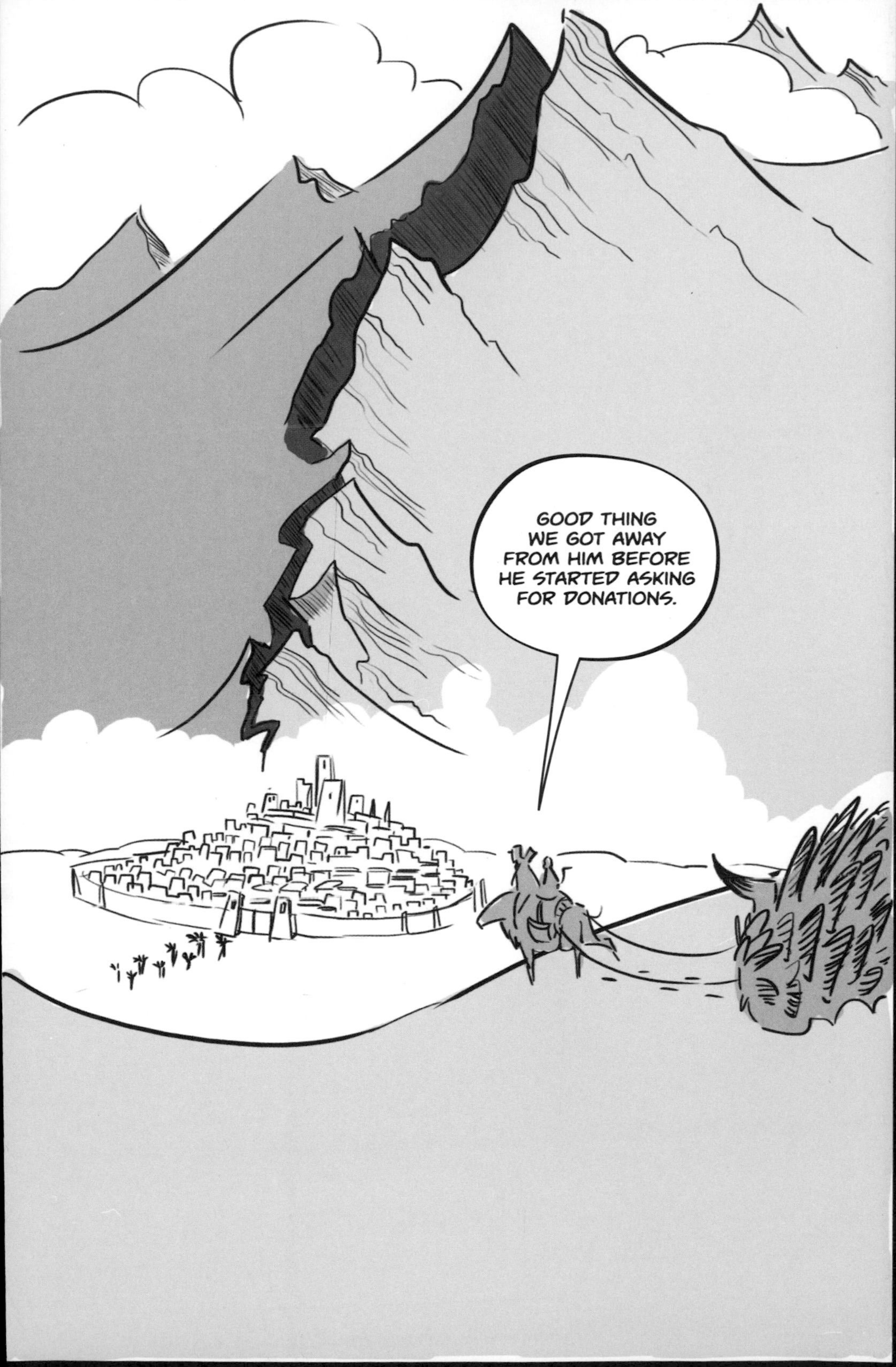
GOOD THING WE GOT AWAY FROM HIM BEFORE HE STARTED ASKING FOR DONATIONS.

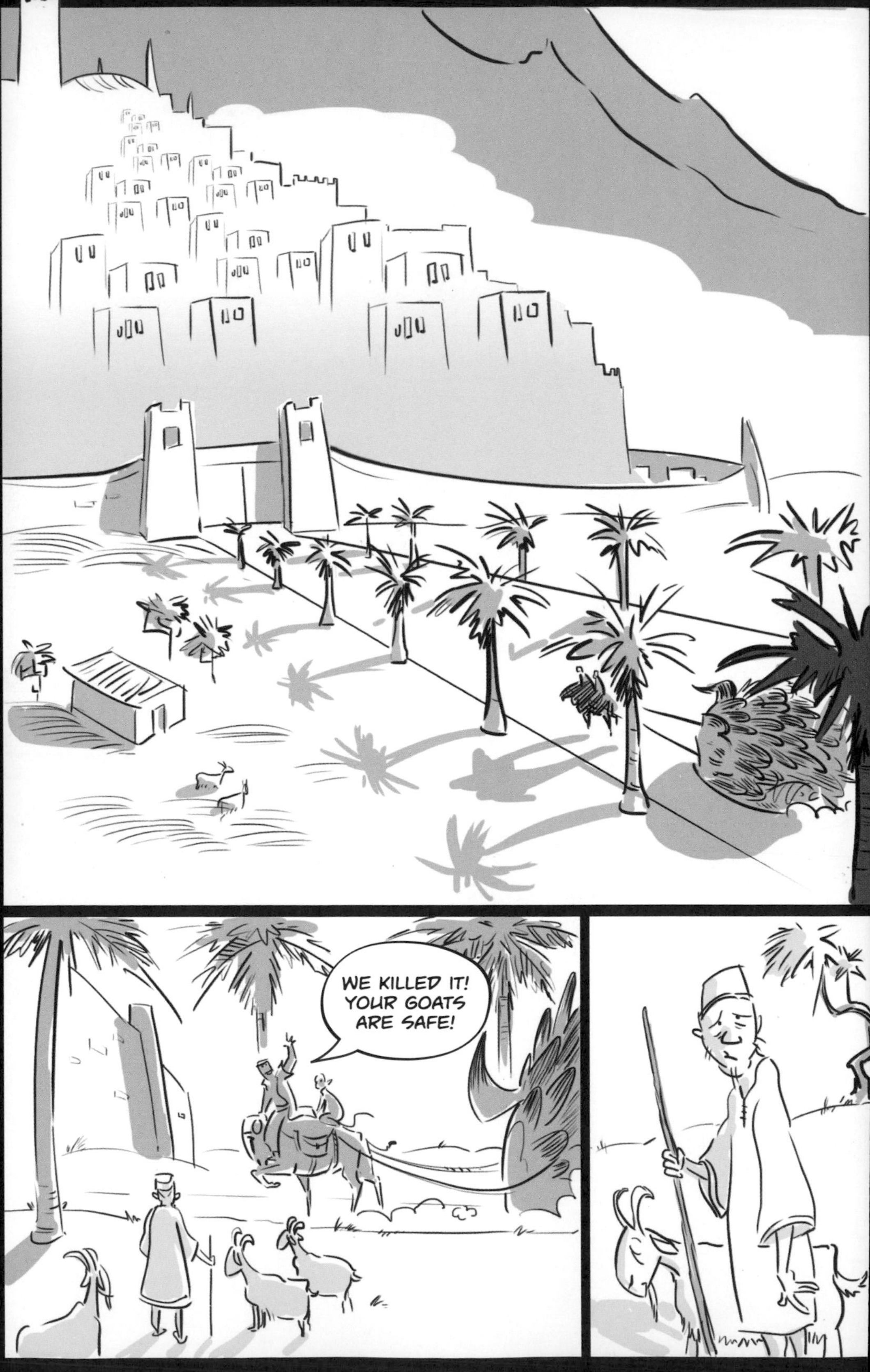
WE KILLED IT! YOUR GOATS ARE SAFE!

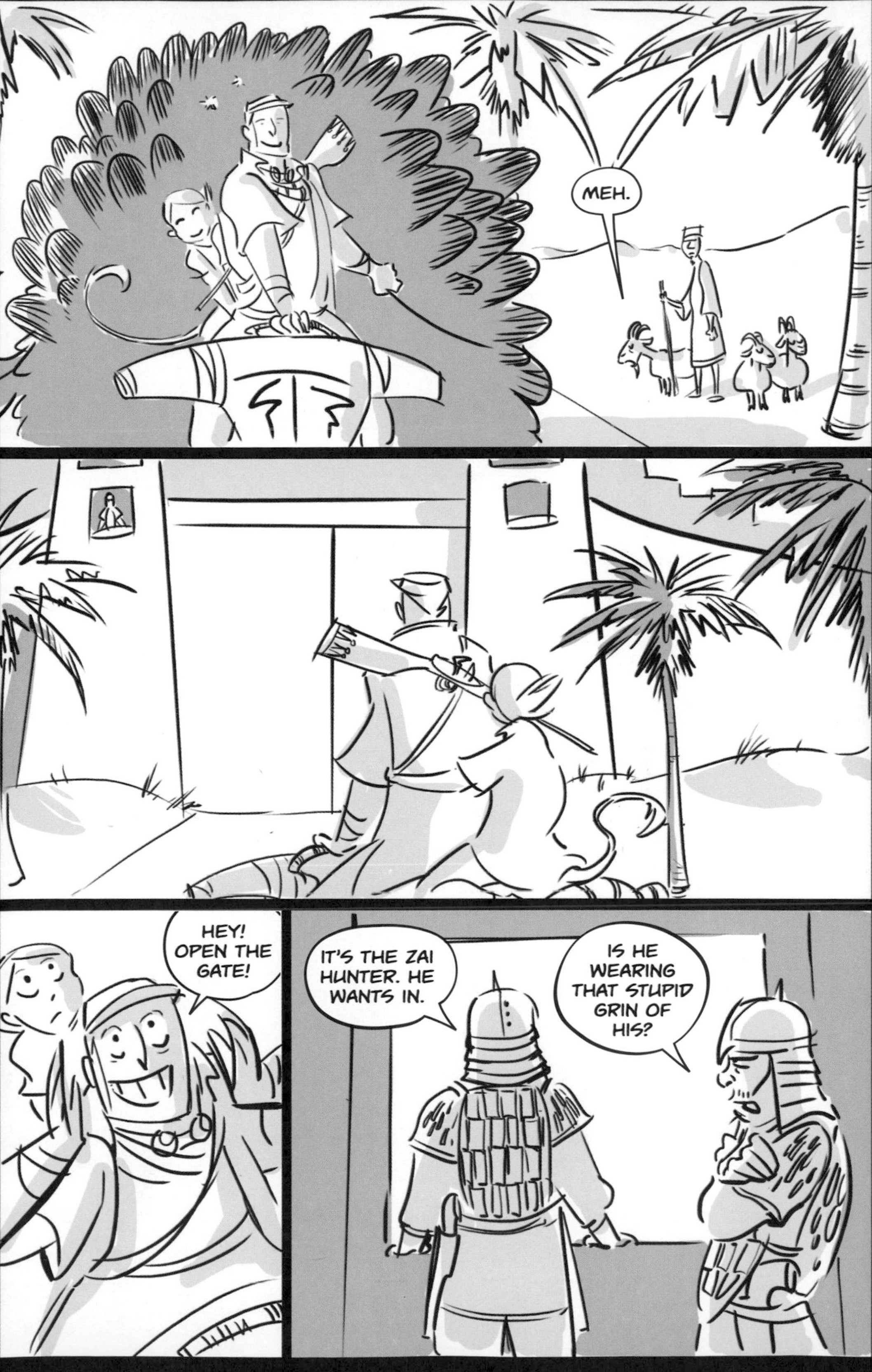
MEH.
HEY! OPEN THE GATE!
IT'S THE ZAI HUNTER. HE WANTS IN.
IS HE WEARING THAT STUPID GRIN OF HIS?

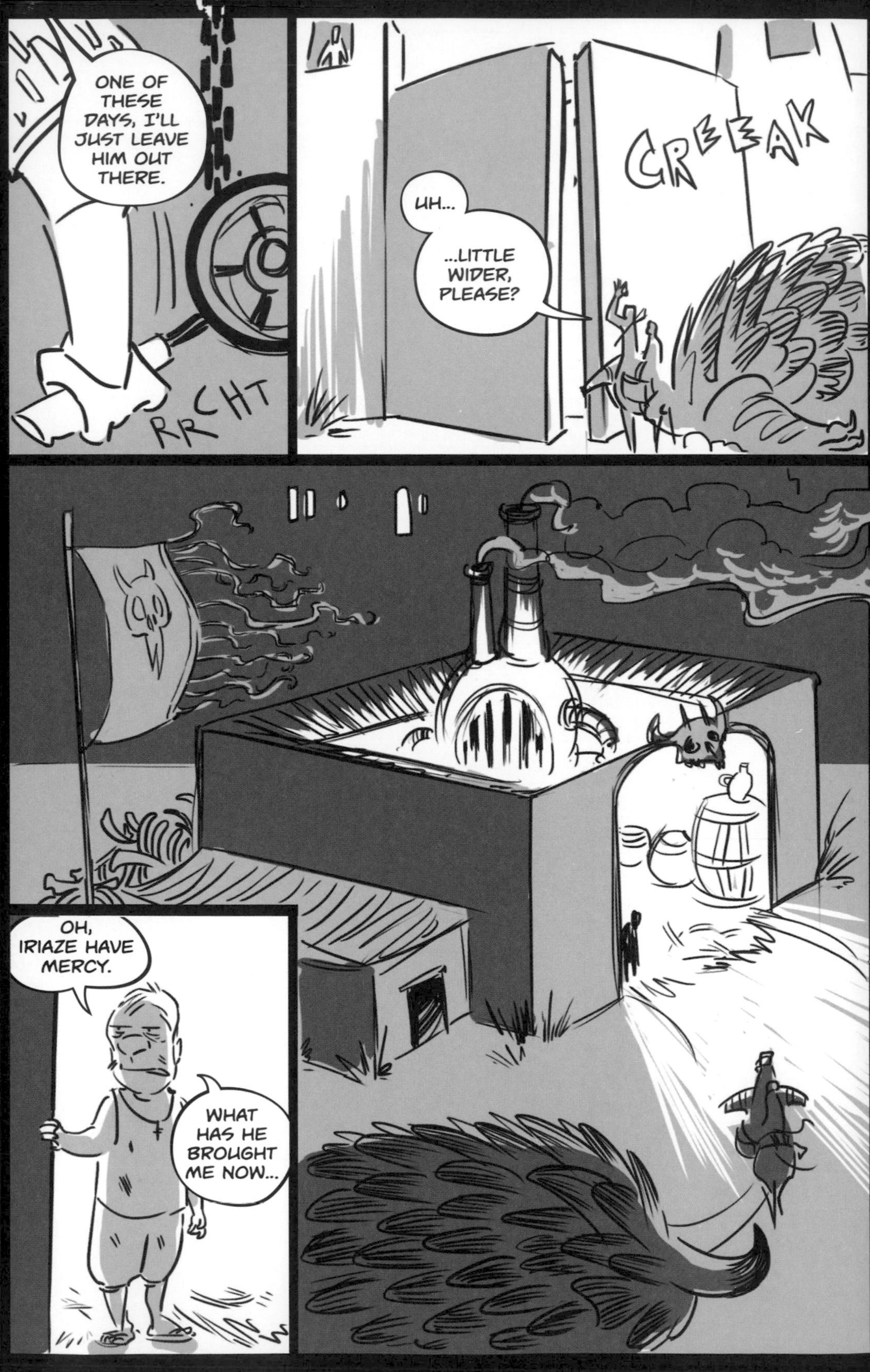

ONE OF THESE DAYS, I'LL JUST LEAVE HIM OUT THERE.
RRCHT
CREEAK
UH...
...LITTLE WIDER, PLEASE?
OH, IRIAZE HAVE MERCY.
WHAT HAS HE BROUGHT ME NOW...

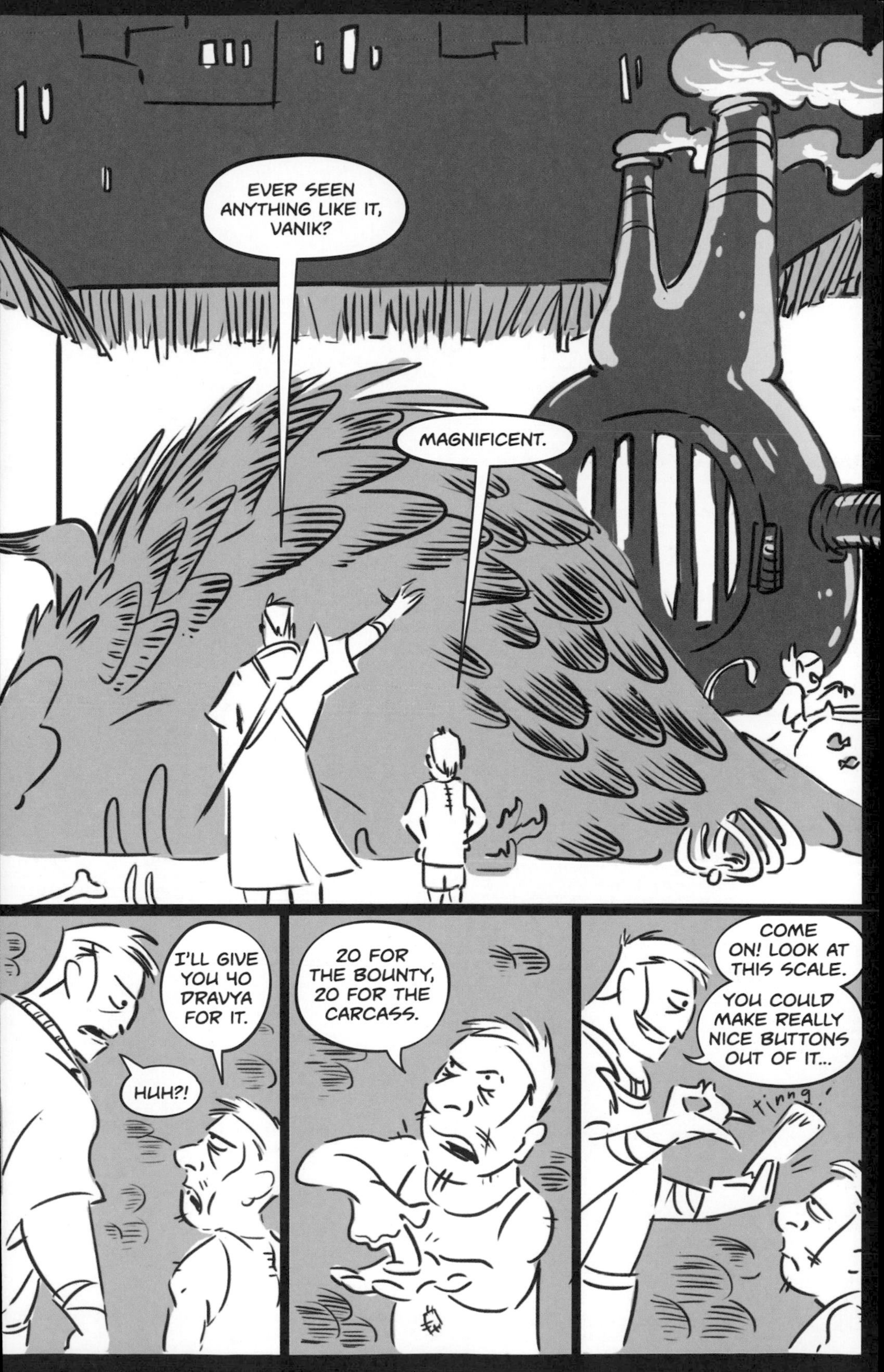
EVER SEEN ANYTHING LIKE IT, VANIK?
MAGNIFICENT.
I'LL GIVE YOU 40 DRAVYA FOR IT.
HUH?!
20 FOR THE BOUNTY, 20 FOR THE CARCASS.
COME ON! LOOK AT THIS SCALE.
YOU COULD MAKE REALLY NICE BUTTONS OUT OF IT...
tinng!

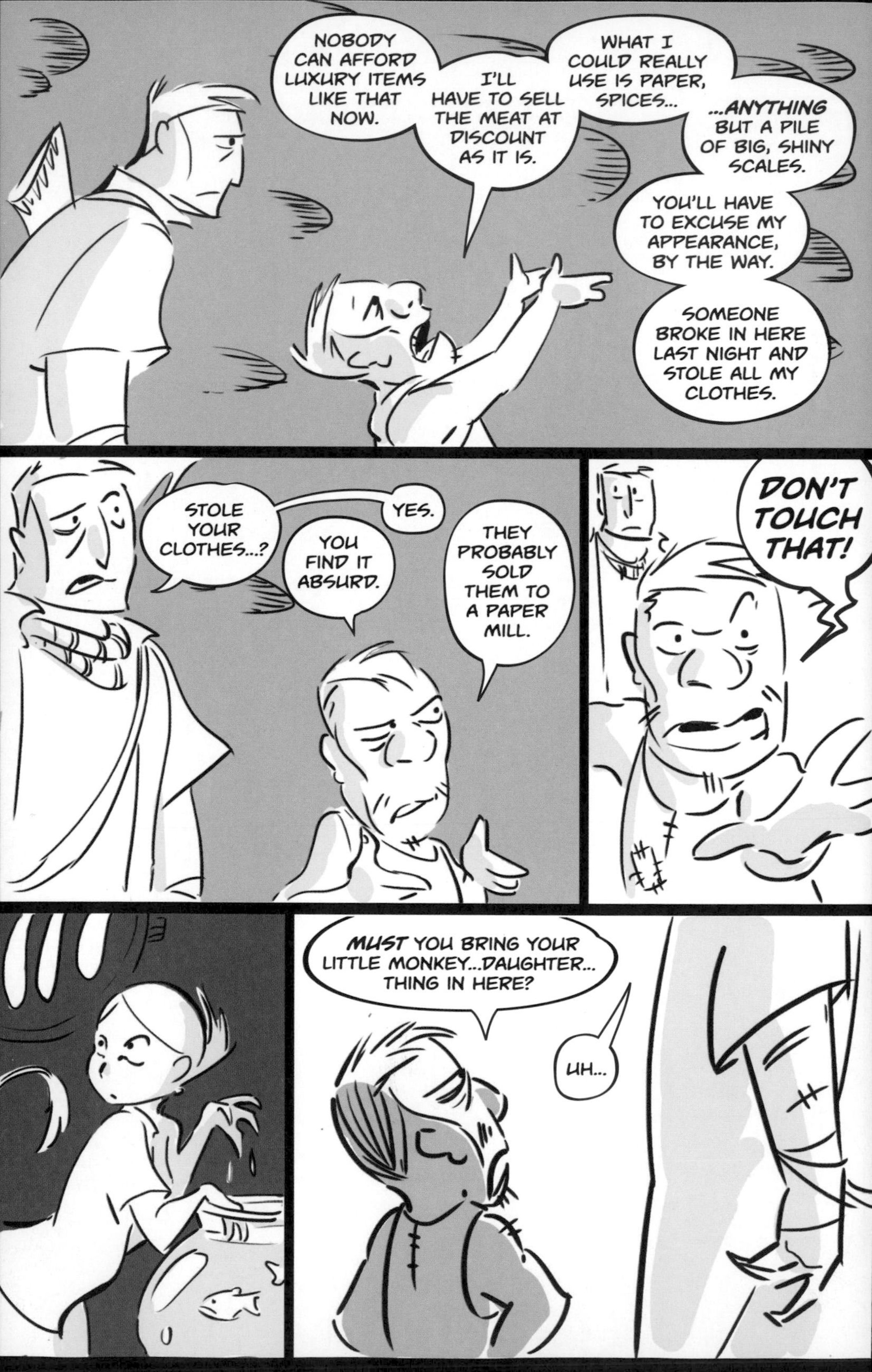
NOBODY CAN AFFORD LUXURY ITEMS LIKE THAT NOW.
I'LL HAVE TO SELL THE MEAT AT DISCOUNT AS IT IS.
WHAT I COULD REALLY USE IS PAPER, SPICES...
...ANYTHING BUT A PILE OF BIG, SHINY SCALES.
YOU'LL HAVE TO EXCUSE MY APPEARANCE, BY THE WAY.
SOMEONE BROKE IN HERE LAST NIGHT AND STOLE ALL MY CLOTHES.
STOLE YOUR CLOTHES...?
YES.
YOU FIND IT ABSURD.
THEY PROBABLY SOLD THEM TO A PAPER MILL.
DON'T TOUCH THAT!
MUST YOU BRING YOUR LITTLE MONKEY...DAUGHTER... THING IN HERE?
UH...

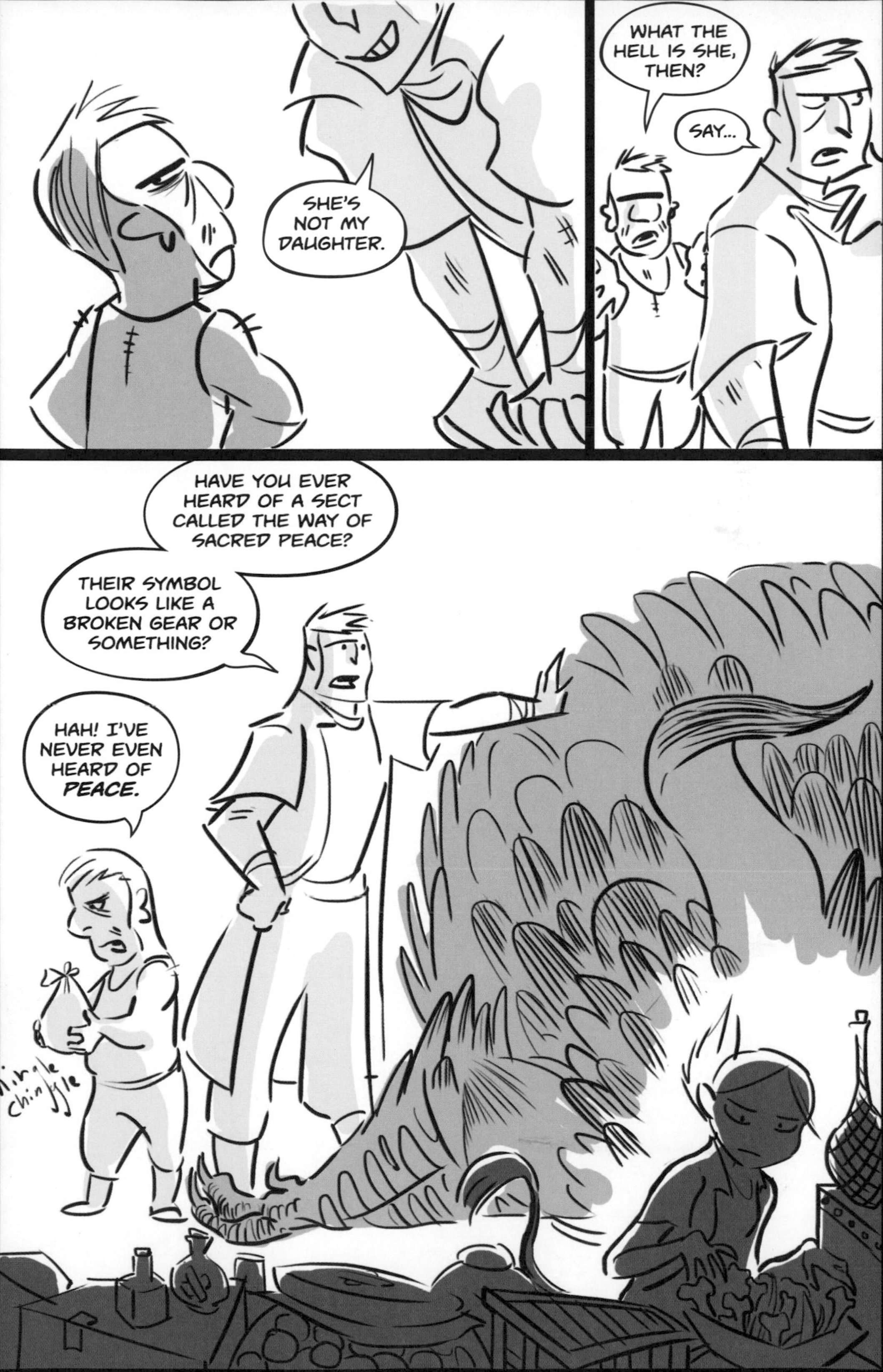
SHE'S NOT MY DAUGHTER.
WHAT THE HELL IS SHE, THEN?
SAY...
HAVE YOU EVER HEARD OF A SECT CALLED THE WAY OF SACRED PEACE?
THEIR SYMBOL LOOKS LIKE A BROKEN GEAR OR SOMETHING?
HAH! I'VE NEVER EVEN HEARD OF *PEACE.*
chingle

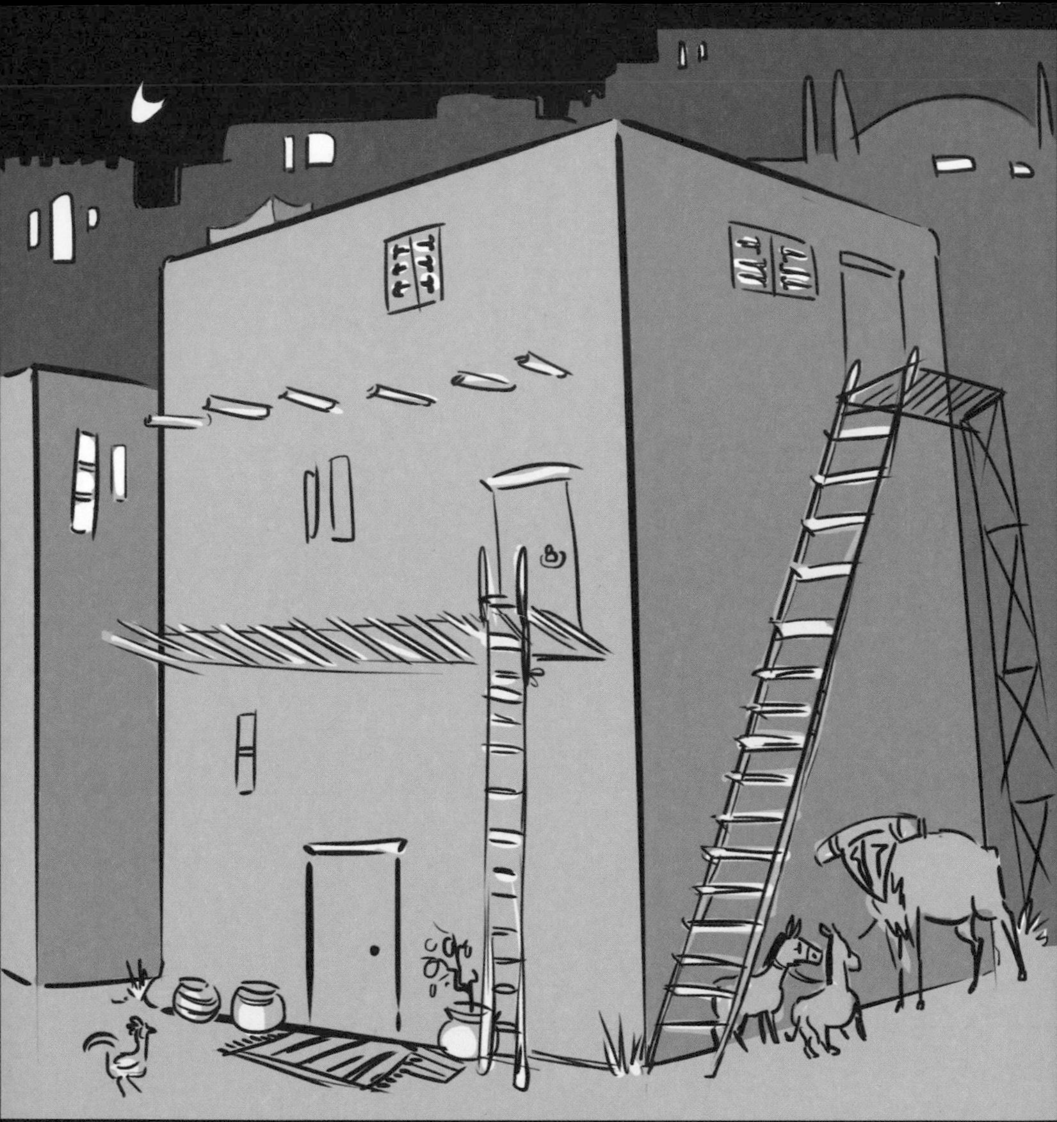

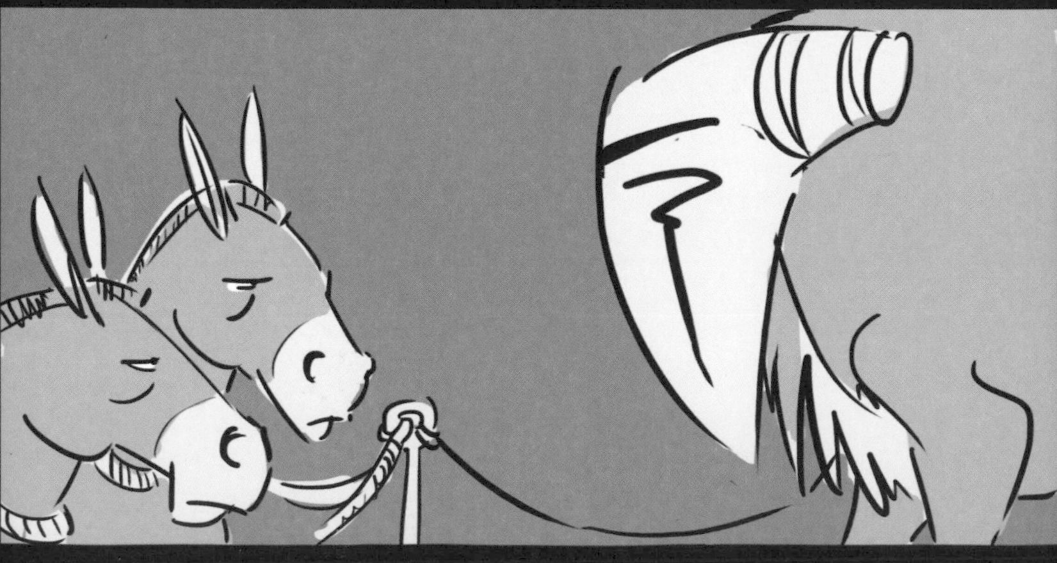

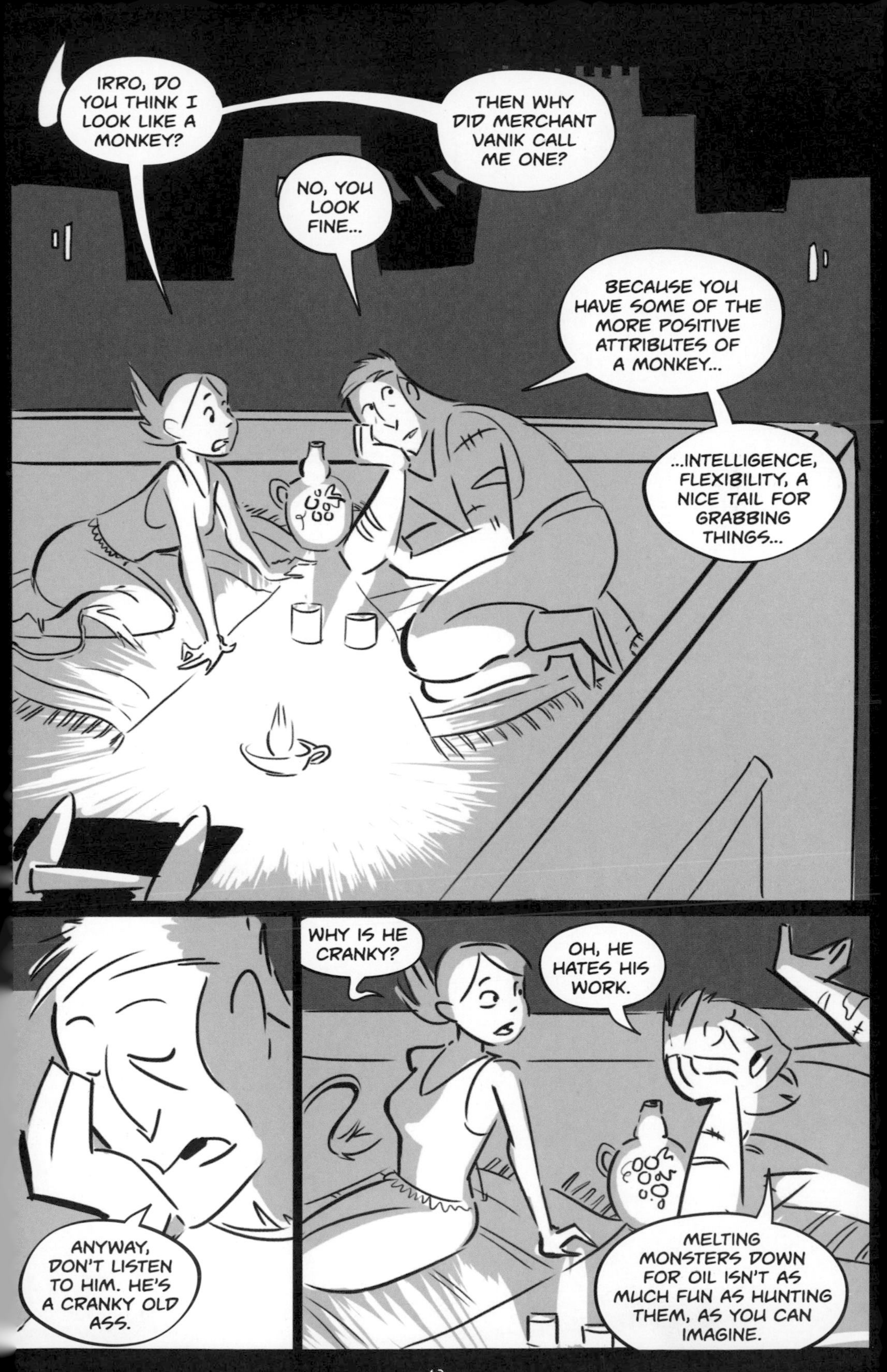
IRRO, DO YOU THINK I LOOK LIKE A MONKEY?
NO, YOU LOOK FINE...
THEN WHY DID MERCHANT VANIK CALL ME ONE?
BECAUSE YOU HAVE SOME OF THE MORE POSITIVE ATTRIBUTES OF A MONKEY...
...INTELLIGENCE, FLEXIBILITY, A NICE TAIL FOR GRABBING THINGS...
ANYWAY, DON'T LISTEN TO HIM. HE'S A CRANKY OLD ASS.
WHY IS HE CRANKY?
OH, HE HATES HIS WORK.
MELTING MONSTERS DOWN FOR OIL ISN'T AS MUCH FUN AS HUNTING THEM, AS YOU CAN IMAGINE.

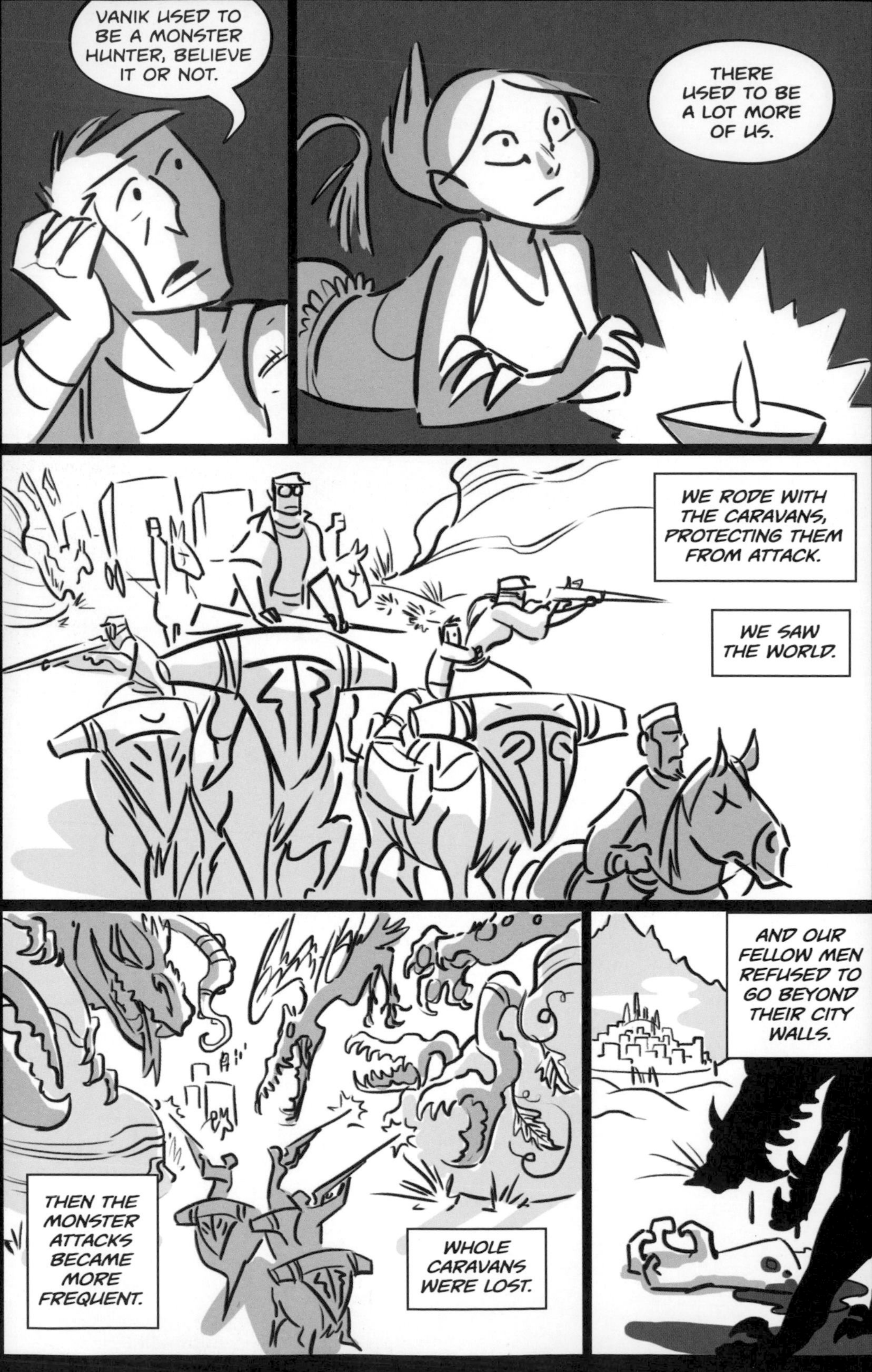
VANIK USED TO BE A MONSTER HUNTER, BELIEVE IT OR NOT.
THERE USED TO BE A LOT MORE OF US.
WE RODE WITH THE CARAVANS, PROTECTING THEM FROM ATTACK.
WE SAW THE WORLD.
THEN THE MONSTER ATTACKS BECAME MORE FREQUENT.
WHOLE CARAVANS WERE LOST.
AND OUR FELLOW MEN REFUSED TO GO BEYOND THEIR CITY WALLS.

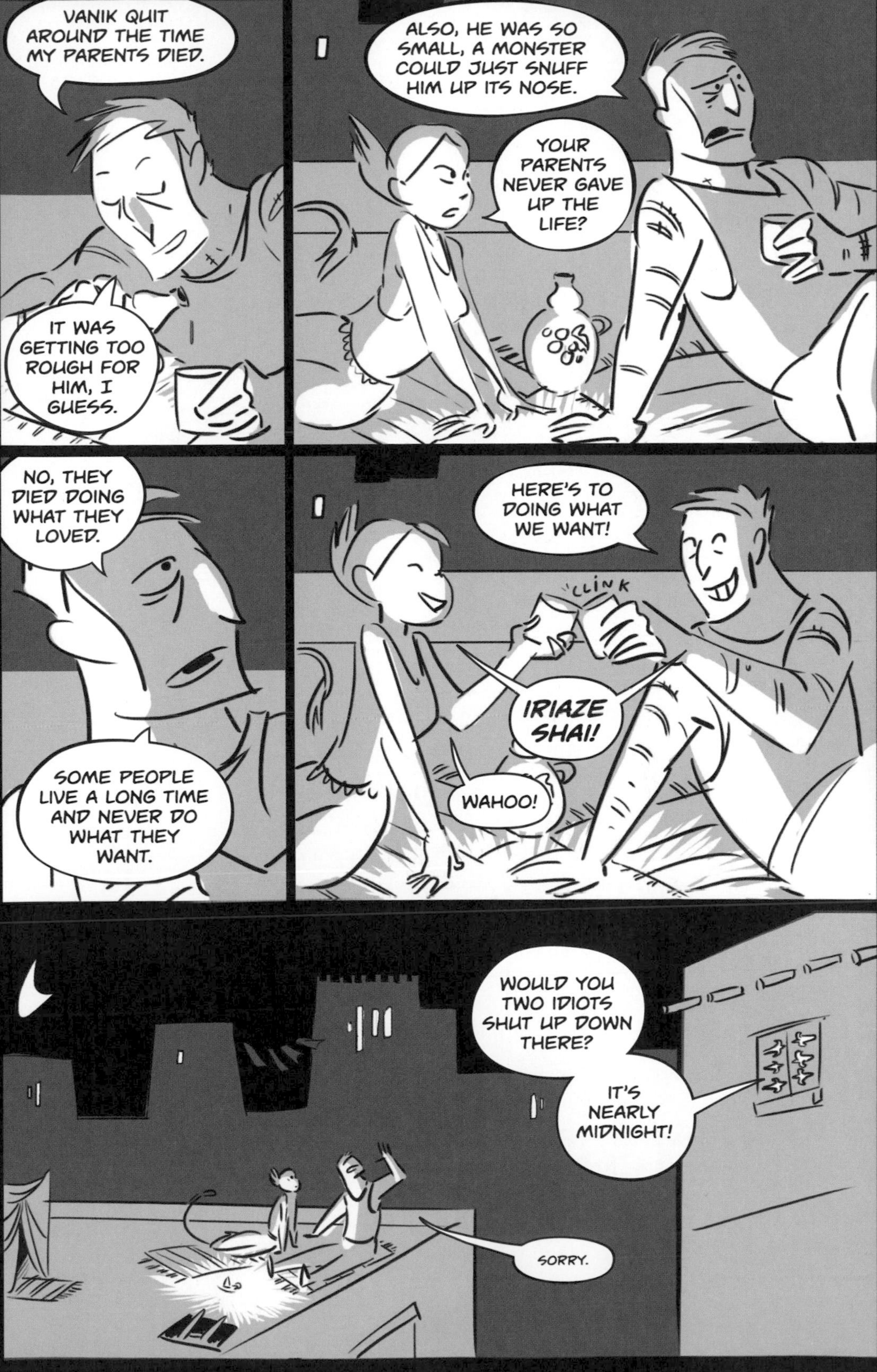
VANIK QUIT AROUND THE TIME MY PARENTS DIED.
IT WAS GETTING TOO ROUGH FOR HIM, I GUESS.
ALSO, HE WAS SO SMALL, A MONSTER COULD JUST SNUFF HIM UP ITS NOSE.
YOUR PARENTS NEVER GAVE UP THE LIFE?
NO, THEY DIED DOING WHAT THEY LOVED.
SOME PEOPLE LIVE A LONG TIME AND NEVER DO WHAT THEY WANT.
HERE'S TO DOING WHAT WE WANT!
CLINK
IRIAZE SHAI!
WAHOO!
WOULD YOU TWO IDIOTS SHUT UP DOWN THERE?
IT'S NEARLY MIDNIGHT!
SORRY.

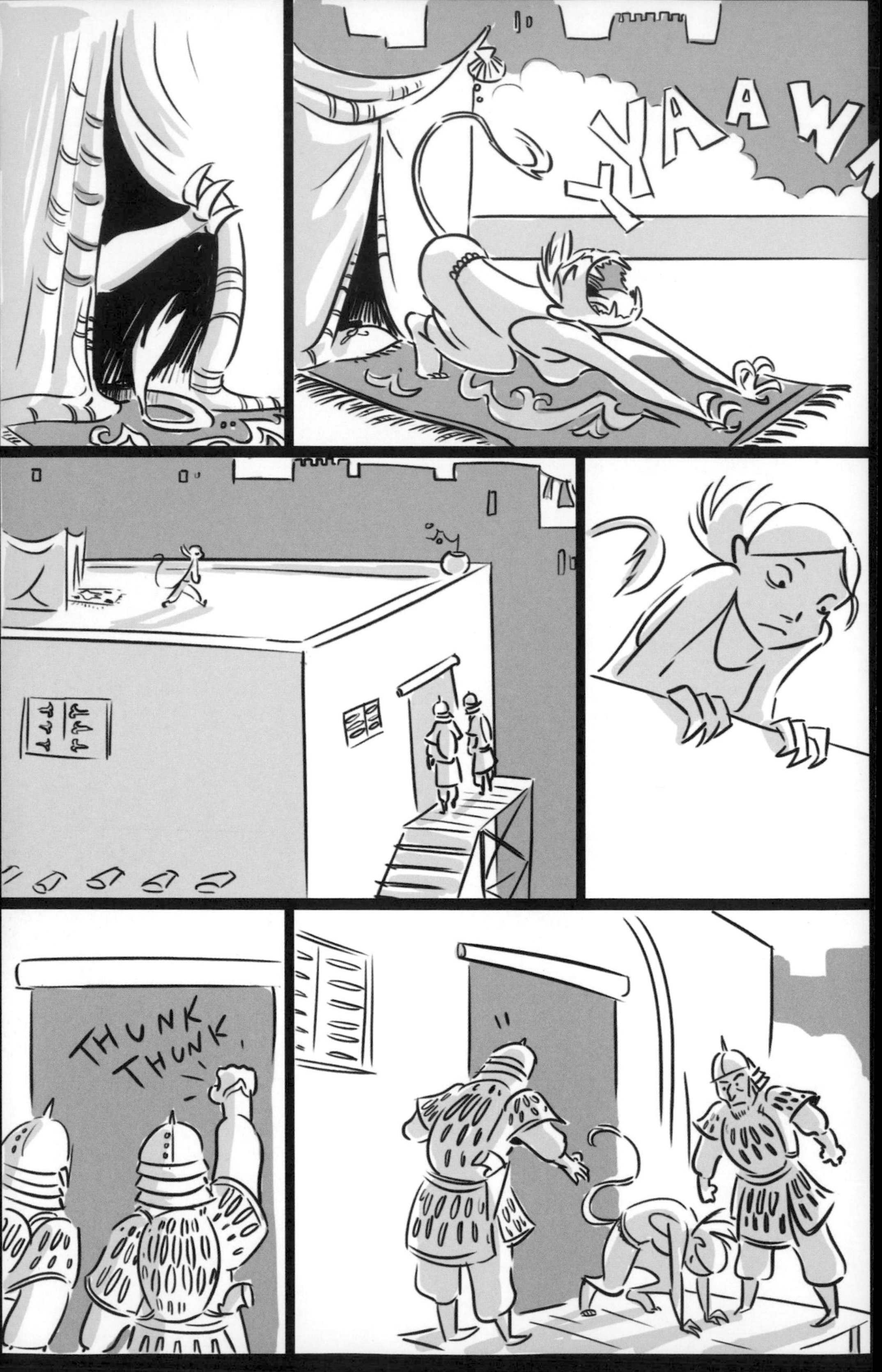
YAAWN
THUNK
THUNK

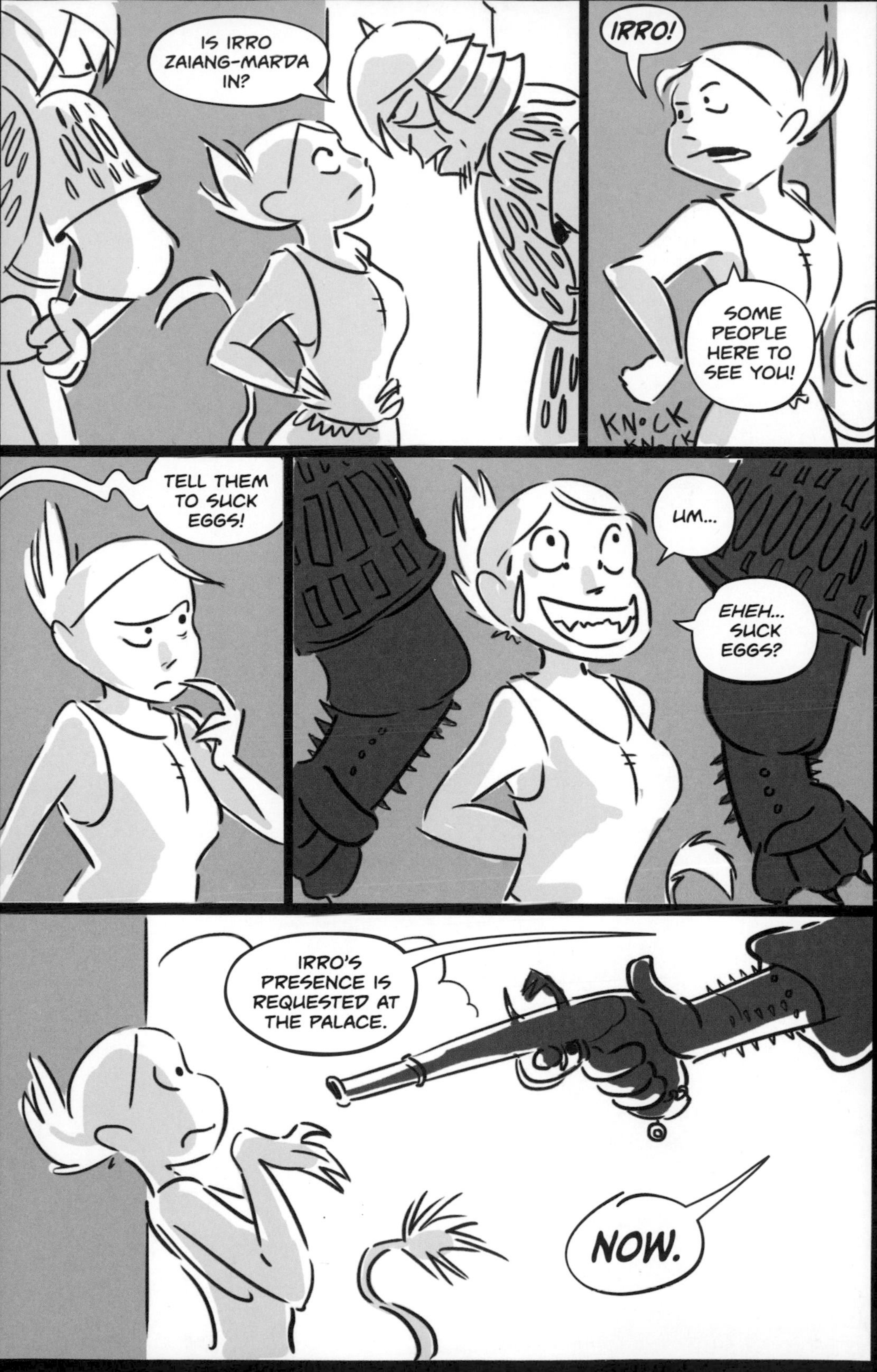
IS IRRO ZAIANG-MARDA IN?
IRRO!
SOME PEOPLE HERE TO SEE YOU!
KNOCK
TELL THEM TO SUCK EGGS!
UM...
EHEH... SUCK EGGS?
IRRO'S PRESENCE IS REQUESTED AT THE PALACE.
NOW.

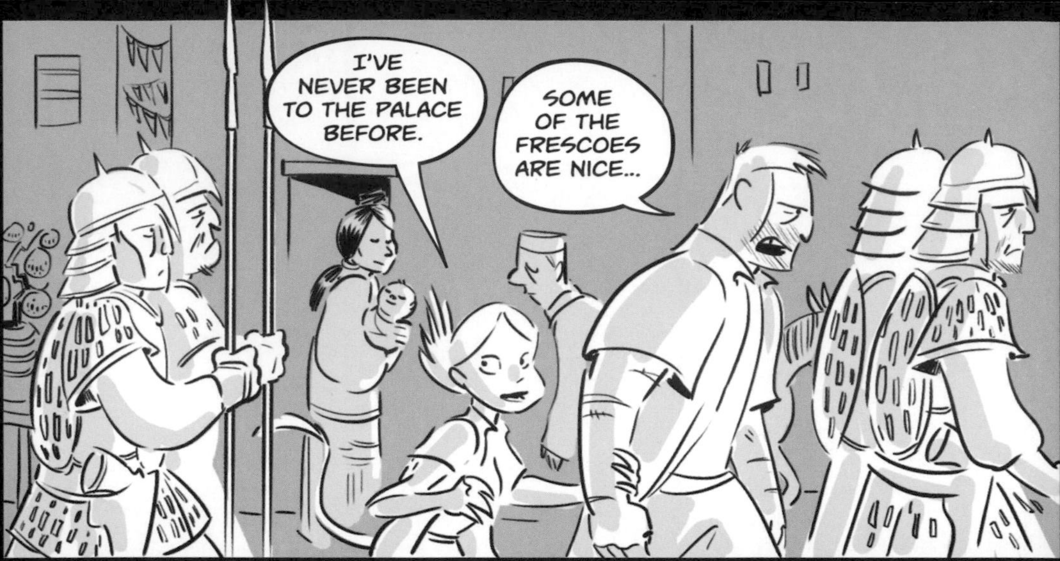
I'VE NEVER BEEN TO THE PALACE BEFORE.
SOME OF THE FRESCOES ARE NICE...

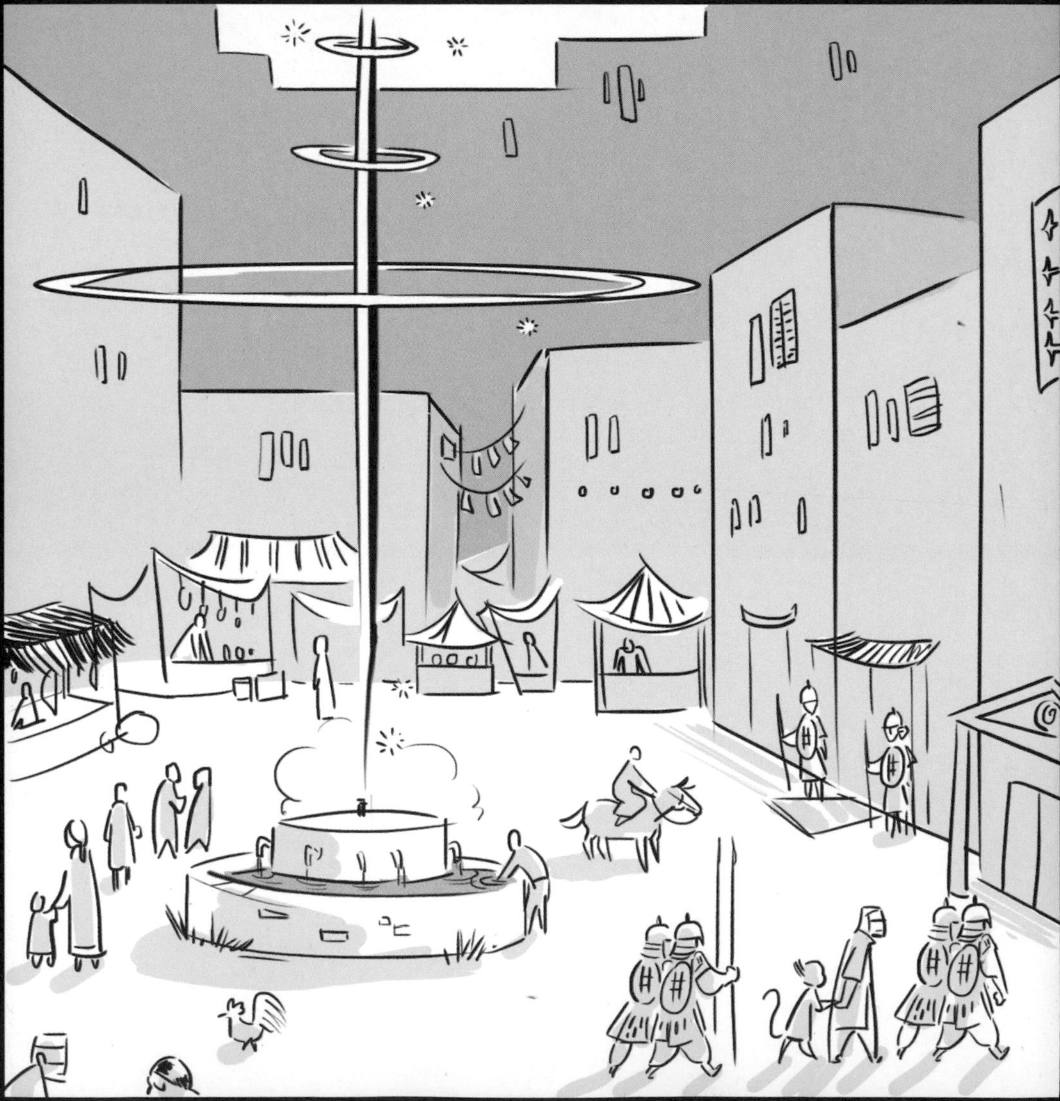

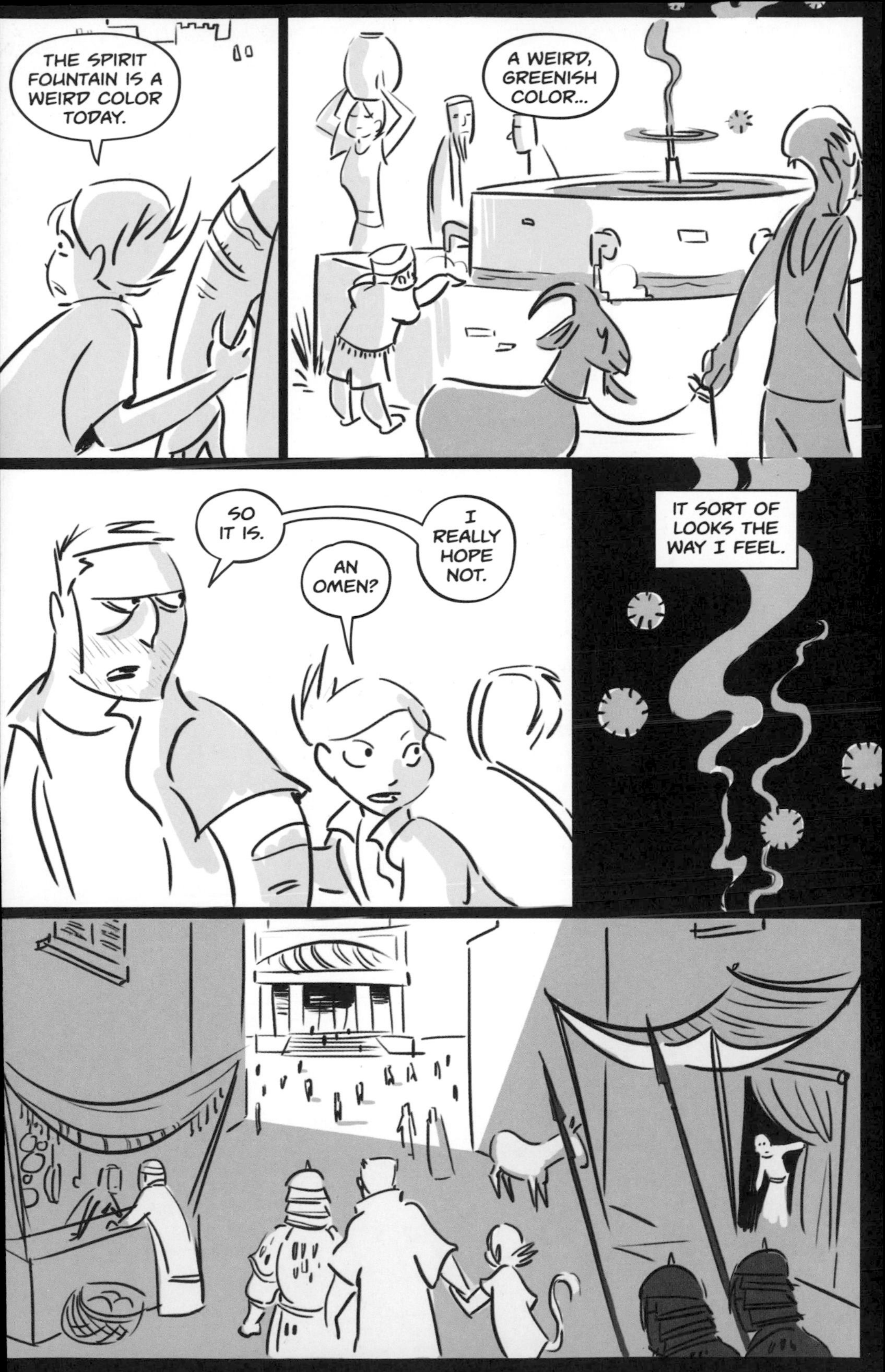
THE SPIRIT FOUNTAIN IS A WEIRD COLOR TODAY.
A WEIRD, GREENISH COLOR...
SO IT IS.
AN OMEN?
I REALLY HOPE NOT.
IT SORT OF LOOKS THE WAY I FEEL.

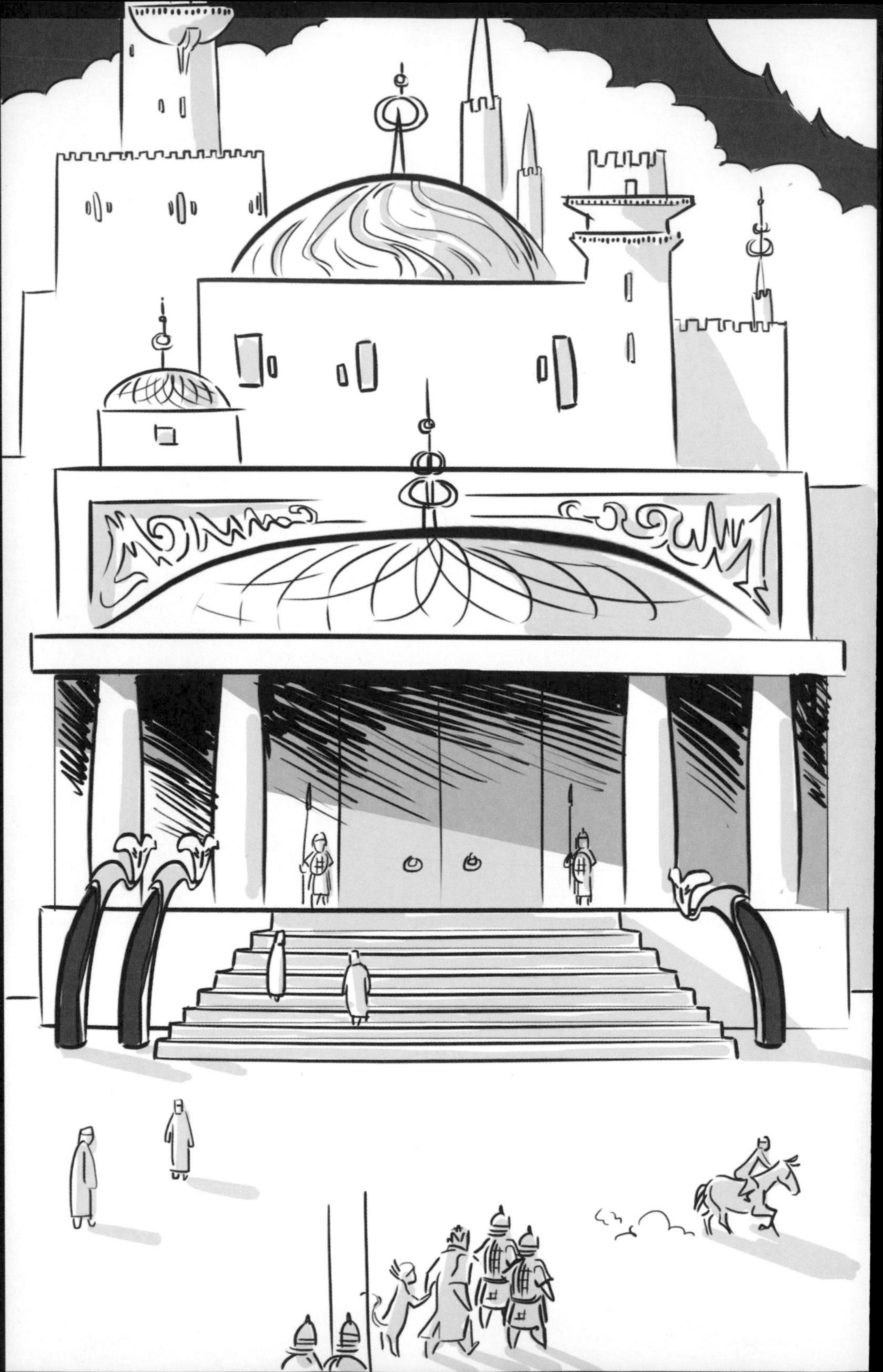

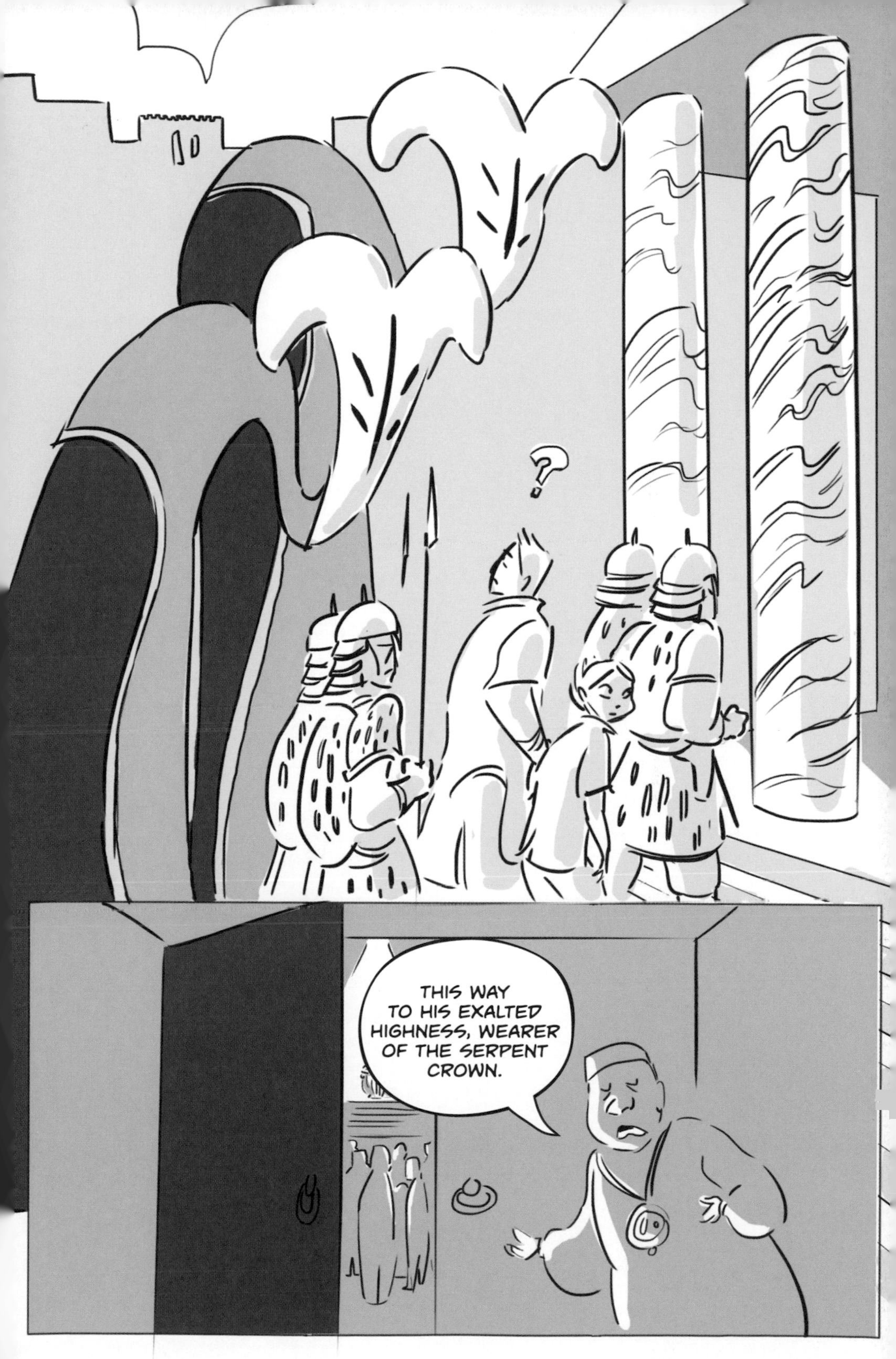
?
THIS WAY TO HIS EXALTED HIGHNESS, WEARER OF THE SERPENT CROWN.

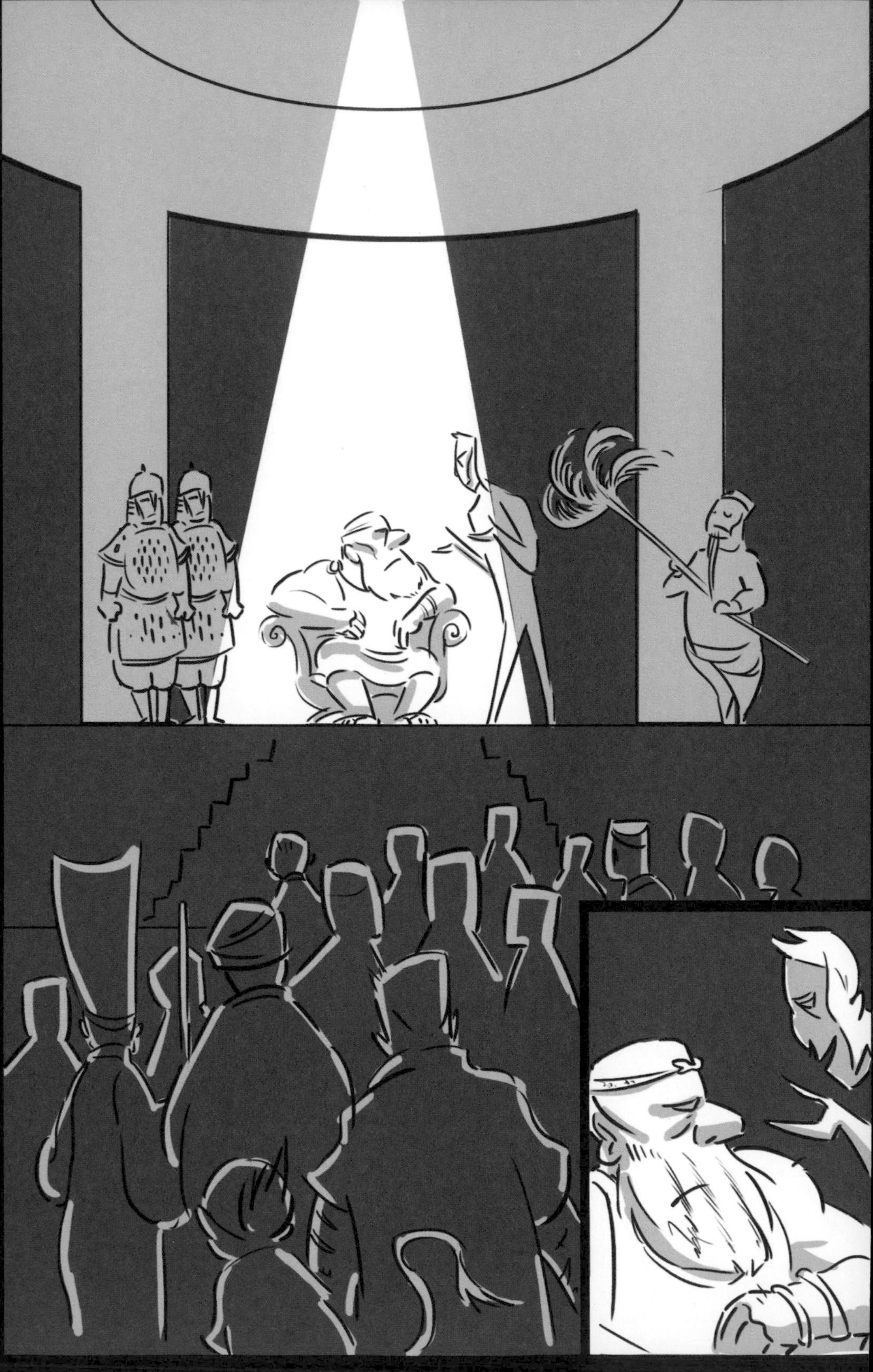

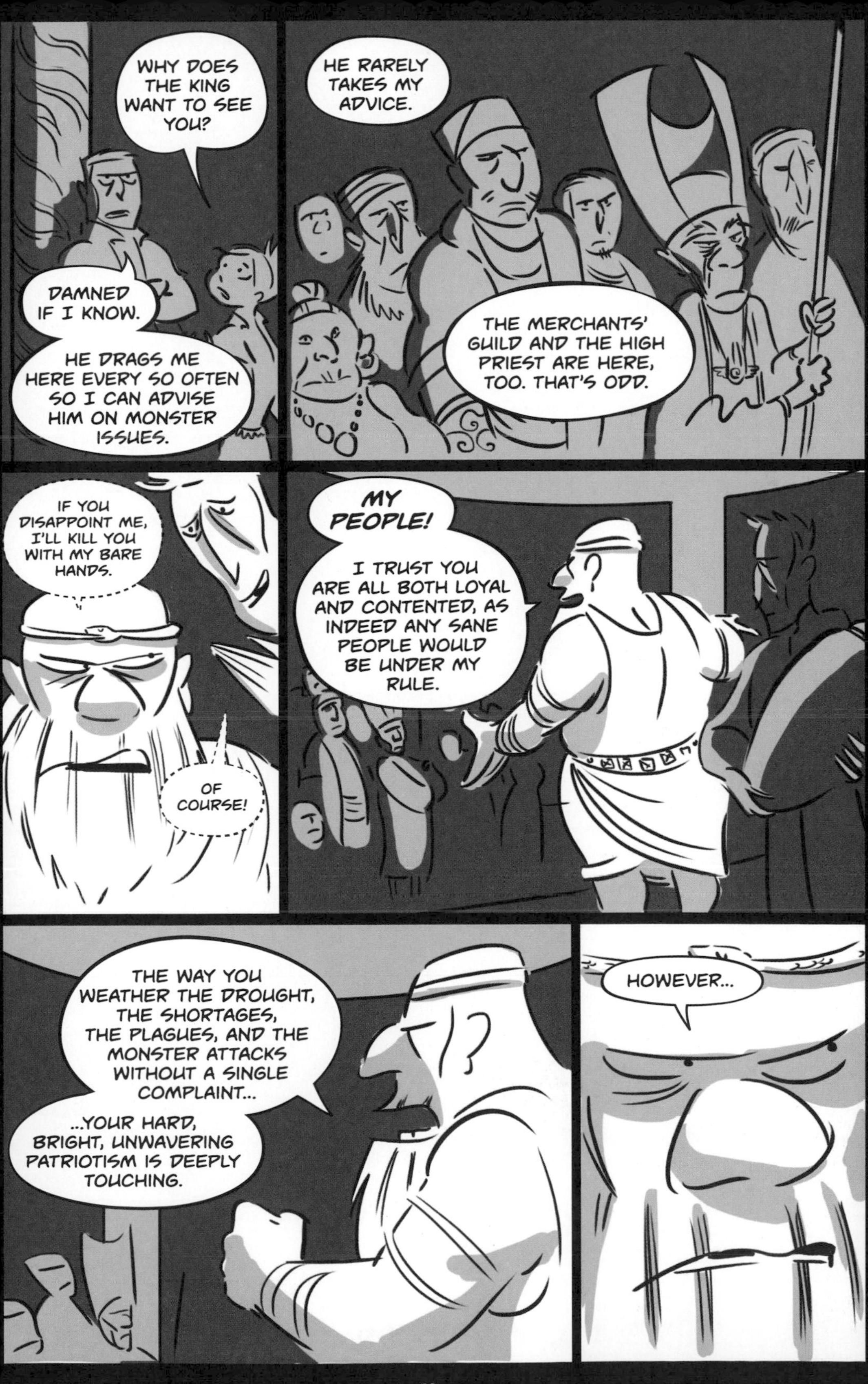
WHY DOES THE KING WANT TO SEE YOU?
DAMNED IF I KNOW.
HE DRAGS ME HERE EVERY SO OFTEN SO I CAN ADVISE HIM ON MONSTER ISSUES.
HE RARELY TAKES MY ADVICE.
THE MERCHANTS' GUILD AND THE HIGH PRIEST ARE HERE, TOO. THAT'S ODD.
IF YOU DISAPPOINT ME, I'LL KILL YOU WITH MY BARE HANDS.
OF COURSE!
MY PEOPLE!
I TRUST YOU ARE ALL BOTH LOYAL AND CONTENTED, AS INDEED ANY SANE PEOPLE WOULD BE UNDER MY RULE.
THE WAY YOU WEATHER THE DROUGHT, THE SHORTAGES, THE PLAGUES, AND THE MONSTER ATTACKS WITHOUT A SINGLE COMPLAINT...
...YOUR HARD, BRIGHT, UNWAVERING PATRIOTISM IS DEEPLY TOUCHING.
HOWEVER...

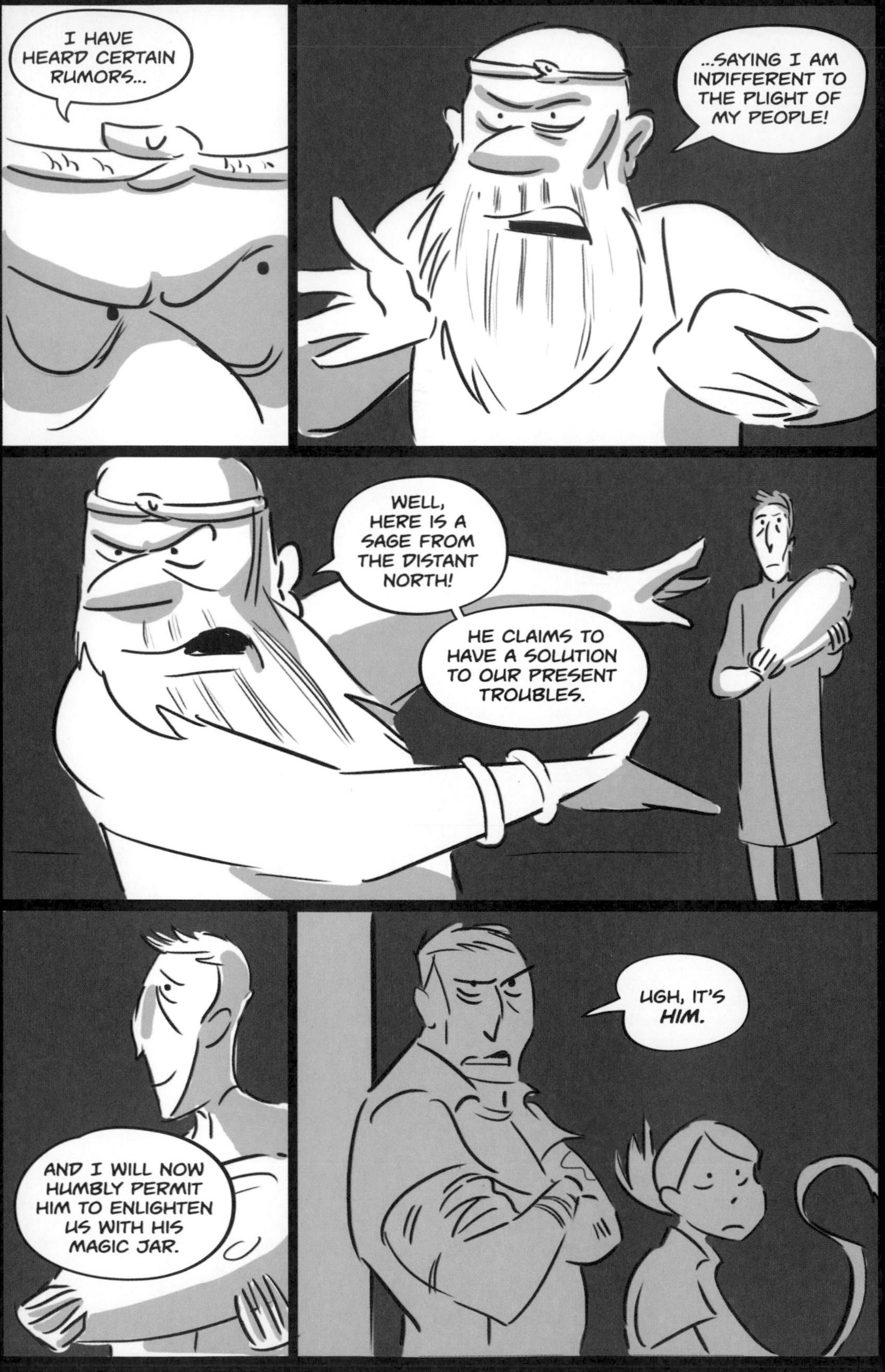
I HAVE HEARD CERTAIN RUMORS...
...SAYING I AM INDIFFERENT TO THE PLIGHT OF MY PEOPLE!
WELL, HERE IS A SAGE FROM THE DISTANT NORTH!
HE CLAIMS TO HAVE A SOLUTION TO OUR PRESENT TROUBLES.
AND I WILL NOW HUMBLY PERMIT HIM TO ENLIGHTEN US WITH HIS MAGIC JAR.
UGH, IT'S *HIM.*

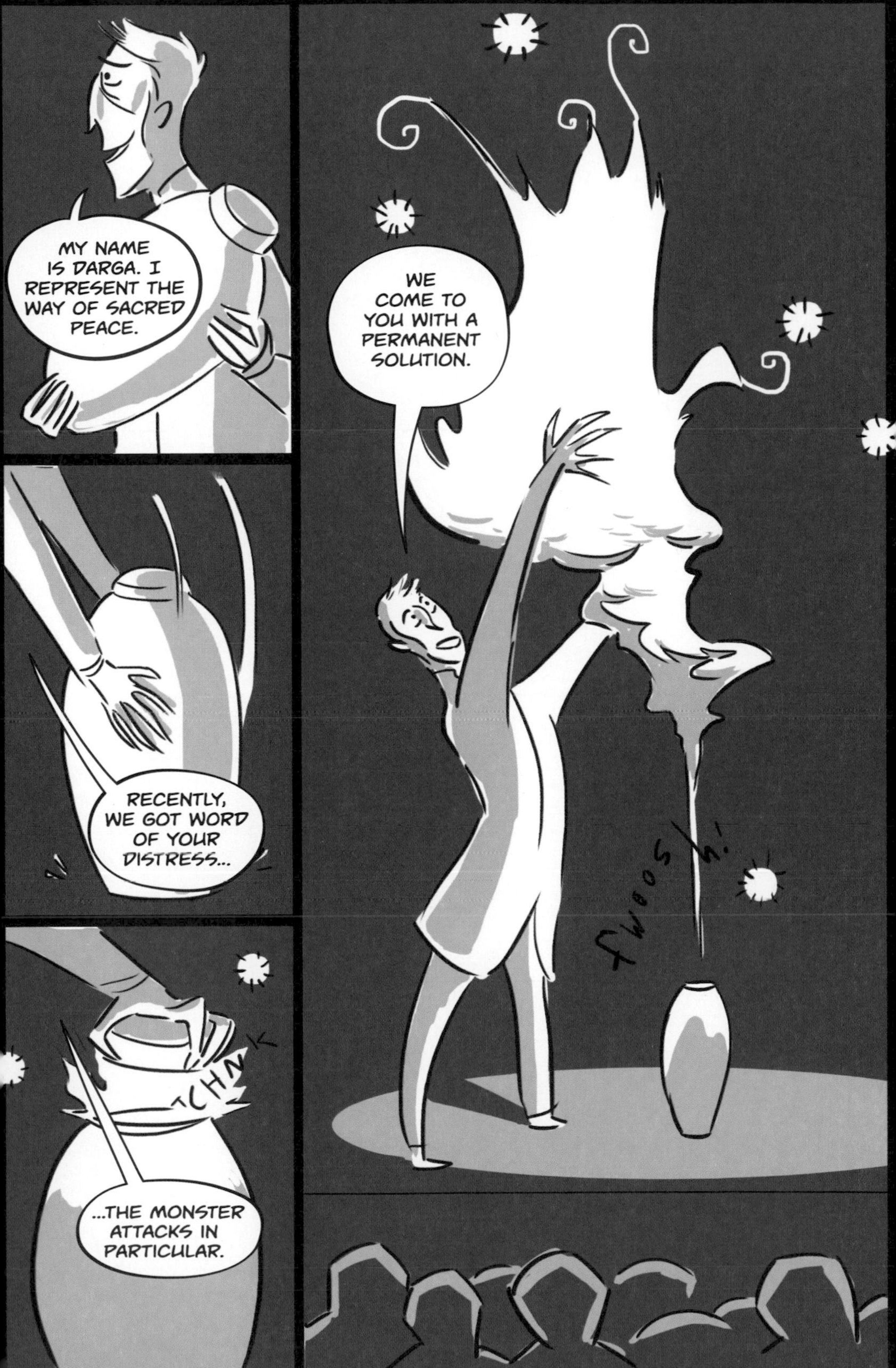
MY NAME IS DARGA. I REPRESENT THE WAY OF SACRED PEACE.
RECENTLY, WE GOT WORD OF YOUR DISTRESS...
...THE MONSTER ATTACKS IN PARTICULAR.
^CHNK
WE COME TO YOU WITH A PERMANENT SOLUTION.
fwoosh!

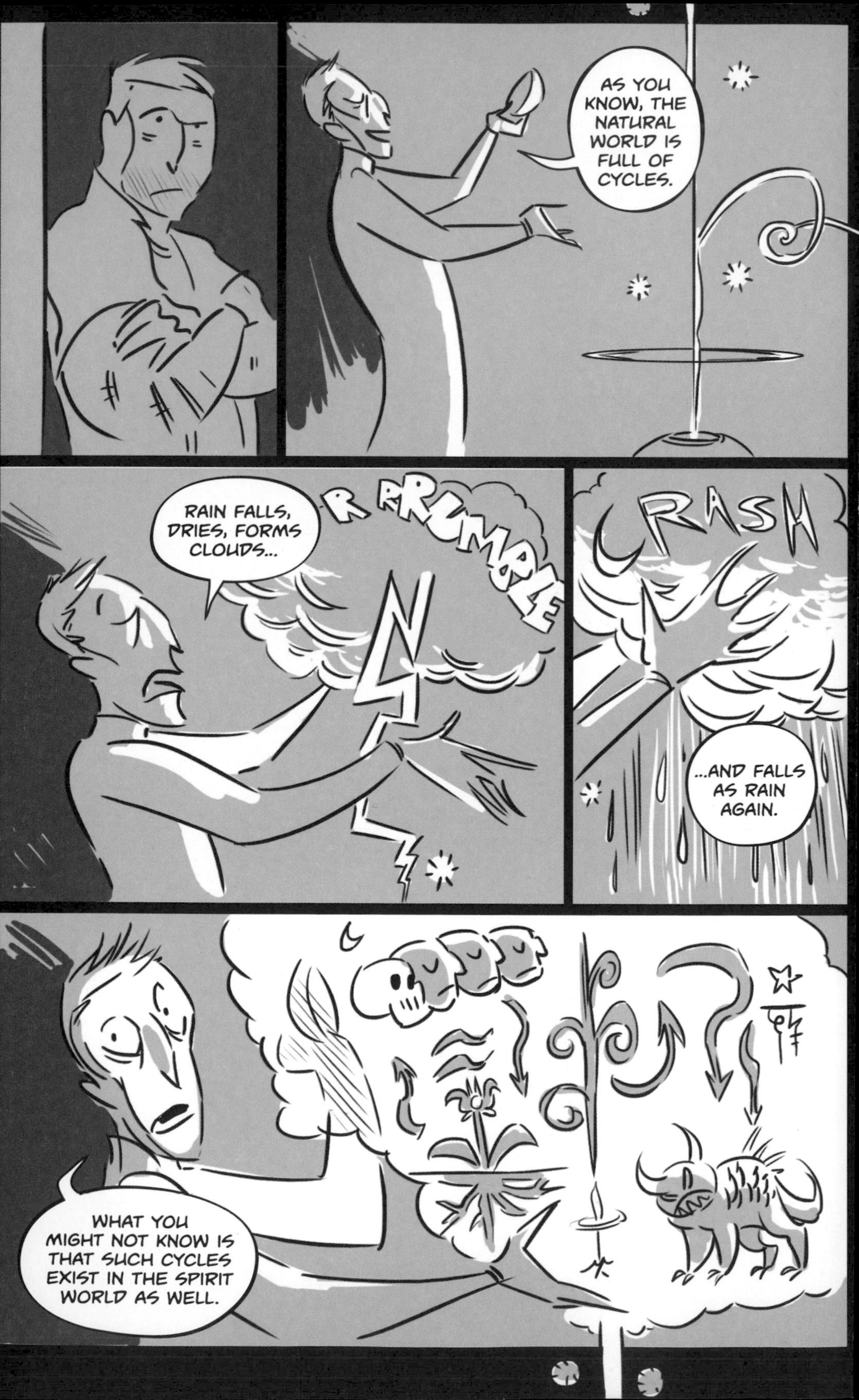
AS YOU KNOW, THE NATURAL WORLD IS FULL OF CYCLES.
RAIN FALLS, DRIES, FORMS CLOUDS...
R RRUMBLE
CRASH
...AND FALLS AS RAIN AGAIN.
WHAT YOU MIGHT NOT KNOW IS THAT SUCH CYCLES EXIST IN THE SPIRIT WORLD AS WELL.

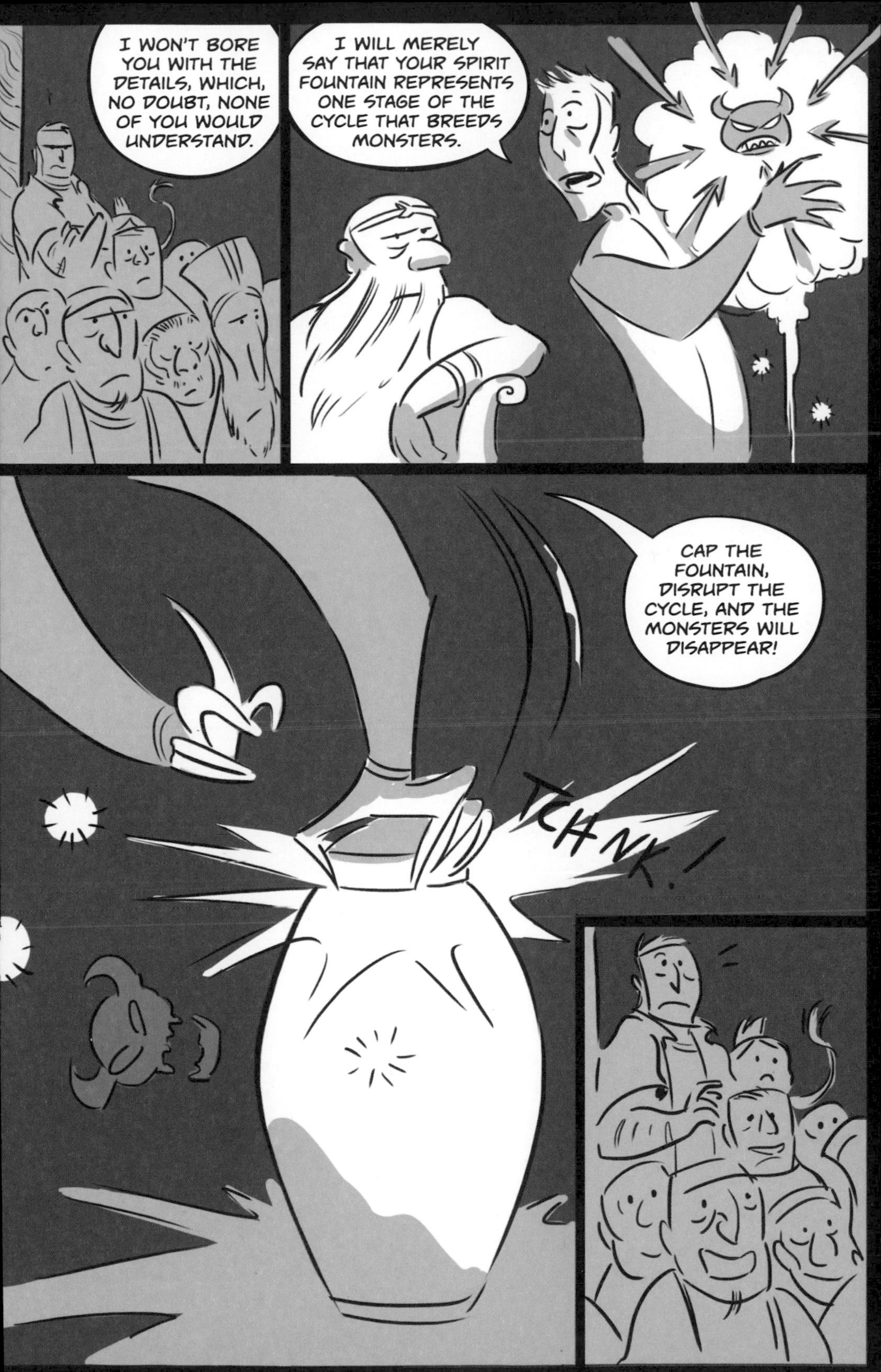
I WON'T BORE YOU WITH THE DETAILS, WHICH, NO DOUBT, NONE OF YOU WOULD UNDERSTAND.
I WILL MERELY SAY THAT YOUR SPIRIT FOUNTAIN REPRESENTS ONE STAGE OF THE CYCLE THAT BREEDS MONSTERS.
CAP THE FOUNTAIN, DISRUPT THE CYCLE, AND THE MONSTERS WILL DISAPPEAR!
TCHNK.!

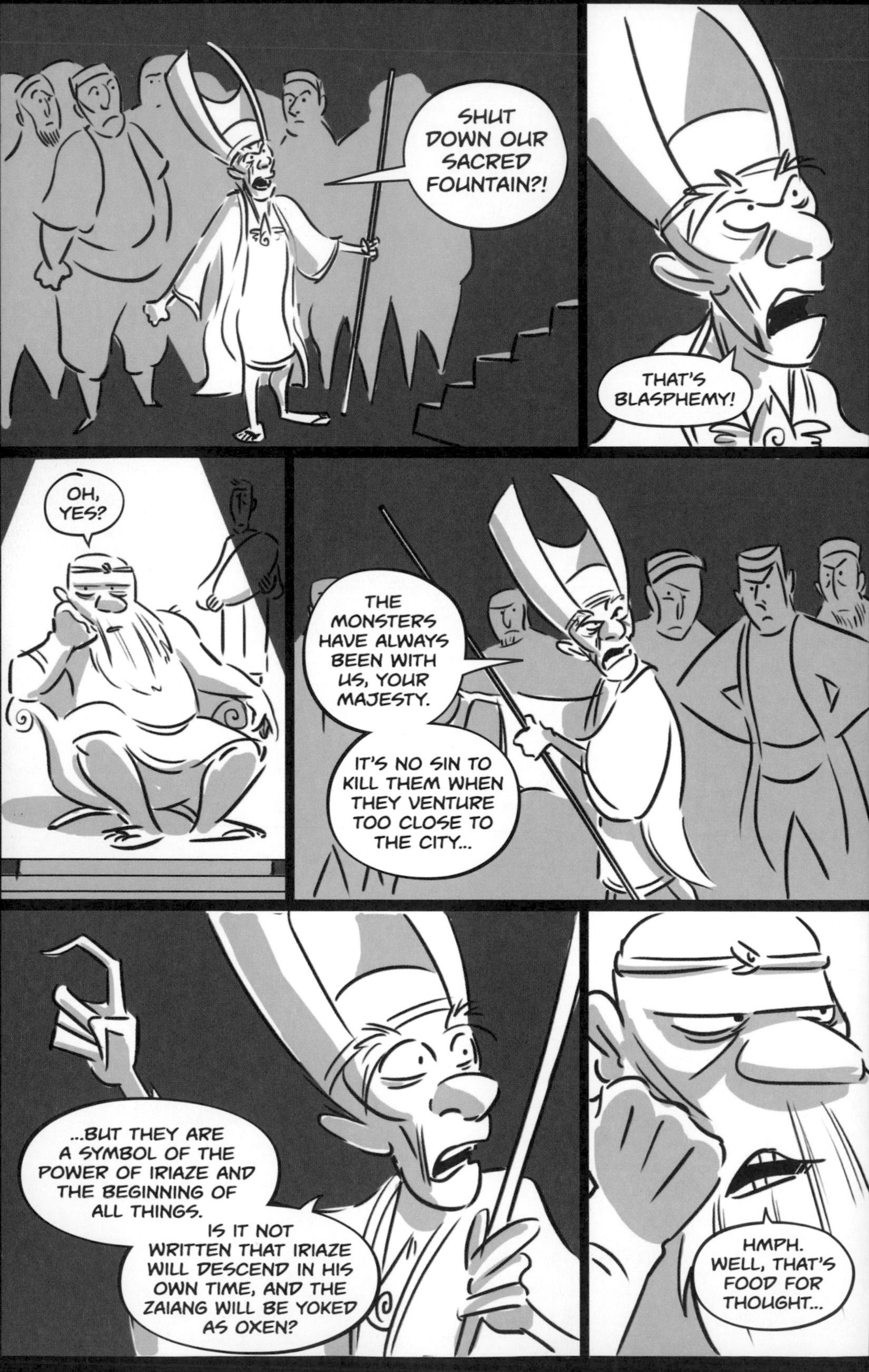
SHUT DOWN OUR SACRED FOUNTAIN?!
THAT'S BLASPHEMY!
OH, YES?
THE MONSTERS HAVE ALWAYS BEEN WITH US, YOUR MAJESTY.
IT'S NO SIN TO KILL THEM WHEN THEY VENTURE TOO CLOSE TO THE CITY...
...BUT THEY ARE A SYMBOL OF THE POWER OF IRIAZE AND THE BEGINNING OF ALL THINGS.
IS IT NOT WRITTEN THAT IRIAZE WILL DESCEND IN HIS OWN TIME, AND THE ZAIANG WILL BE YOKED AS OXEN?
HMPH. WELL, THAT'S FOOD FOR THOUGHT...

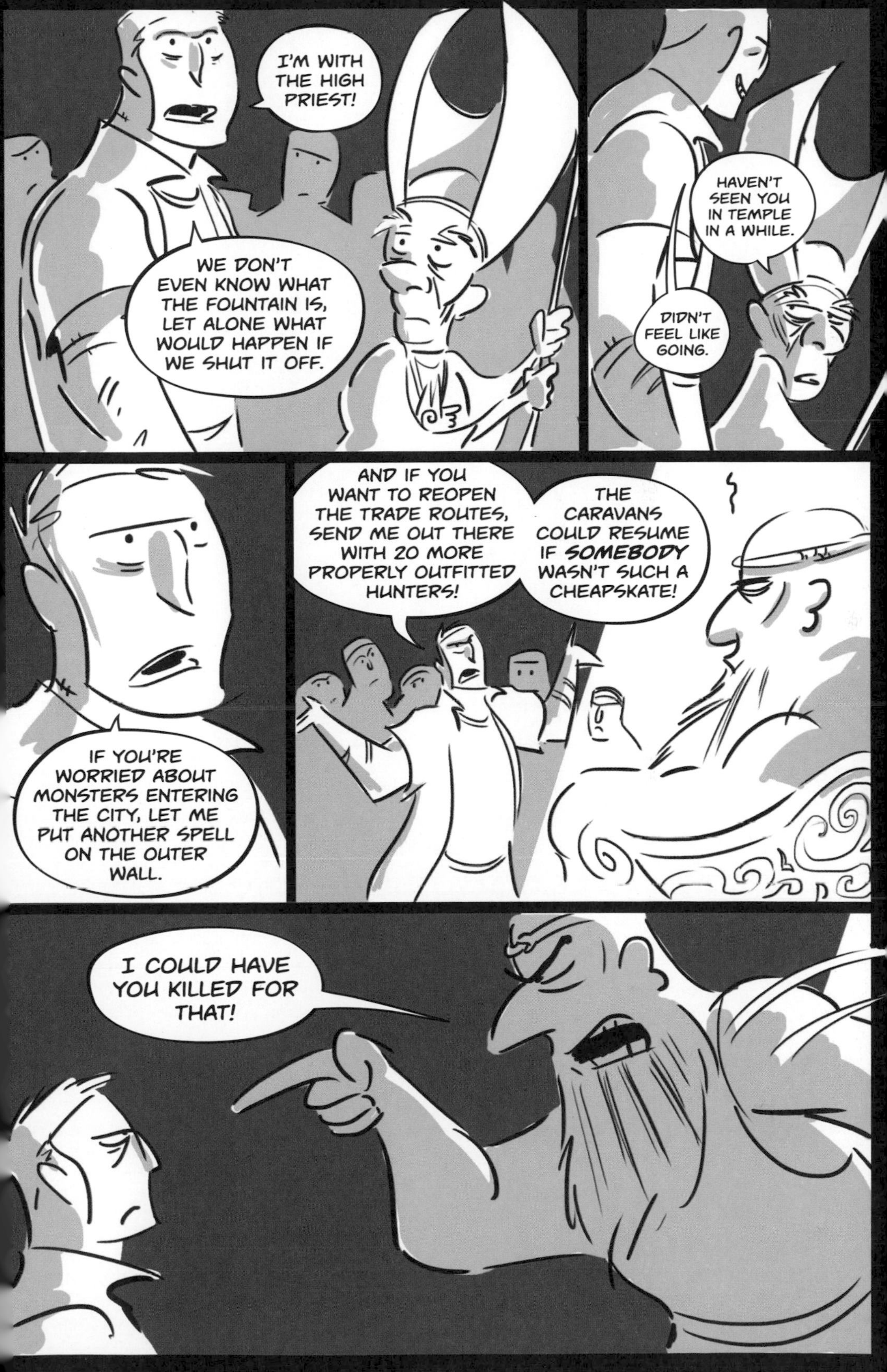
I'M WITH THE HIGH PRIEST!
WE DON'T EVEN KNOW WHAT THE FOUNTAIN IS, LET ALONE WHAT WOULD HAPPEN IF WE SHUT IT OFF.
HAVEN'T SEEN YOU IN TEMPLE IN A WHILE.
DIDN'T FEEL LIKE GOING.
IF YOU'RE WORRIED ABOUT MONSTERS ENTERING THE CITY, LET ME PUT ANOTHER SPELL ON THE OUTER WALL.
AND IF YOU WANT TO REOPEN THE TRADE ROUTES, SEND ME OUT THERE WITH 20 MORE PROPERLY OUTFITTED HUNTERS!
THE CARAVANS COULD RESUME IF SOMEBODY WASN'T SUCH A CHEAPSKATE!
I COULD HAVE YOU KILLED FOR THAT!

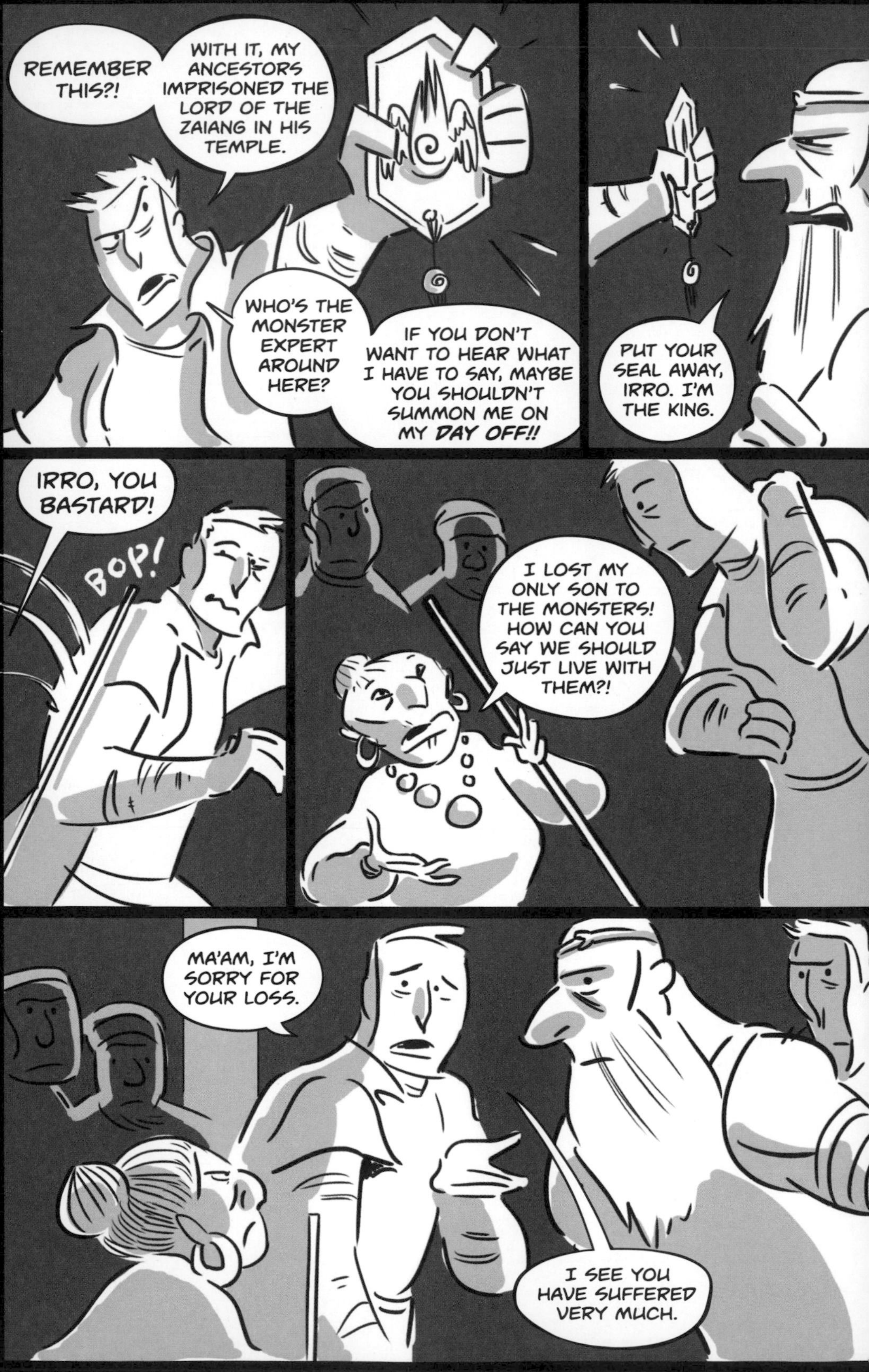
REMEMBER THIS?!
WITH IT, MY ANCESTORS IMPRISONED THE LORD OF THE ZAIANG IN HIS TEMPLE.
WHO'S THE MONSTER EXPERT AROUND HERE?
IF YOU DON'T WANT TO HEAR WHAT I HAVE TO SAY, MAYBE YOU SHOULDN'T SUMMON ME ON MY DAY OFF!!
PUT YOUR SEAL AWAY, IRRO. I'M THE KING.
IRRO, YOU BASTARD!
BOP!
I LOST MY ONLY SON TO THE MONSTERS! HOW CAN YOU SAY WE SHOULD JUST LIVE WITH THEM?!
MA'AM, I'M SORRY FOR YOUR LOSS.
I SEE YOU HAVE SUFFERED VERY MUCH.

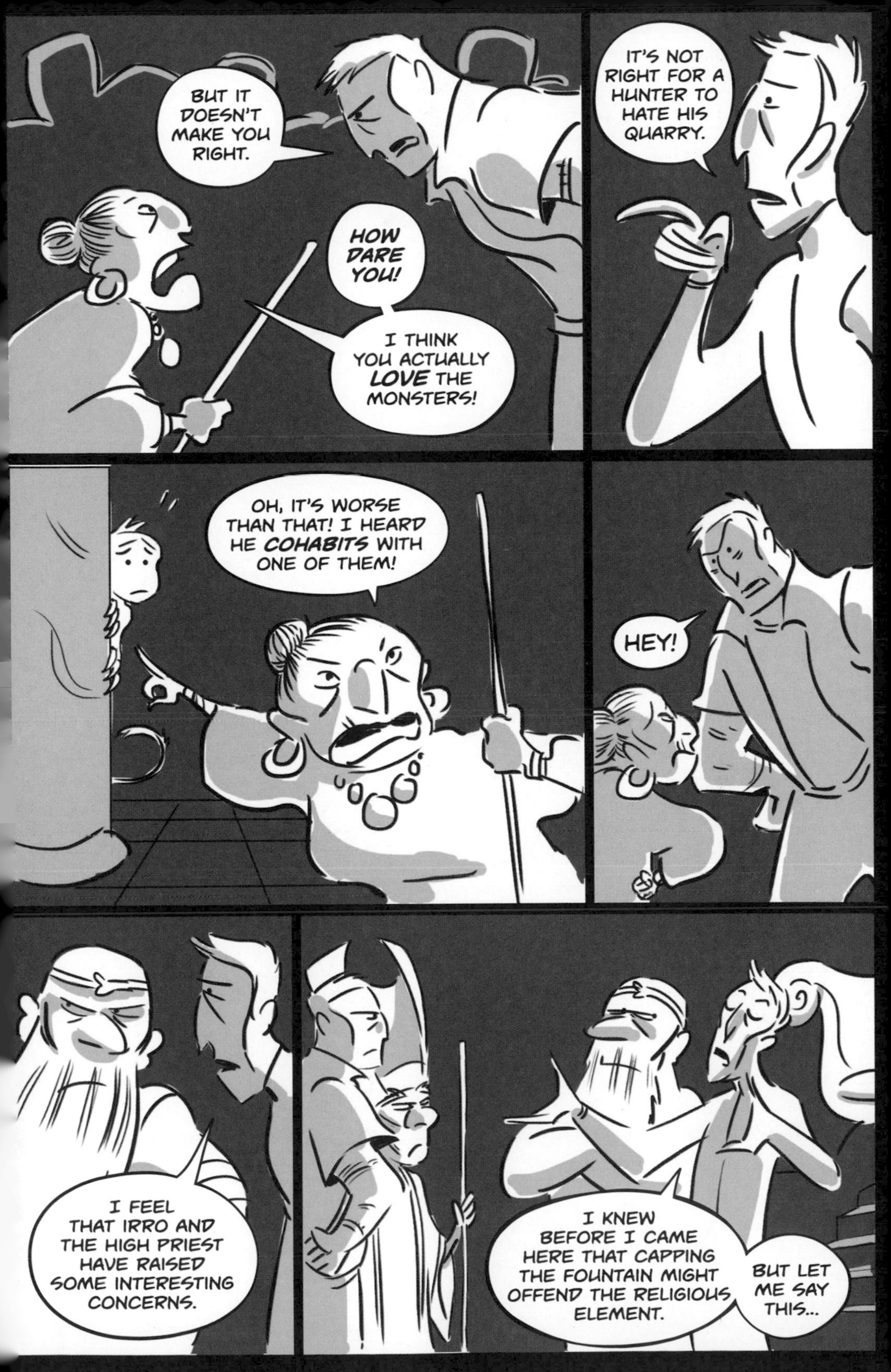
BUT IT DOESN'T MAKE YOU RIGHT.
HOW DARE YOU!
I THINK YOU ACTUALLY LOVE THE MONSTERS!
IT'S NOT RIGHT FOR A HUNTER TO HATE HIS QUARRY.
OH, IT'S WORSE THAN THAT! I HEARD HE COHABITS WITH ONE OF THEM!
HEY!
I FEEL THAT IRRO AND THE HIGH PRIEST HAVE RAISED SOME INTERESTING CONCERNS.
I KNEW BEFORE I CAME HERE THAT CAPPING THE FOUNTAIN MIGHT OFFEND THE RELIGIOUS ELEMENT.
BUT LET ME SAY THIS...

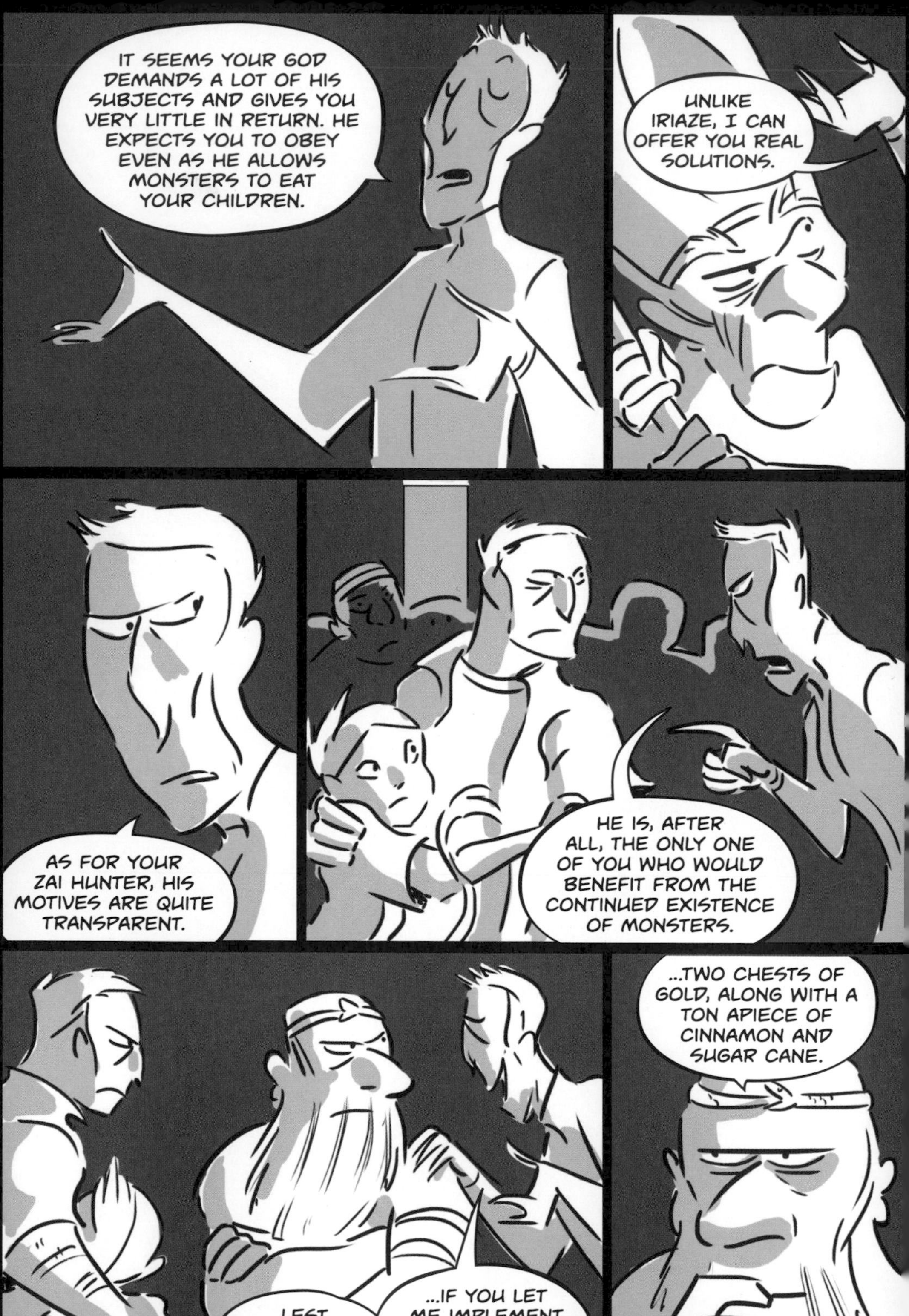
IT SEEMS YOUR GOD DEMANDS A LOT OF HIS SUBJECTS AND GIVES YOU VERY LITTLE IN RETURN. HE EXPECTS YOU TO OBEY EVEN AS HE ALLOWS MONSTERS TO EAT YOUR CHILDREN.
UNLIKE IRIAZE, I CAN OFFER YOU REAL SOLUTIONS.
AS FOR YOUR ZAI HUNTER, HIS MOTIVES ARE QUITE TRANSPARENT.
HE IS, AFTER ALL, THE ONLY ONE OF YOU WHO WOULD BENEFIT FROM THE CONTINUED EXISTENCE OF MONSTERS.
LEST YOU HAVE DOUBTS, YOUR HIGHNESS...
...IF YOU LET ME IMPLEMENT MY PLAN, I WILL DONATE TO YOUR CITY...
...TWO CHESTS OF GOLD, ALONG WITH A TON APIECE OF CINNAMON AND SUGAR CANE.

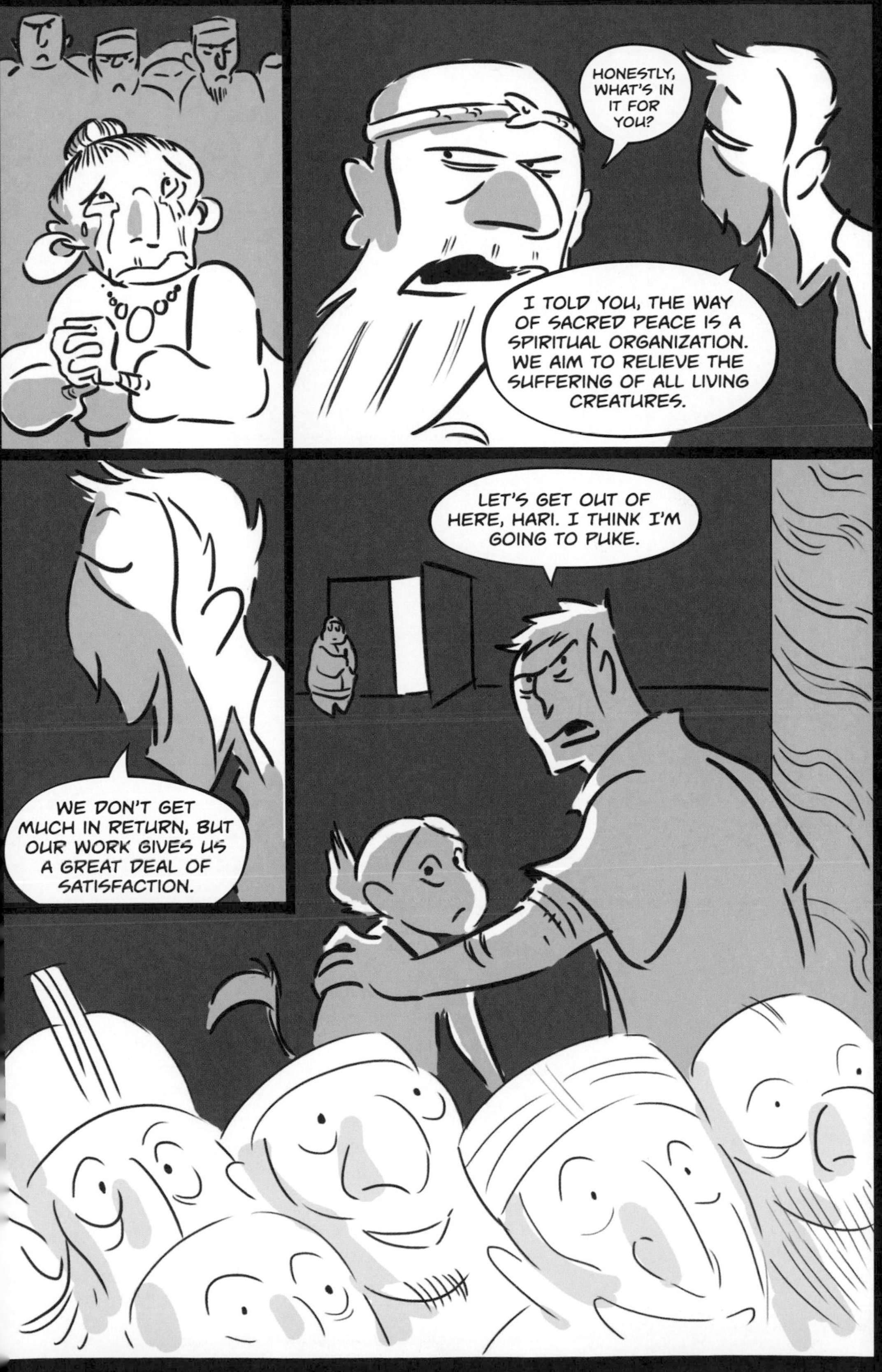
HONESTLY, WHAT'S IN IT FOR YOU?
I TOLD YOU, THE WAY OF SACRED PEACE IS A SPIRITUAL ORGANIZATION. WE AIM TO RELIEVE THE SUFFERING OF ALL LIVING CREATURES.
WE DON'T GET MUCH IN RETURN, BUT OUR WORK GIVES US A GREAT DEAL OF SATISFACTION.
LET'S GET OUT OF HERE, HARI. I THINK I'M GOING TO PUKE.

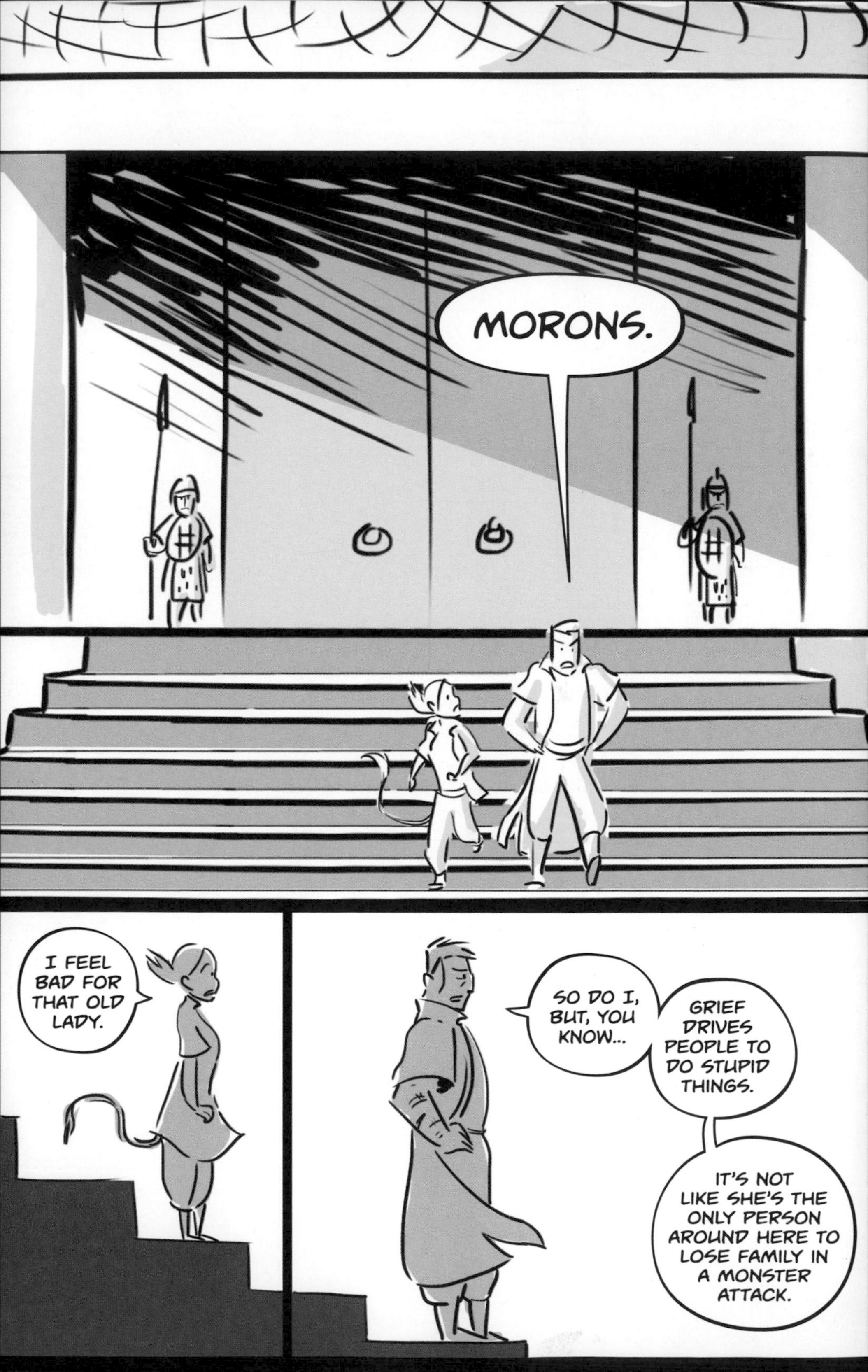
MORONS.
I FEEL BAD FOR THAT OLD LADY.
SO DO I, BUT, YOU KNOW...
GRIEF DRIVES PEOPLE TO DO STUPID THINGS.
IT'S NOT LIKE SHE'S THE ONLY PERSON AROUND HERE TO LOSE FAMILY IN A MONSTER ATTACK.

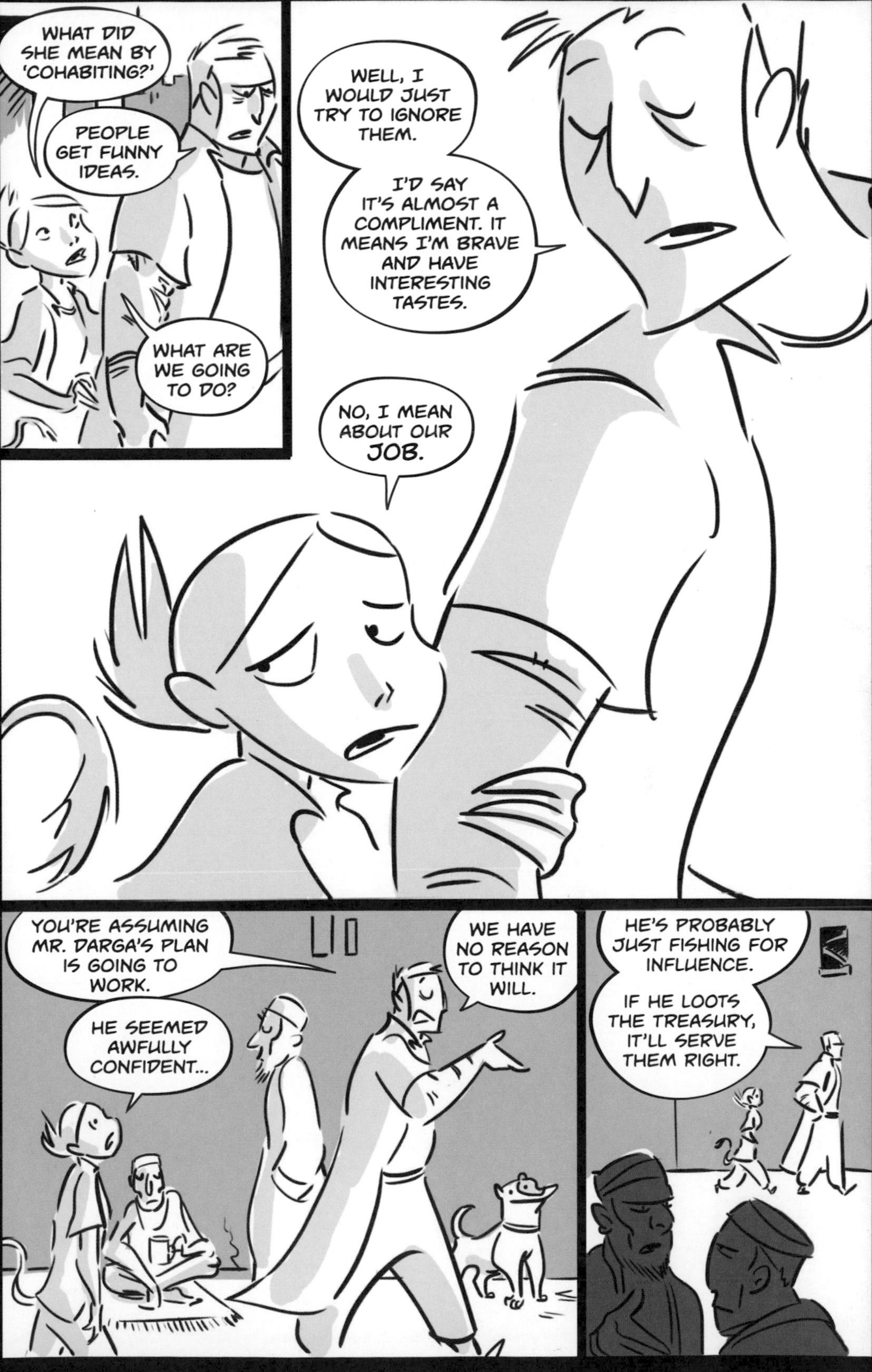
WHAT DID SHE MEAN BY 'COHABITING?'
PEOPLE GET FUNNY IDEAS.
WHAT ARE WE GOING TO DO?
WELL, I WOULD JUST TRY TO IGNORE THEM.
I'D SAY IT'S ALMOST A COMPLIMENT. IT MEANS I'M BRAVE AND HAVE INTERESTING TASTES.
NO, I MEAN ABOUT OUR JOB.
YOU'RE ASSUMING MR. DARGA'S PLAN IS GOING TO WORK.
HE SEEMED AWFULLY CONFIDENT...
WE HAVE NO REASON TO THINK IT WILL.
HE'S PROBABLY JUST FISHING FOR INFLUENCE.
IF HE LOOTS THE TREASURY, IT'LL SERVE THEM RIGHT.

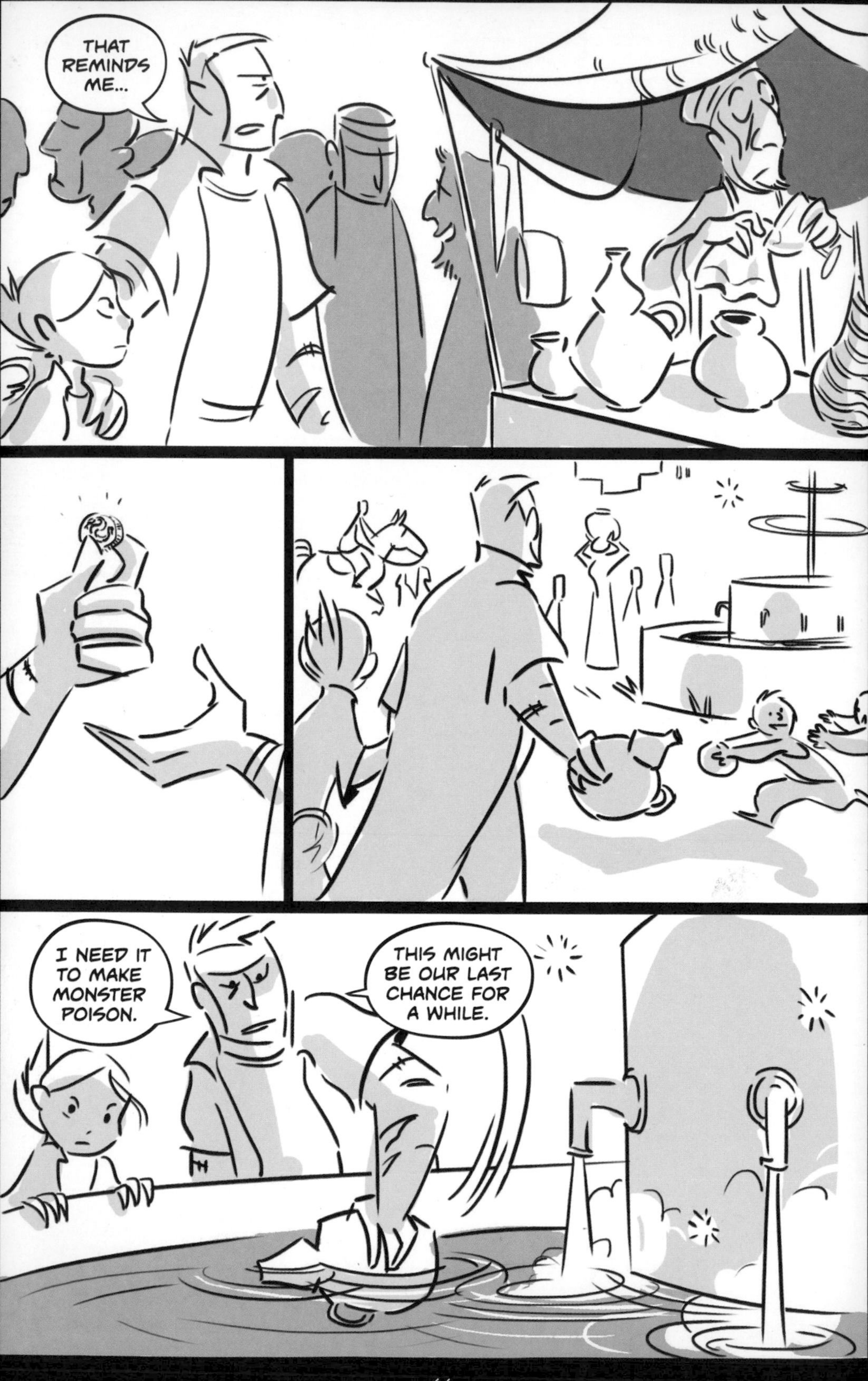
THAT REMINDS ME...
I NEED IT TO MAKE MONSTER POISON.
THIS MIGHT BE OUR LAST CHANCE FOR A WHILE.

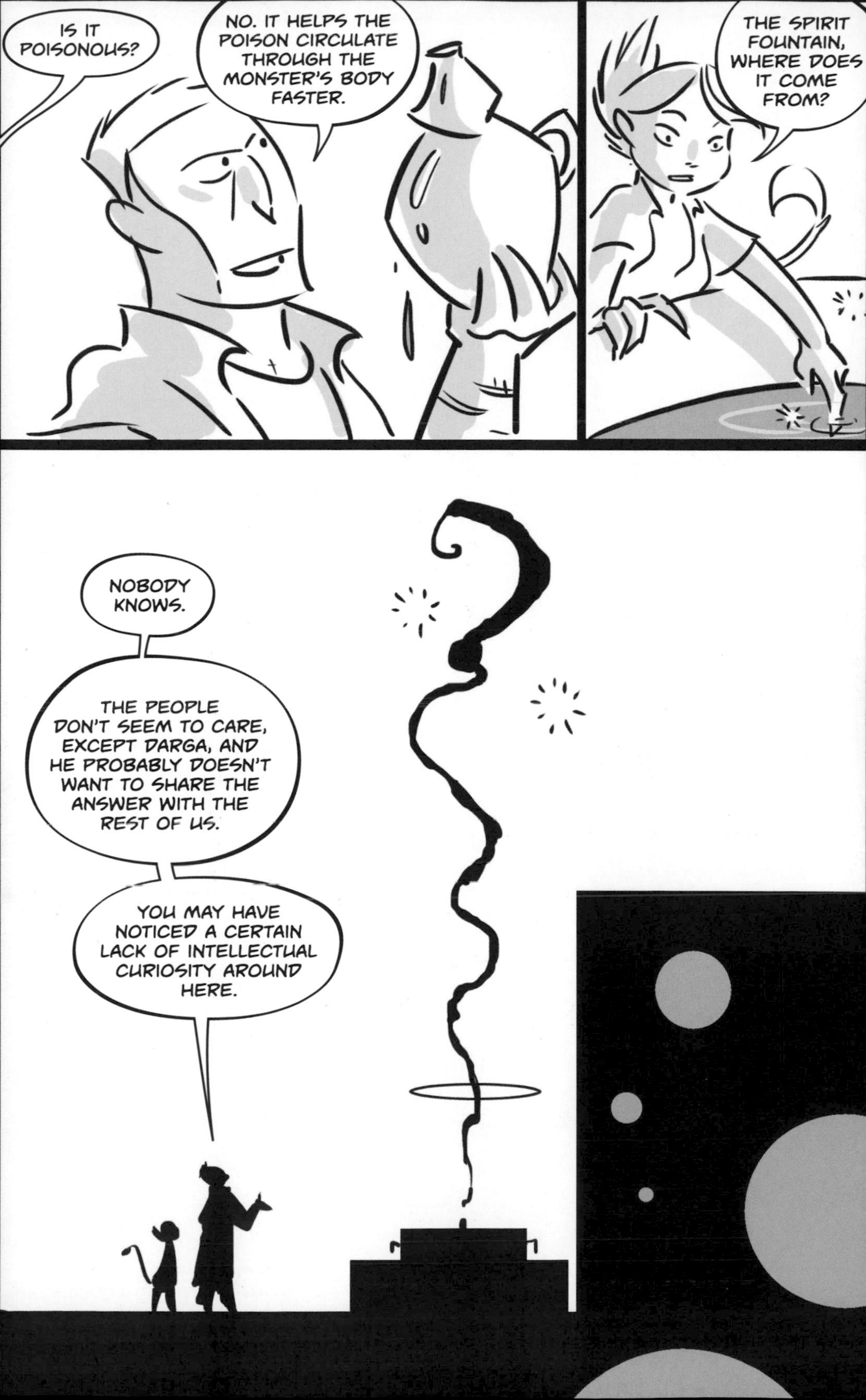
IS IT POISONOUS?
NO. IT HELPS THE POISON CIRCULATE THROUGH THE MONSTER'S BODY FASTER.
THE SPIRIT FOUNTAIN, WHERE DOES IT COME FROM?
NOBODY KNOWS.
THE PEOPLE DON'T SEEM TO CARE, EXCEPT DARGA, AND HE PROBABLY DOESN'T WANT TO SHARE THE ANSWER WITH THE REST OF US.
YOU MAY HAVE NOTICED A CERTAIN LACK OF INTELLECTUAL CURIOSITY AROUND HERE.

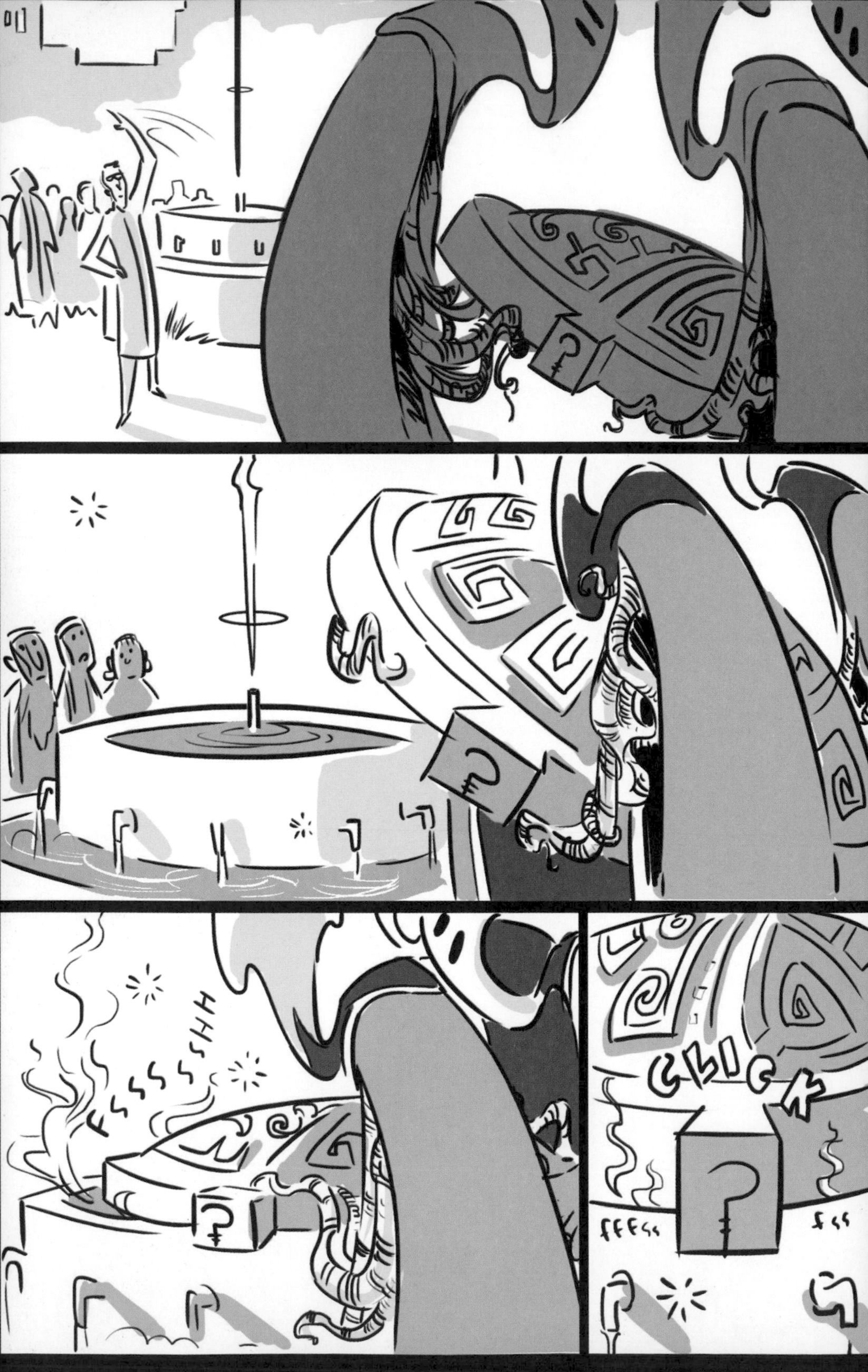
FSSSSSHH
CLICK
FFFss
fss

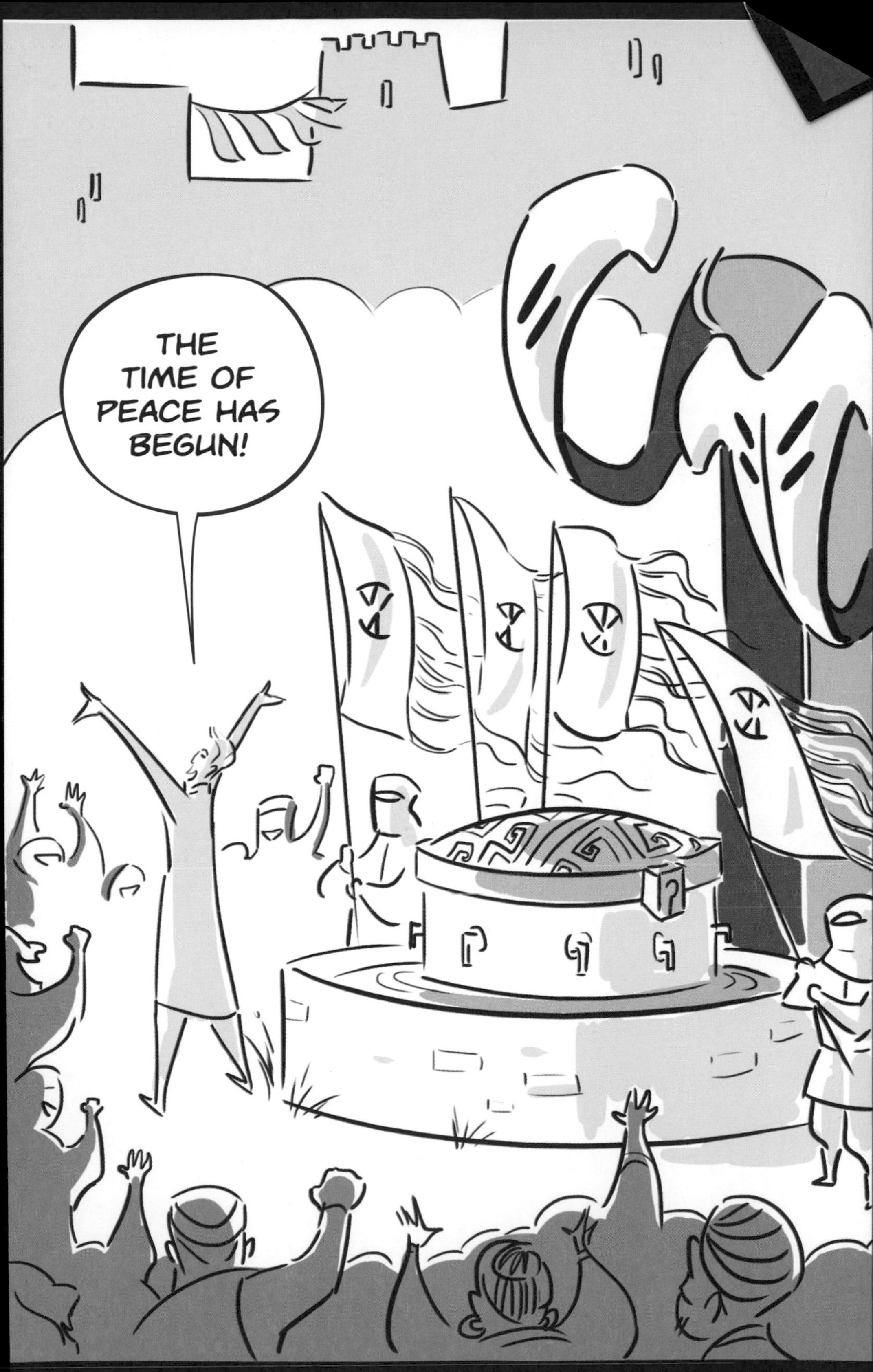
THE TIME OF PEACE HAS BEGUN!

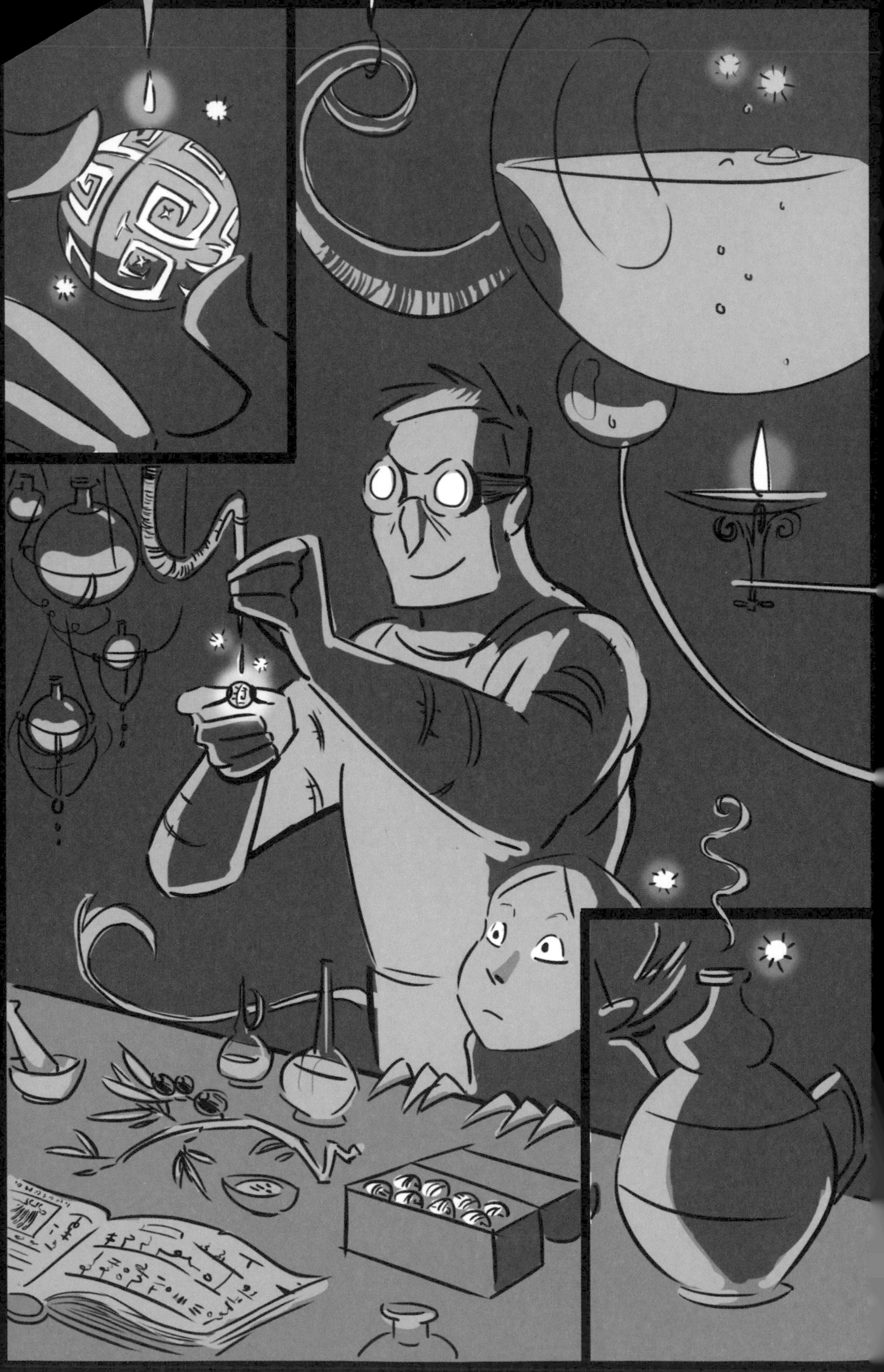

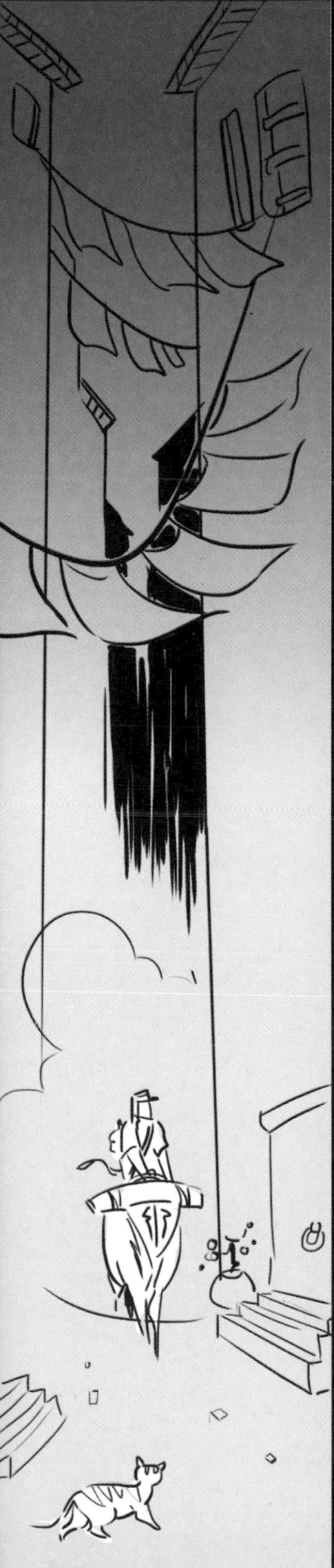

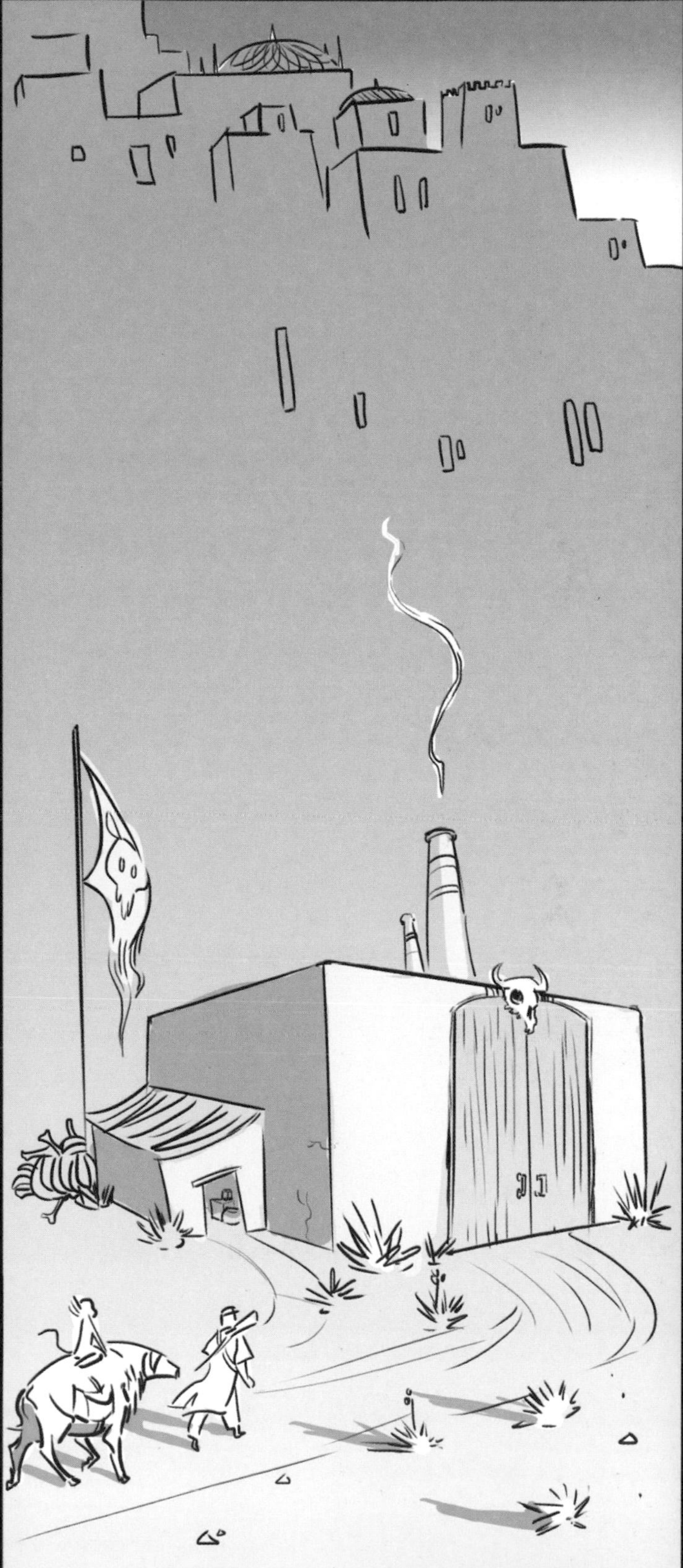

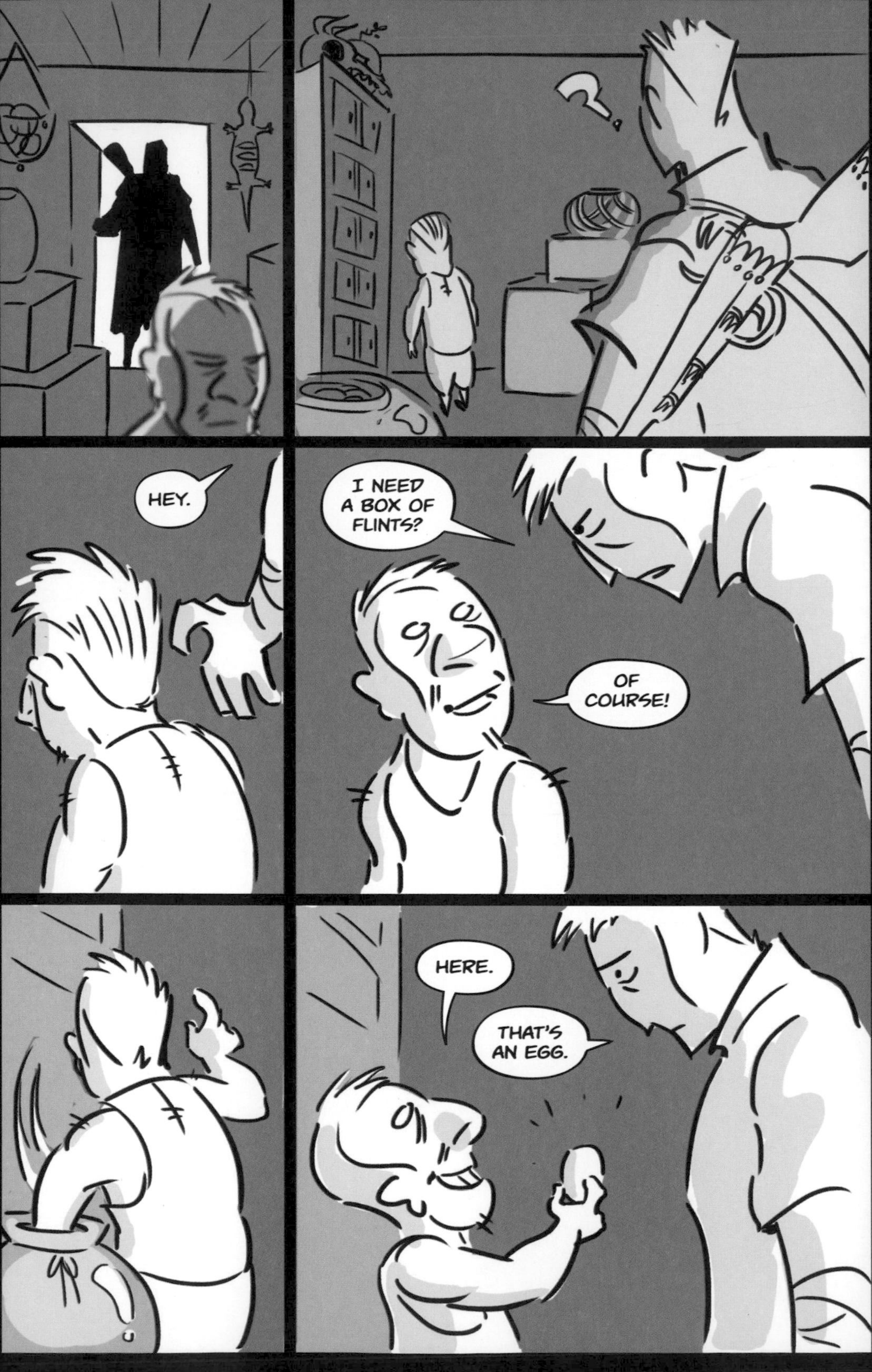
HEY.
I NEED A BOX OF FLINTS?
OF COURSE!
HERE.
THAT'S AN EGG.

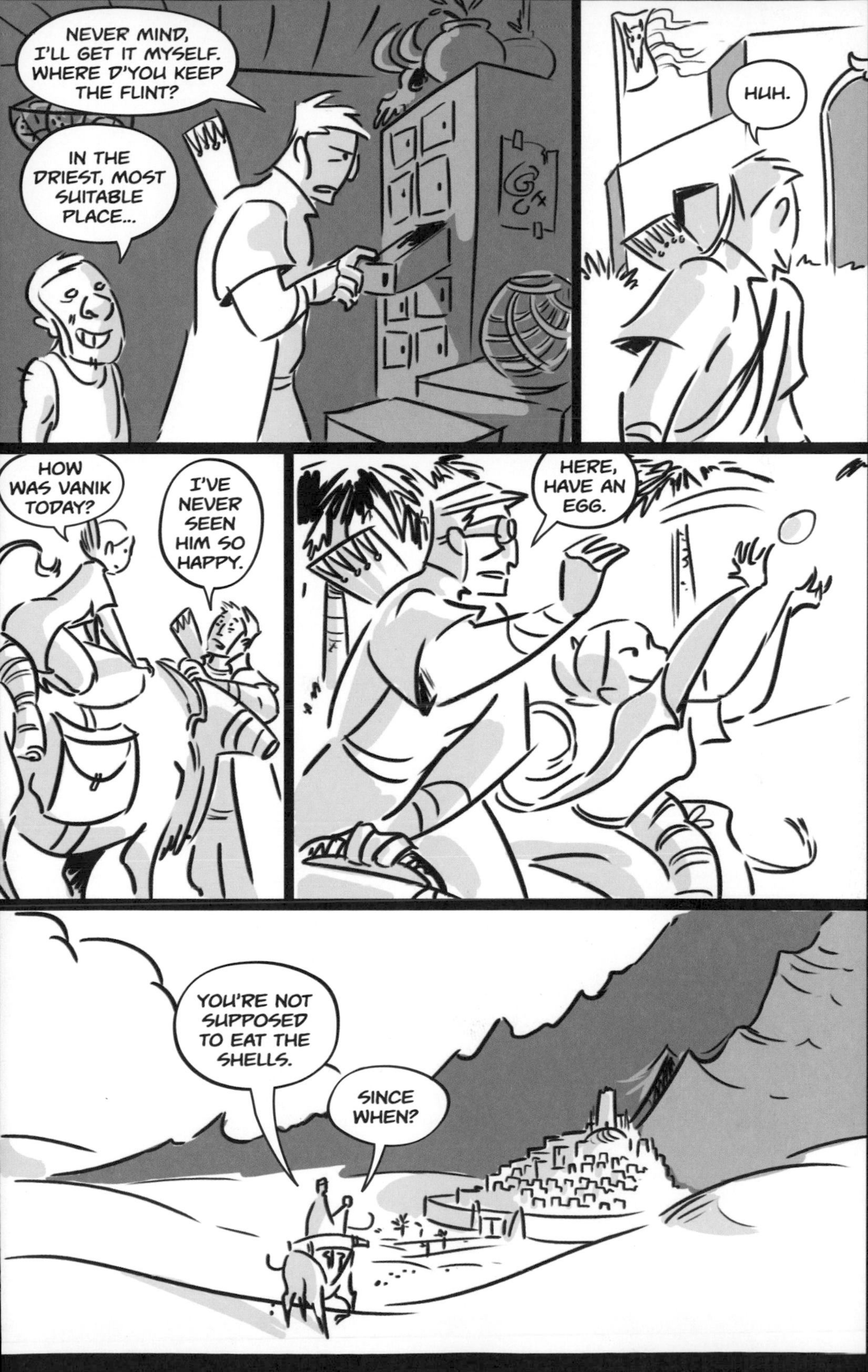
NEVER MIND, I'LL GET IT MYSELF. WHERE D'YOU KEEP THE FLINT?
IN THE DRIEST, MOST SUITABLE PLACE...
HUH.
HOW WAS VANIK TODAY?
I'VE NEVER SEEN HIM SO HAPPY.
HERE, HAVE AN EGG.
YOU'RE NOT SUPPOSED TO EAT THE SHELLS.
SINCE WHEN?

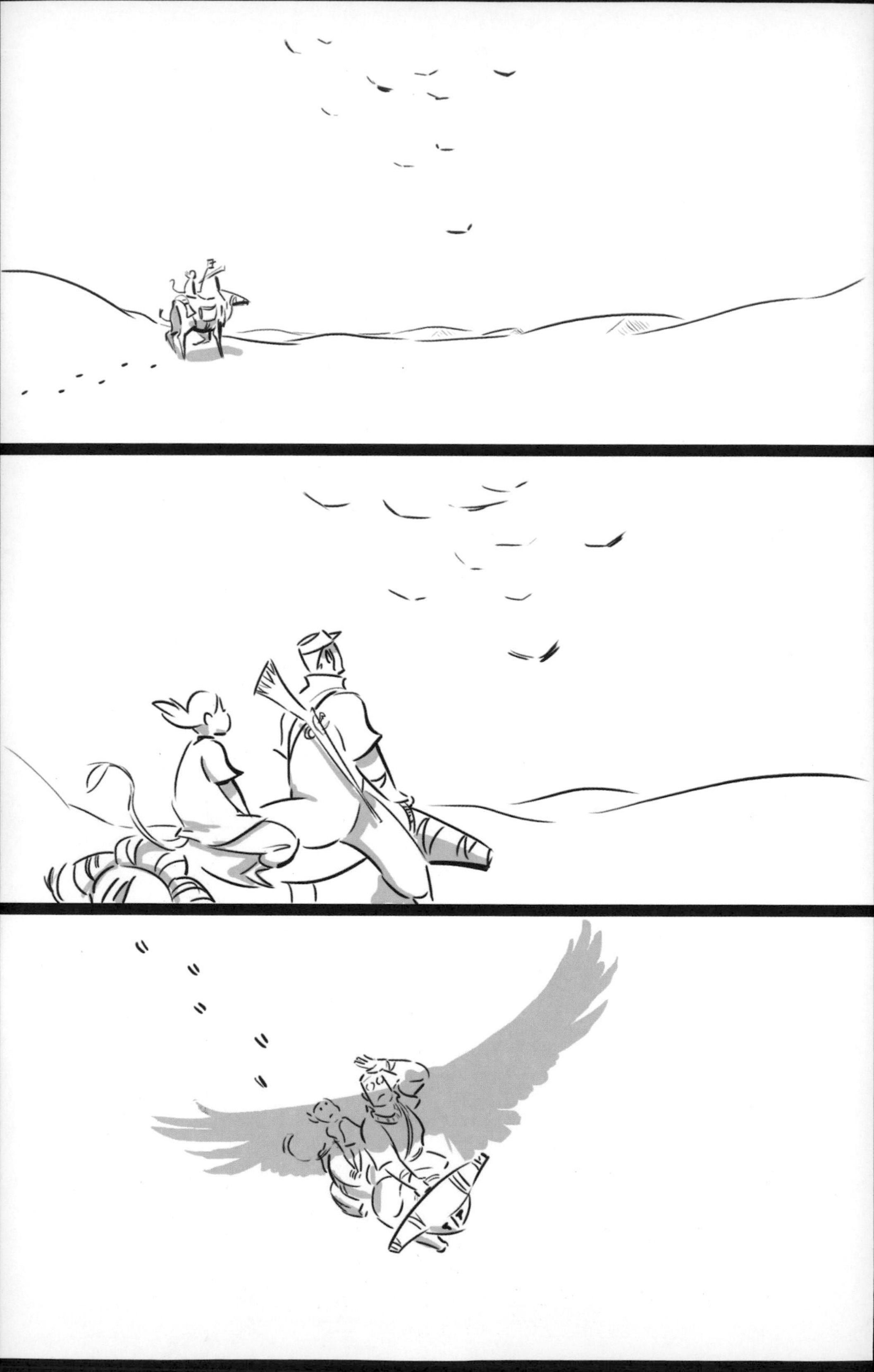

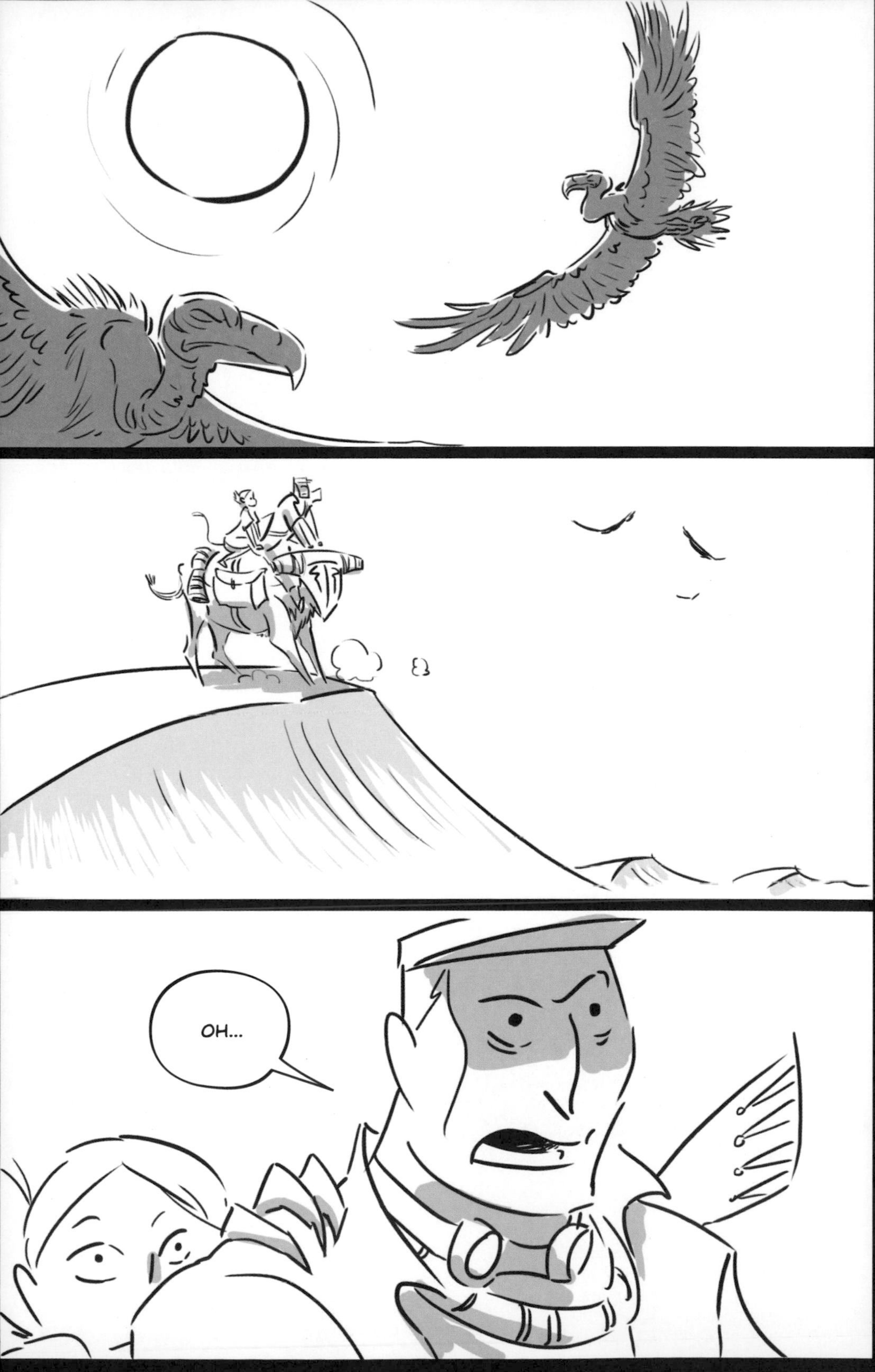
OH...

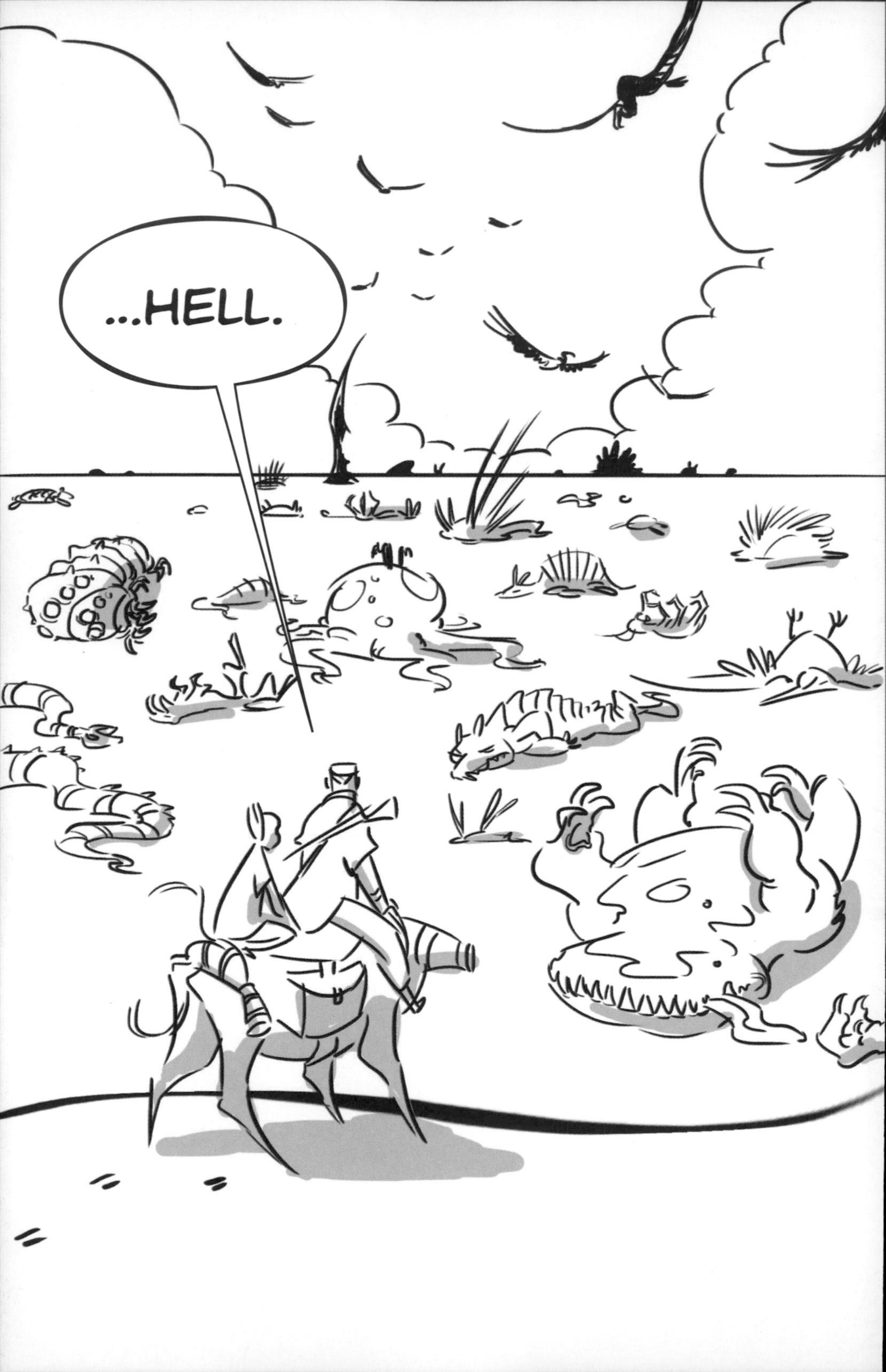
...HELL.

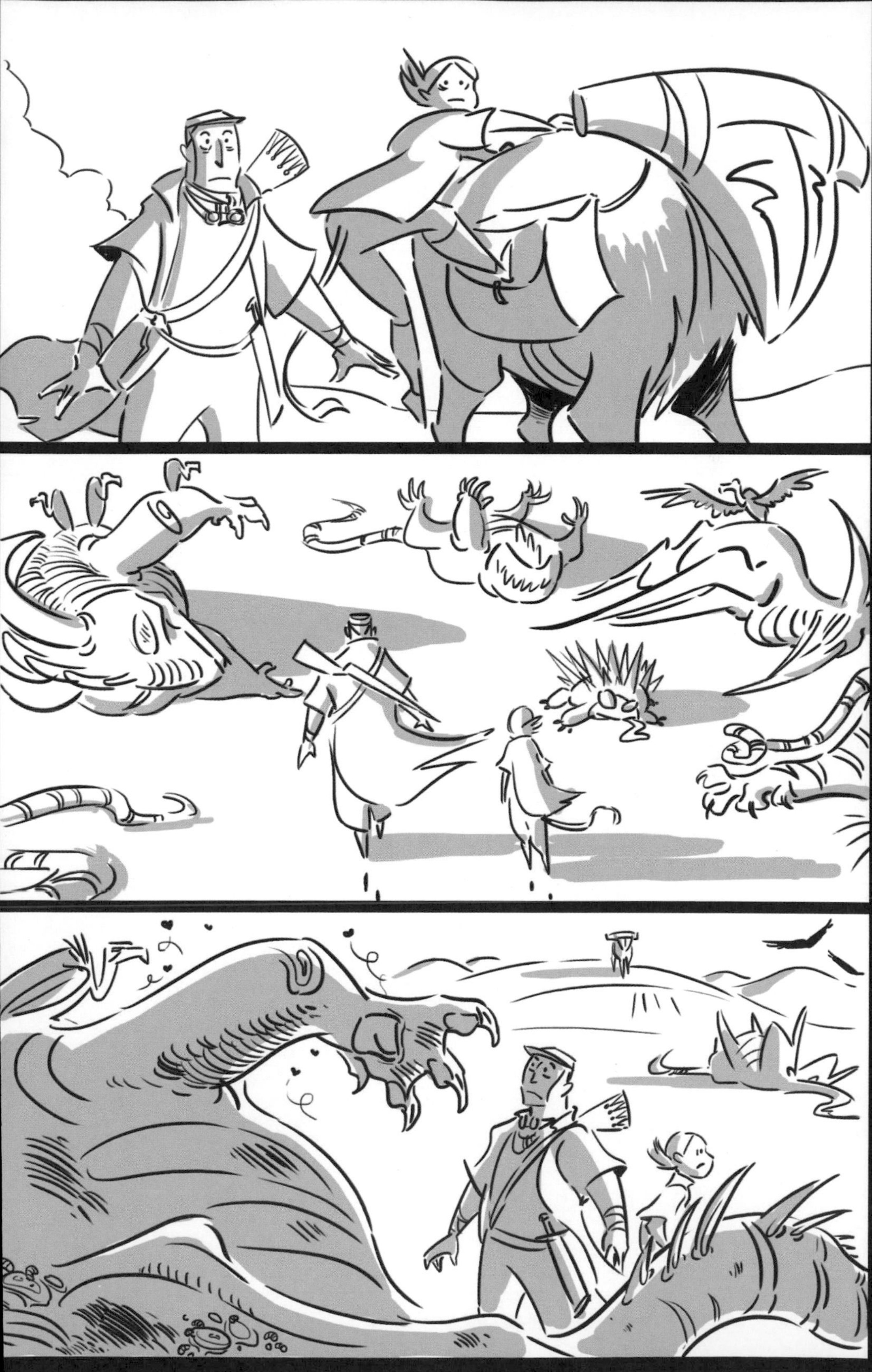

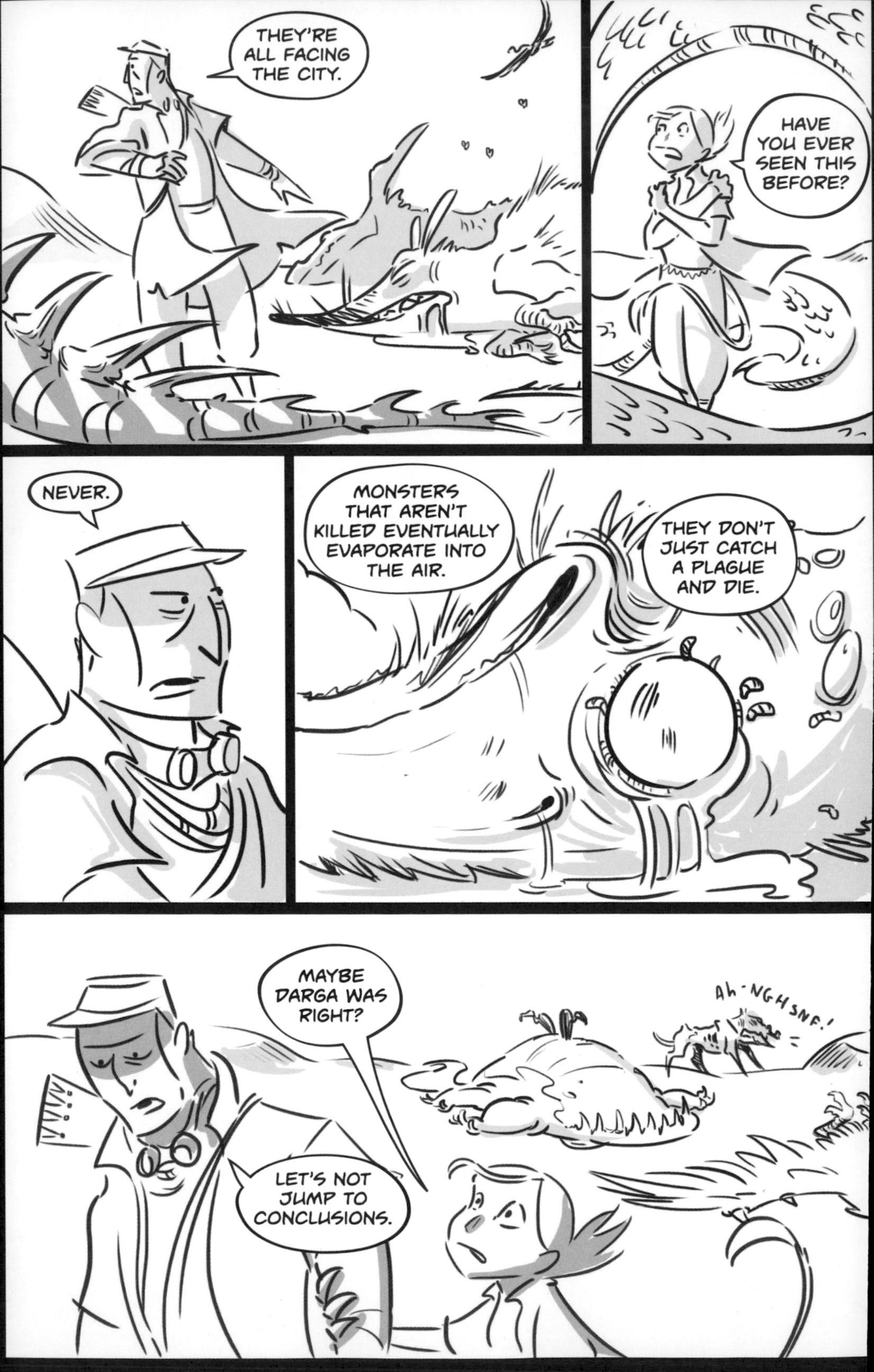
THEY'RE ALL FACING THE CITY.
HAVE YOU EVER SEEN THIS BEFORE?
NEVER.
MONSTERS THAT AREN'T KILLED EVENTUALLY EVAPORATE INTO THE AIR.
THEY DON'T JUST CATCH A PLAGUE AND DIE.
MAYBE DARGA WAS RIGHT?
AH-NGHSNF!
LET'S NOT JUMP TO CONCLUSIONS.

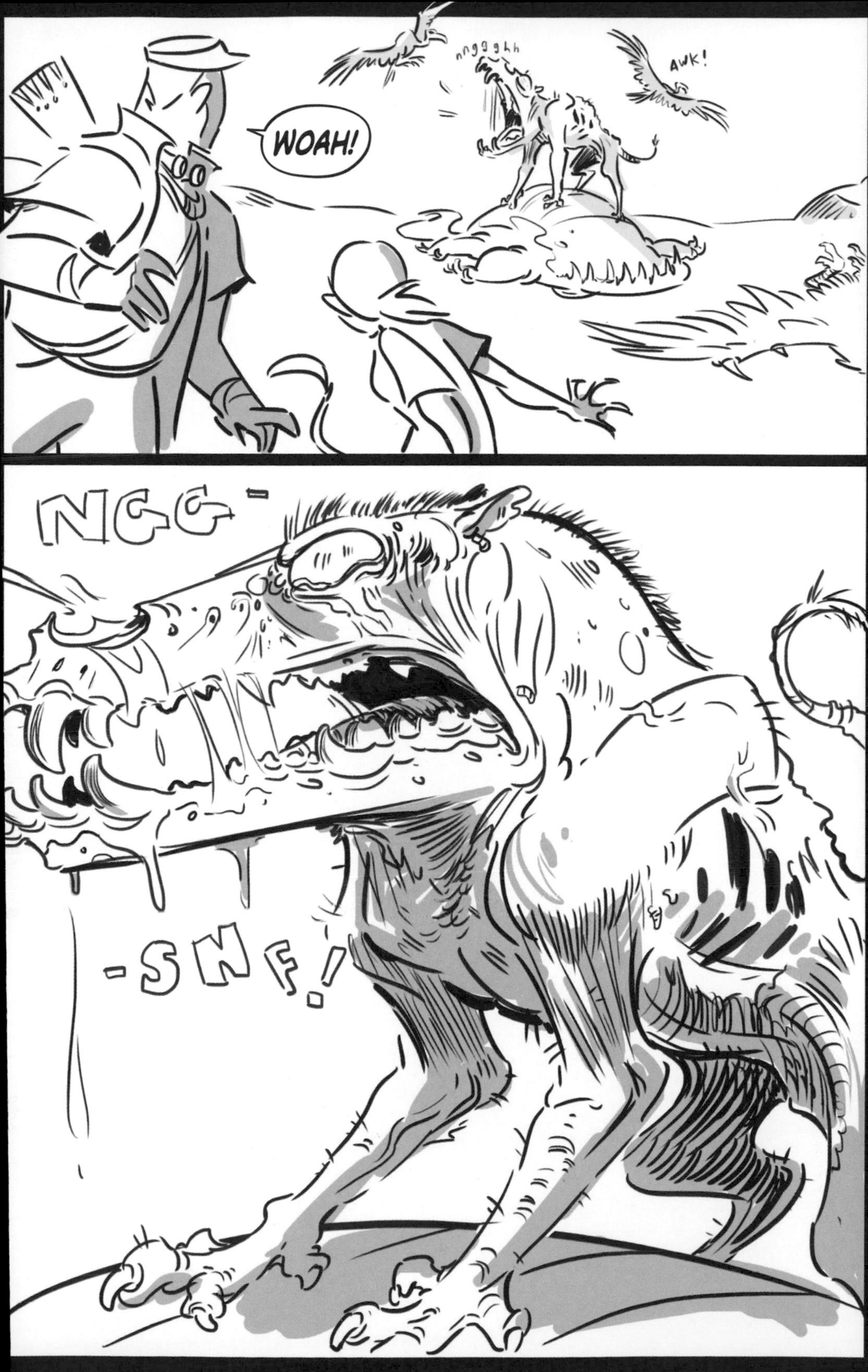
WOAH!
nngggghh
AWK!
NGG-
-SNF!

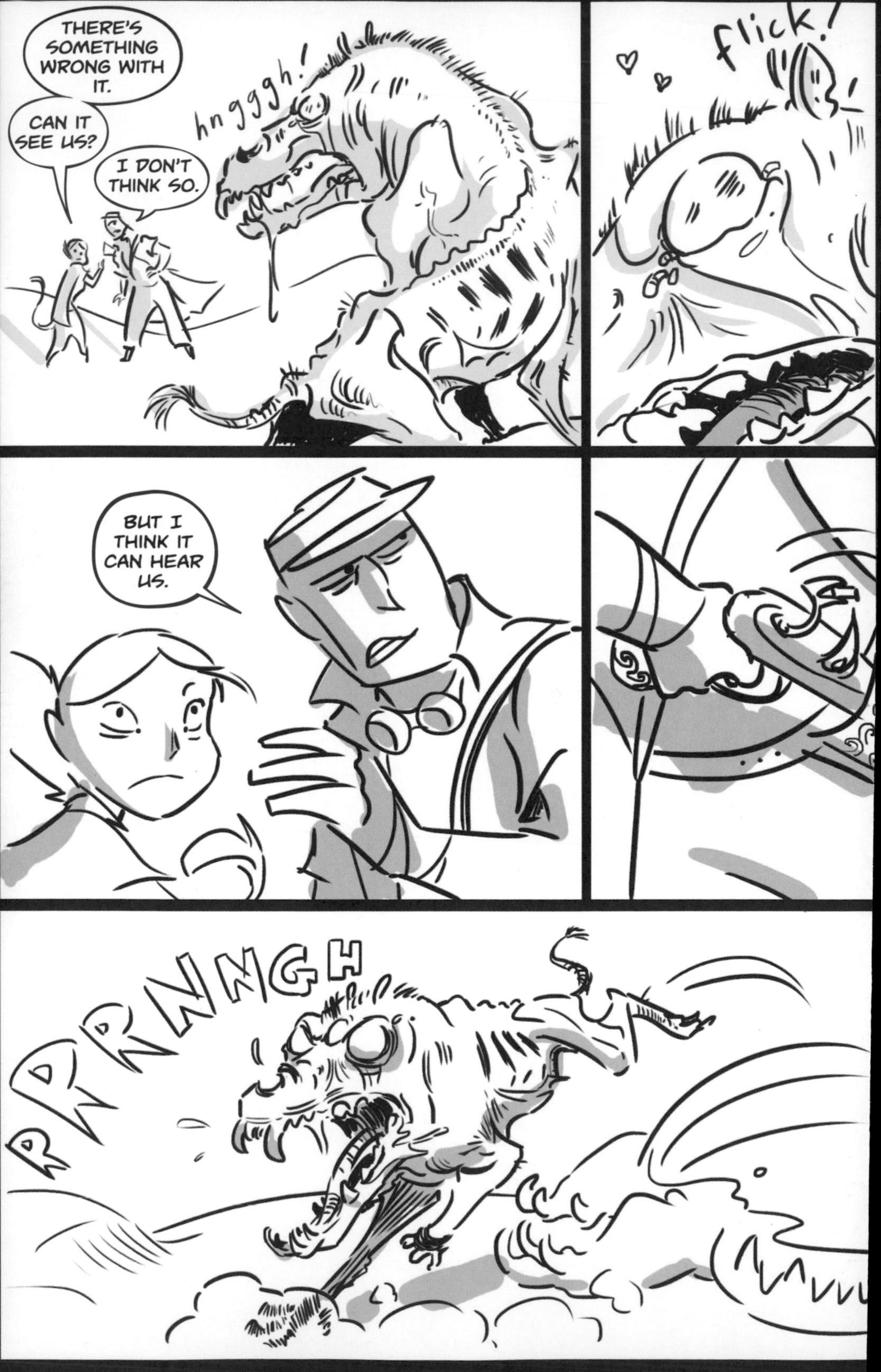
THERE'S SOMETHING WRONG WITH IT.
CAN IT SEE US?
I DON'T THINK SO.
hngggh!
flick!
BUT I THINK IT CAN HEAR US.
PRRNNGH

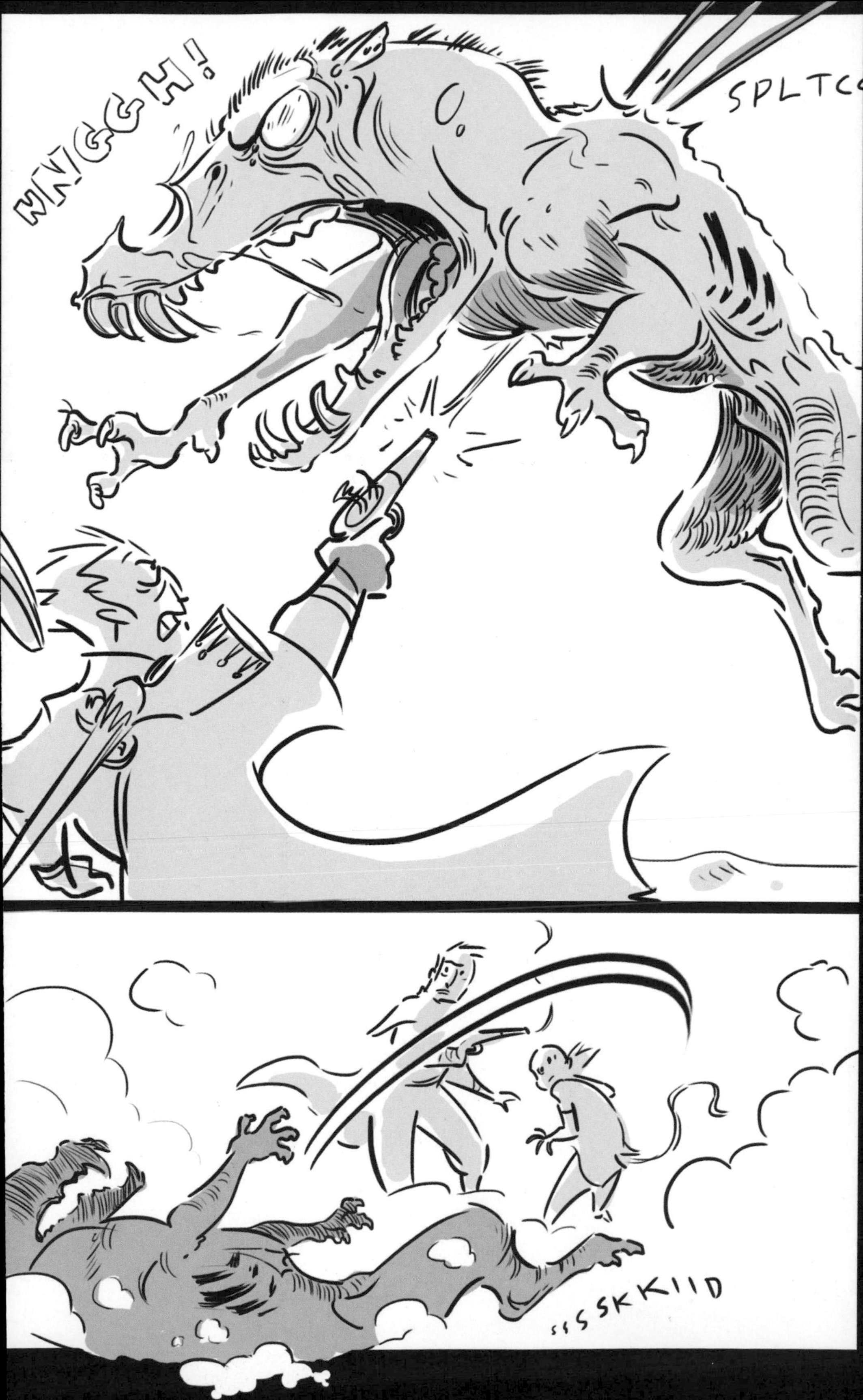
WNIGGH!
SPLTCC
SSSKKIID

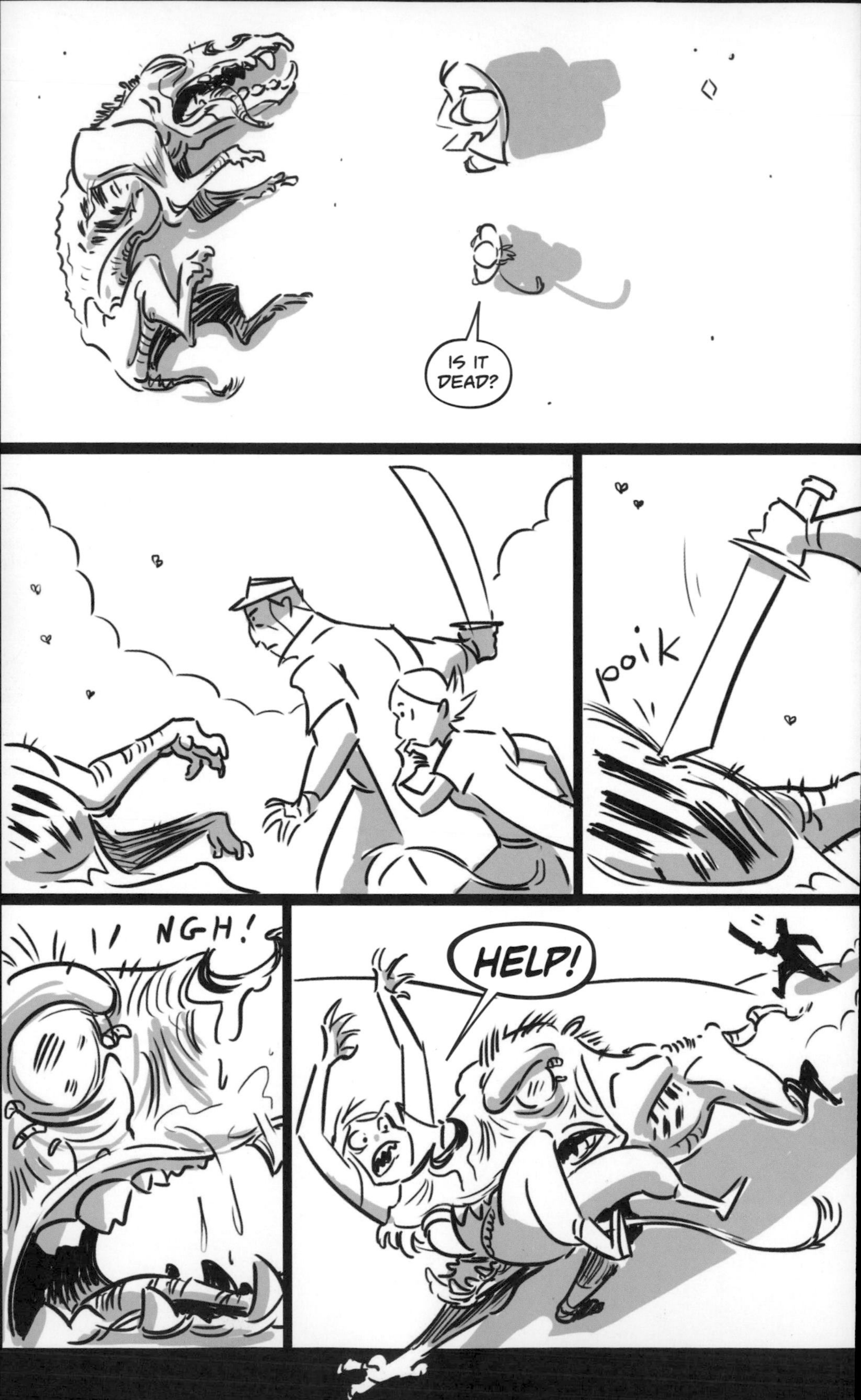
IS IT DEAD?
poik
NGH!
HELP!

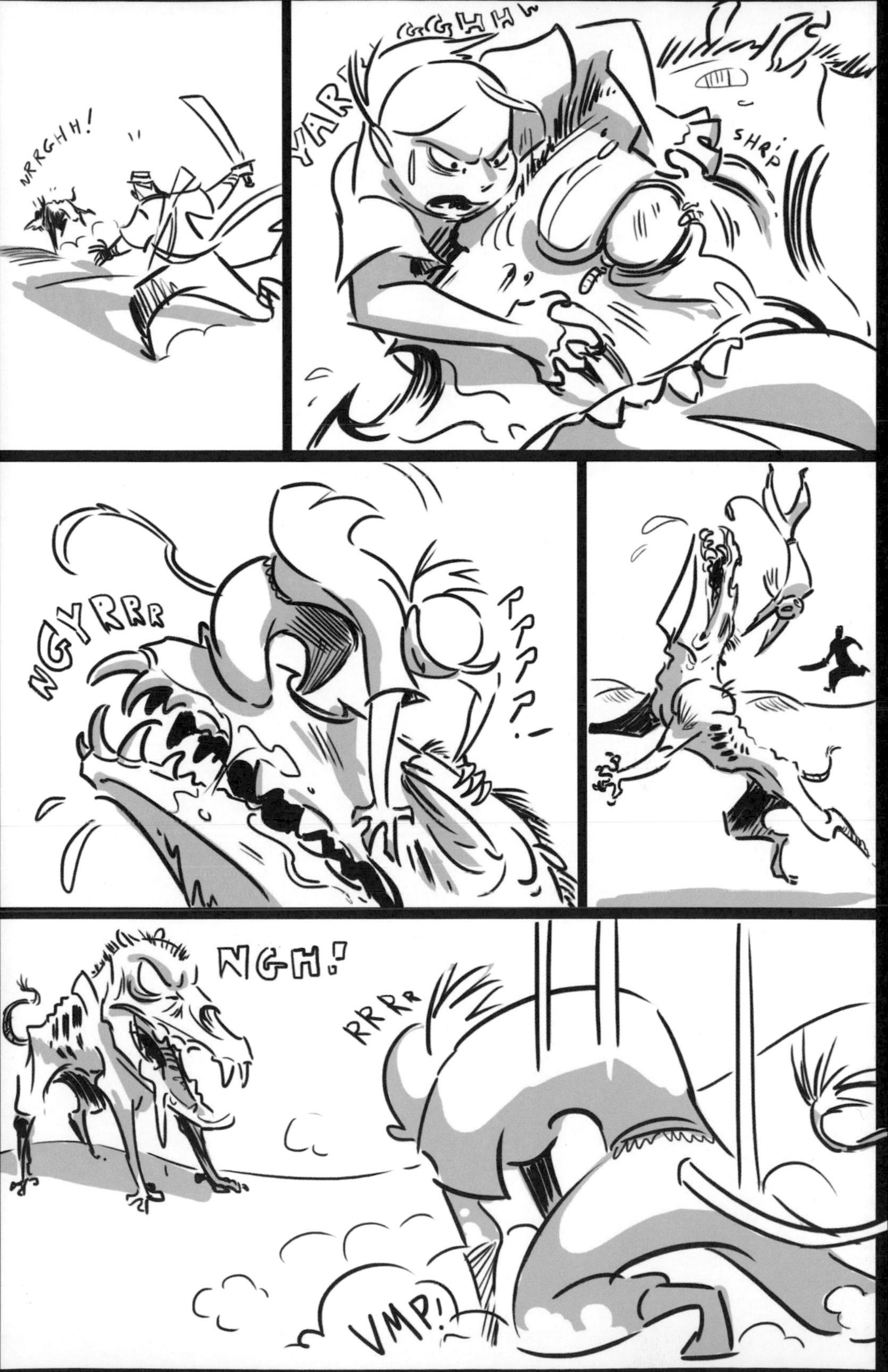
NRRGHH!
YAR
GGHHW
SHRP
NGYRRR
RRRR!
NGH!
RRRR
VMP!

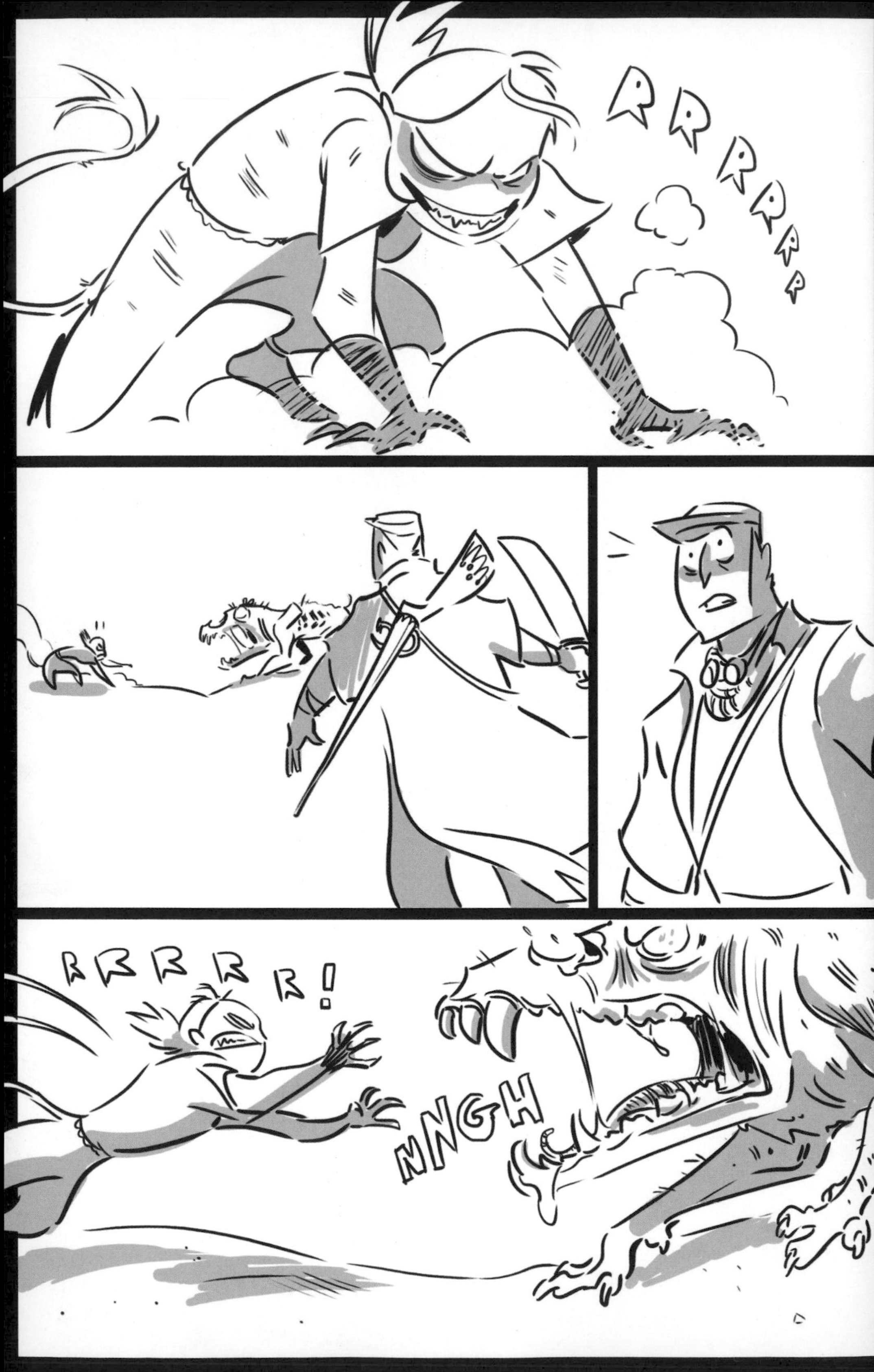
RRRRRRR
RRRRRR!
NNGH

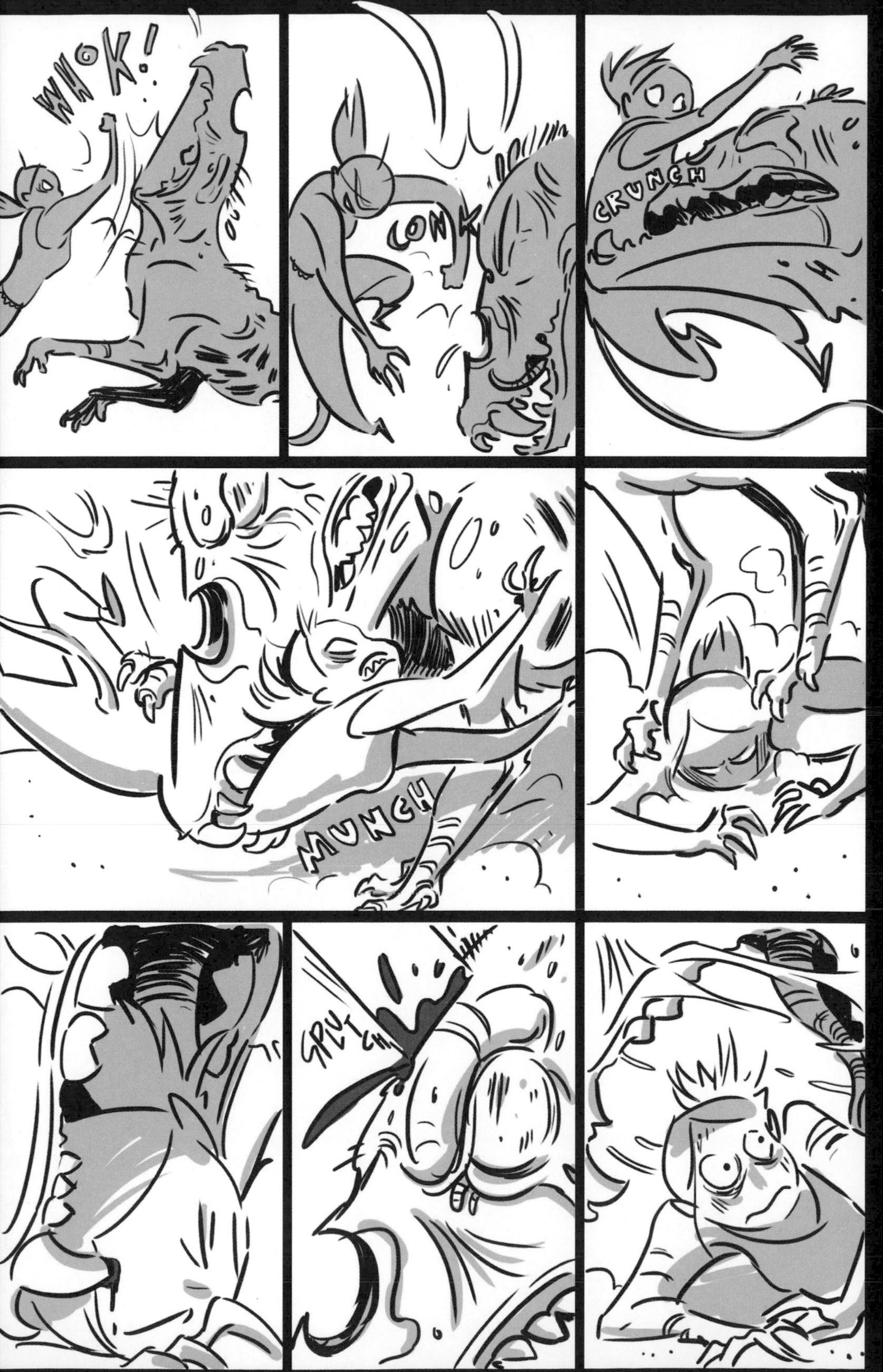
WHOK!
CONK
CRUNCH
MUNCH
SPLUT

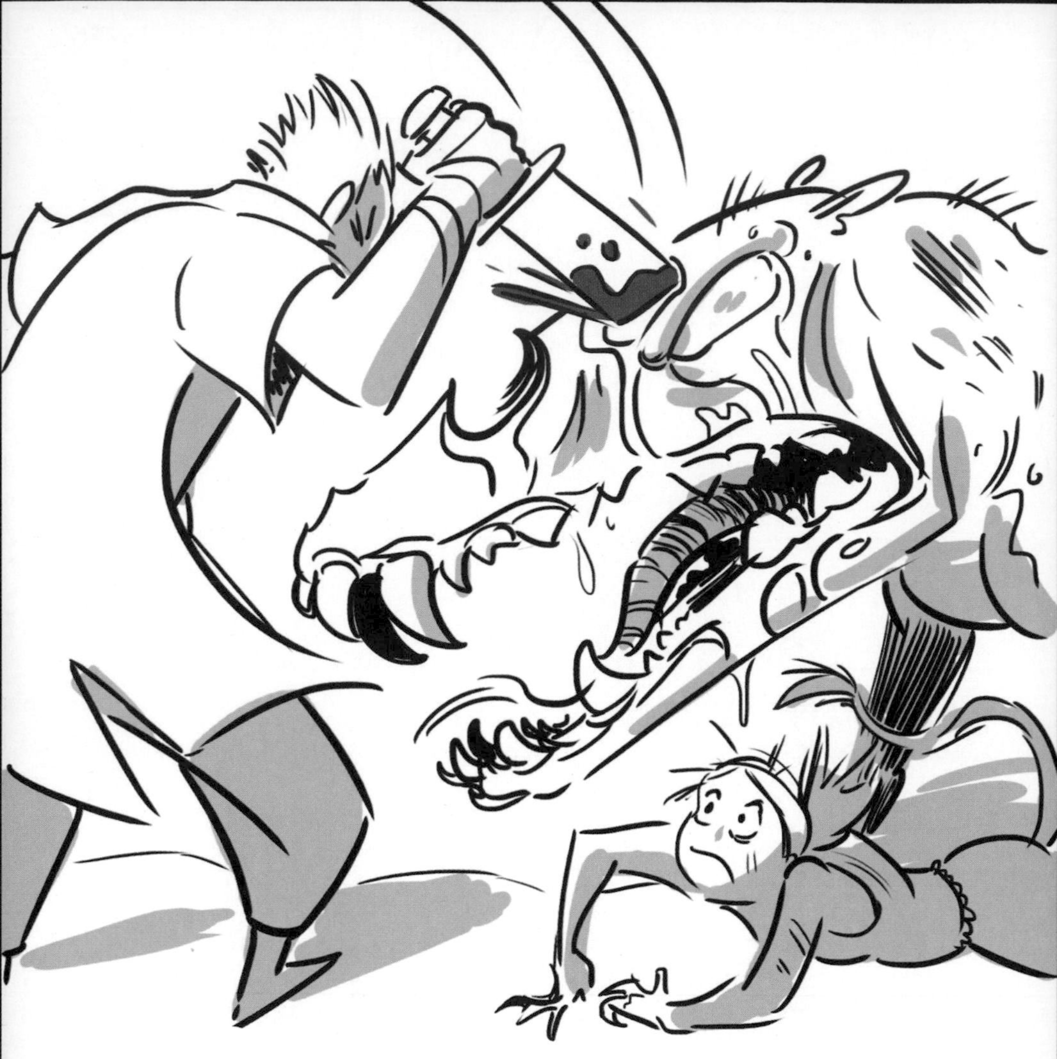

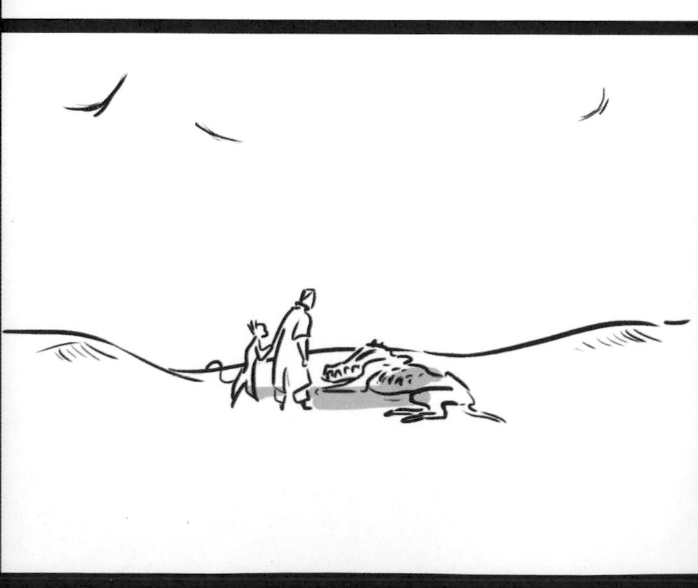

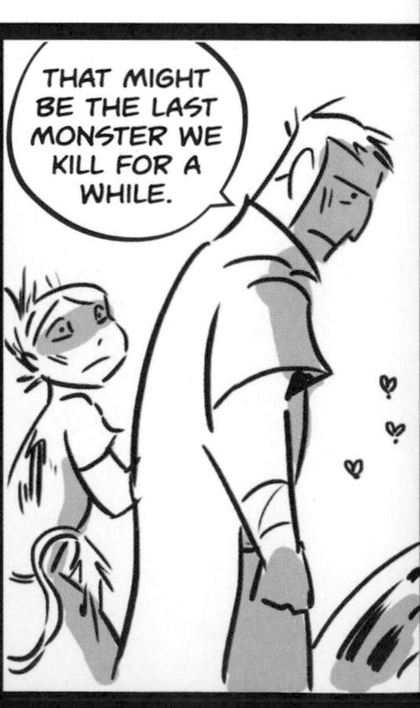
THAT MIGHT BE THE LAST MONSTER WE KILL FOR A WHILE.

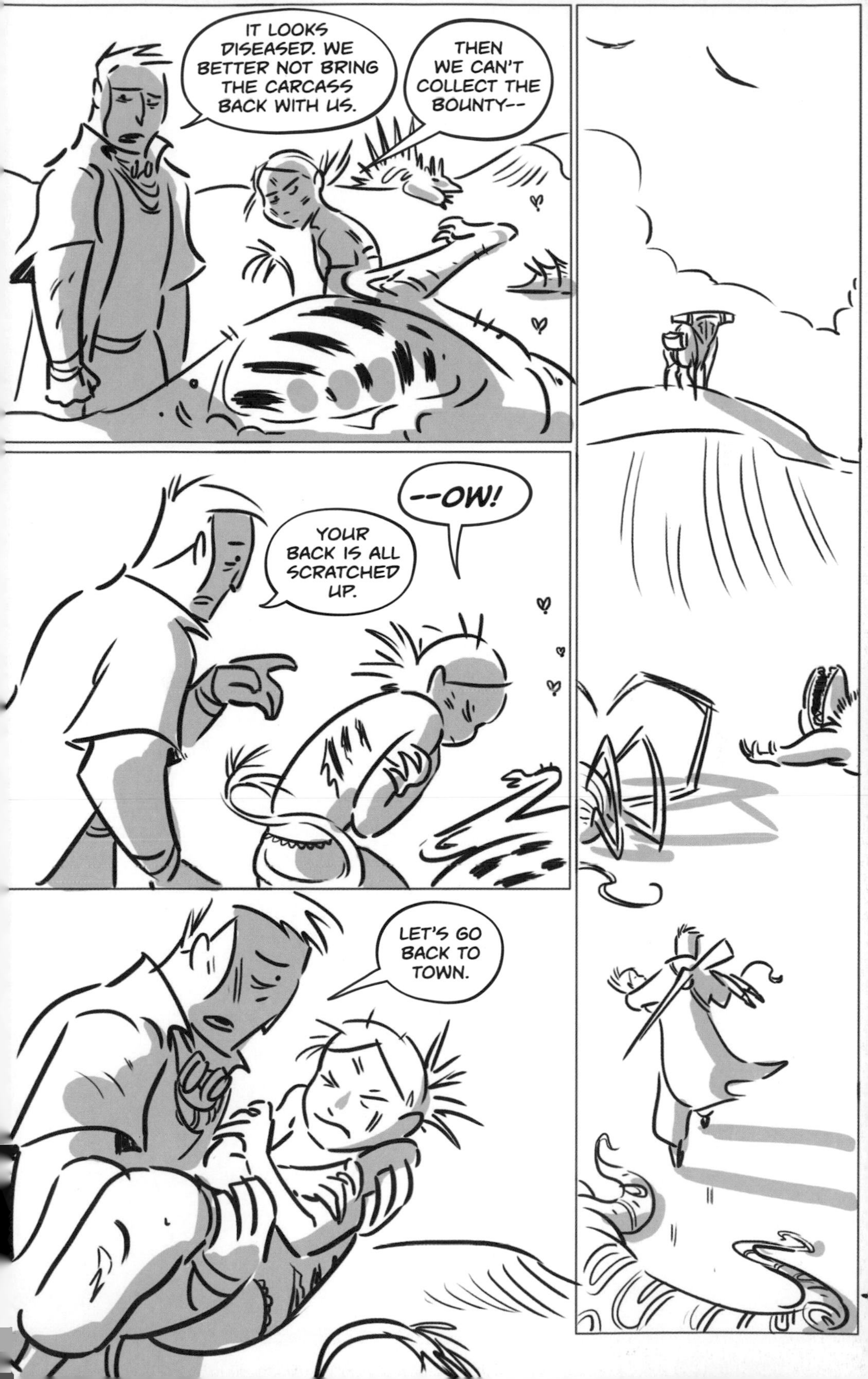
IT LOOKS DISEASED. WE BETTER NOT BRING THE CARCASS BACK WITH US.
THEN WE CAN'T COLLECT THE BOUNTY--
YOUR BACK IS ALL SCRATCHED UP.
--OW!
LET'S GO BACK TO TOWN.

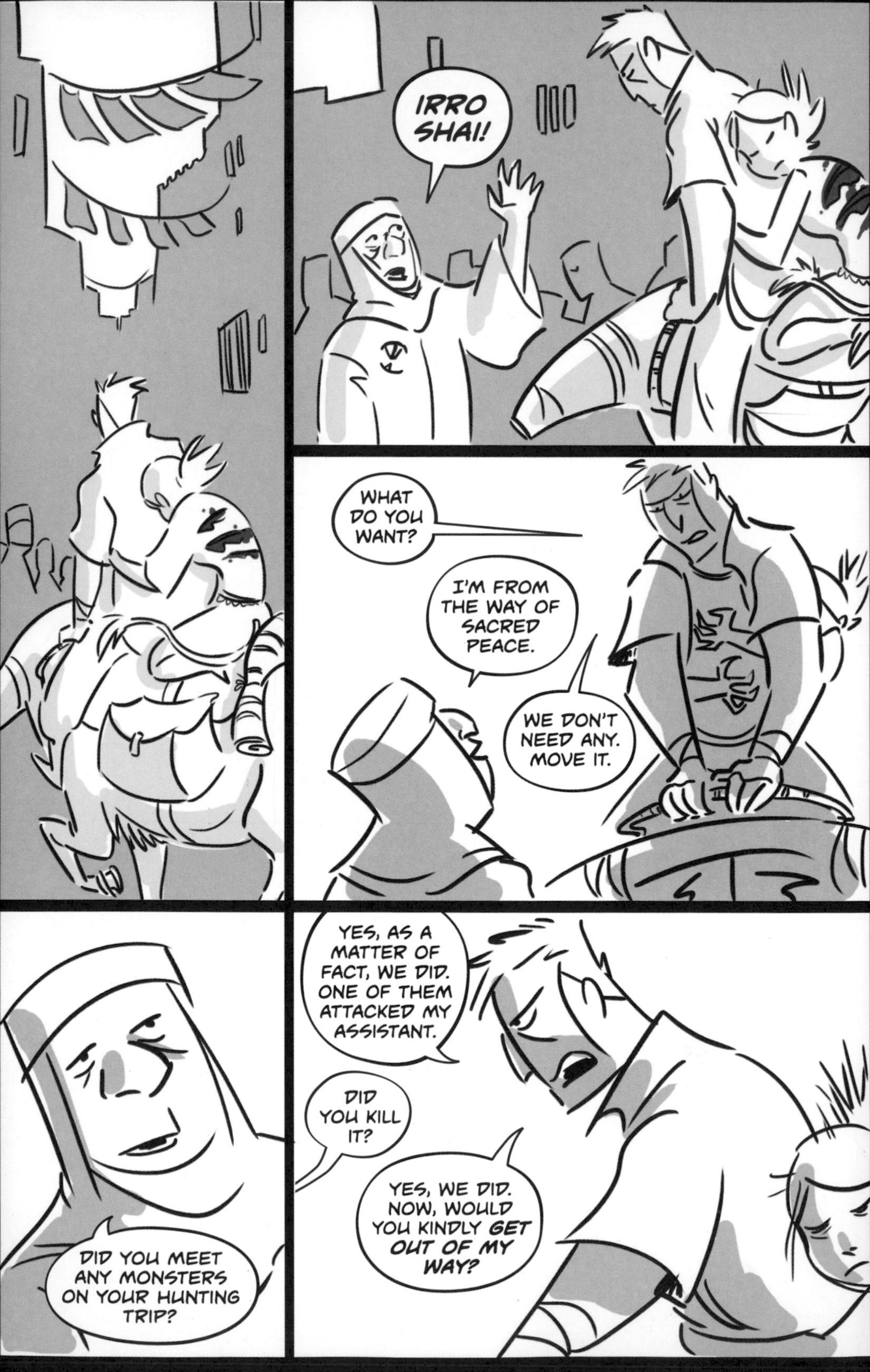
IRRO SHAI!
WHAT DO YOU WANT?
I'M FROM THE WAY OF SACRED PEACE.
WE DON'T NEED ANY. MOVE IT.
DID YOU MEET ANY MONSTERS ON YOUR HUNTING TRIP?
YES, AS A MATTER OF FACT, WE DID. ONE OF THEM ATTACKED MY ASSISTANT.
DID YOU KILL IT?
YES, WE DID. NOW, WOULD YOU KINDLY GET OUT OF MY WAY?

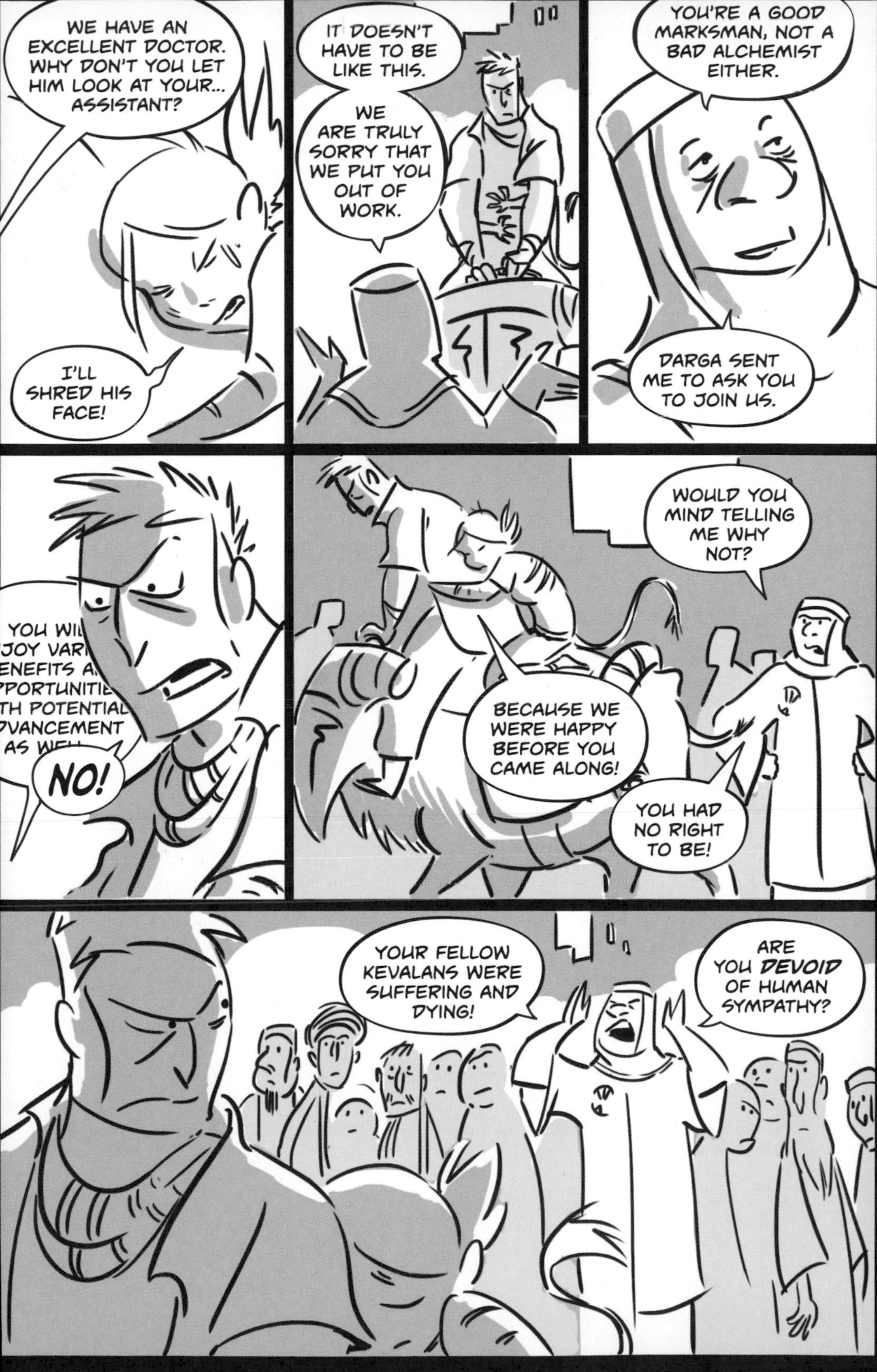
WE HAVE AN EXCELLENT DOCTOR. WHY DON'T YOU LET HIM LOOK AT YOUR... ASSISTANT?
I'LL SHRED HIS FACE!
IT DOESN'T HAVE TO BE LIKE THIS.
WE ARE TRULY SORRY THAT WE PUT YOU OUT OF WORK.
YOU'RE A GOOD MARKSMAN, NOT A BAD ALCHEMIST EITHER.
DARGA SENT ME TO ASK YOU TO JOIN US.
NO!
WOULD YOU MIND TELLING ME WHY NOT?
BECAUSE WE WERE HAPPY BEFORE YOU CAME ALONG!
YOU HAD NO RIGHT TO BE!
YOUR FELLOW KEVALANS WERE SUFFERING AND DYING!
ARE YOU *DEVOID* OF HUMAN SYMPATHY?

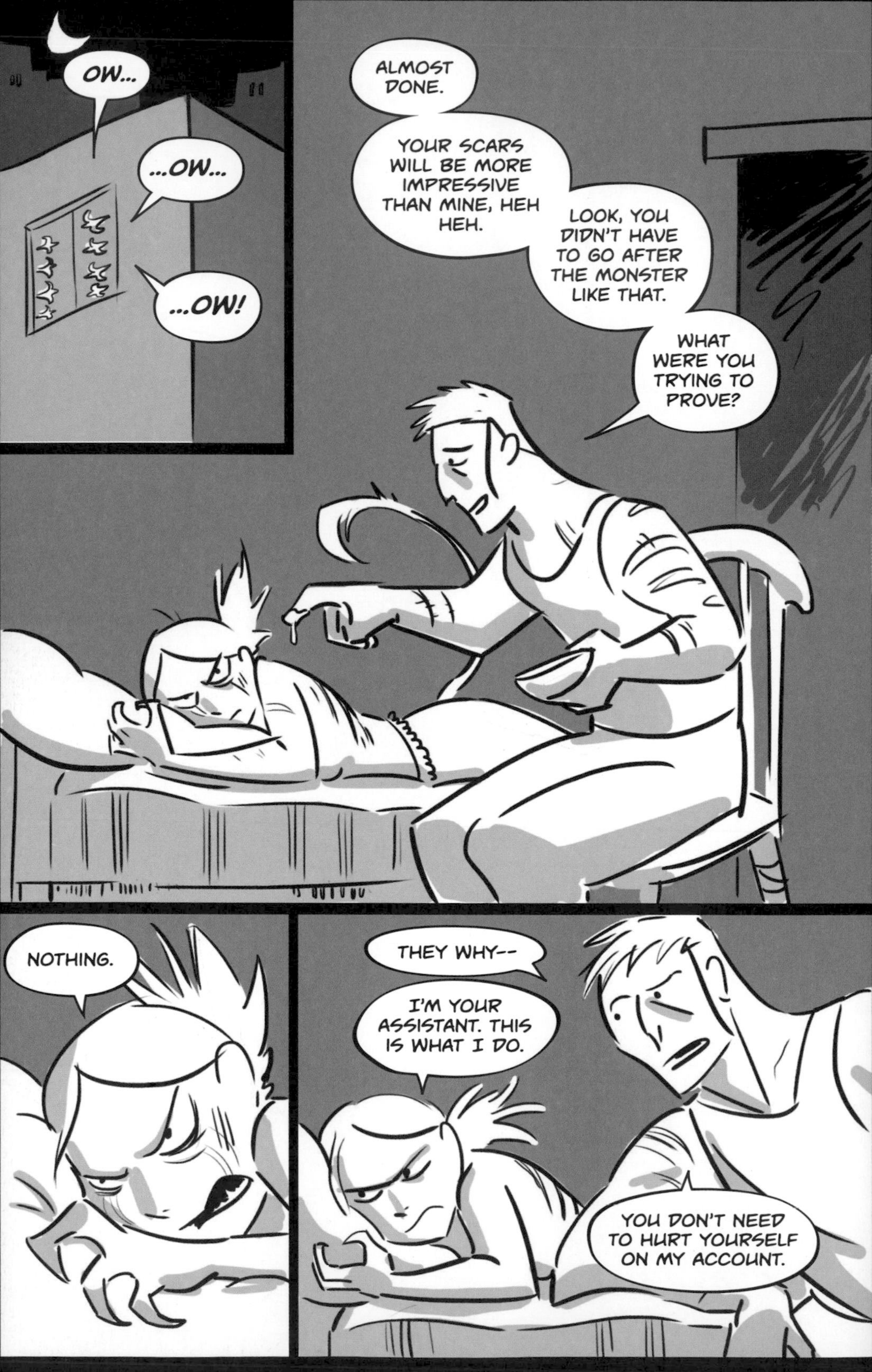
OW...
...OW...
...OW!
ALMOST DONE.
YOUR SCARS WILL BE MORE IMPRESSIVE THAN MINE, HEH HEH.
LOOK, YOU DIDN'T HAVE TO GO AFTER THE MONSTER LIKE THAT.
WHAT WERE YOU TRYING TO PROVE?
NOTHING.
THEY WHY--
I'M YOUR ASSISTANT. THIS IS WHAT I DO.
YOU DON'T NEED TO HURT YOURSELF ON MY ACCOUNT.

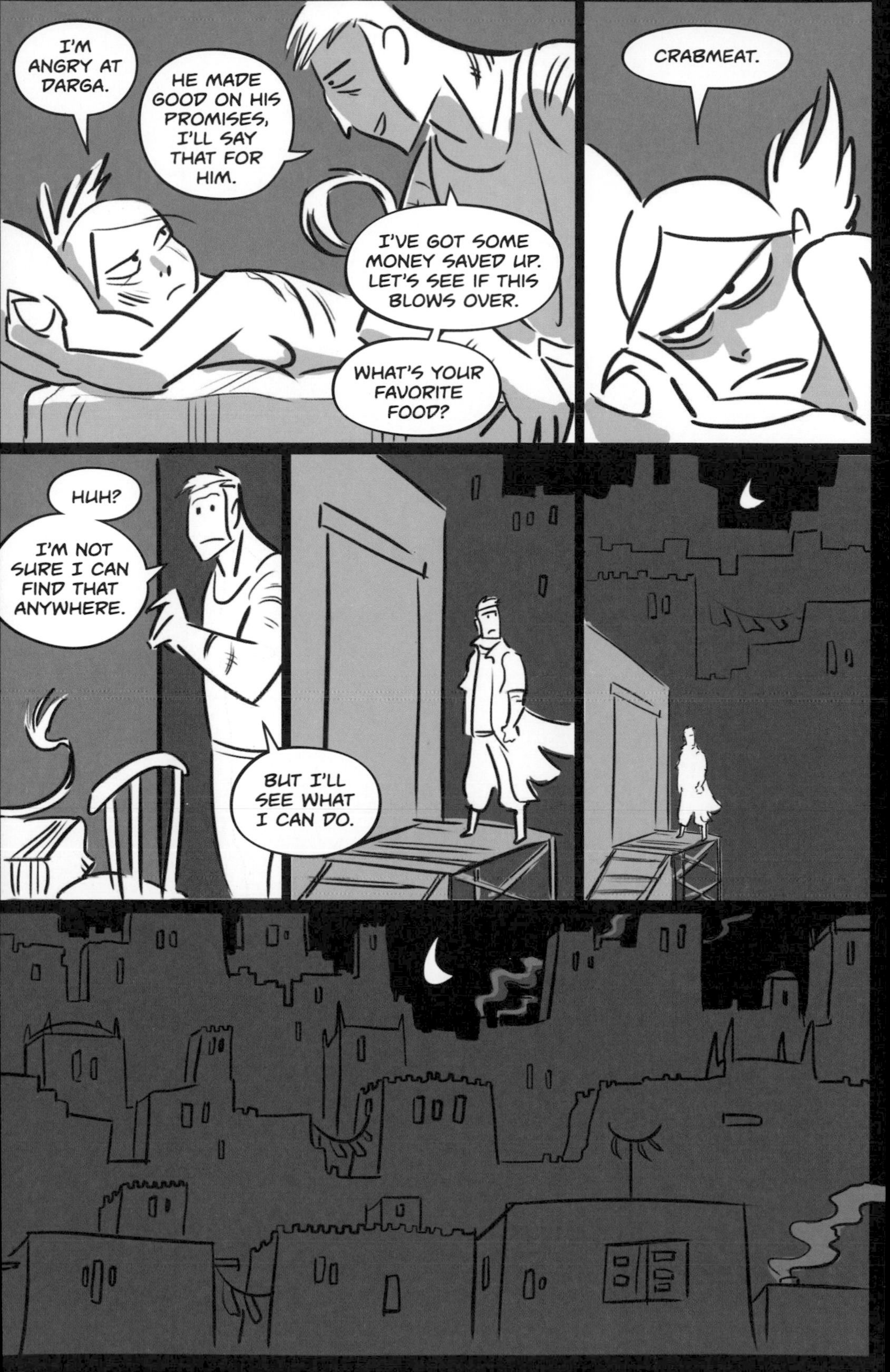
I'M ANGRY AT DARGA.
HE MADE GOOD ON HIS PROMISES, I'LL SAY THAT FOR HIM.
I'VE GOT SOME MONEY SAVED UP. LET'S SEE IF THIS BLOWS OVER.
WHAT'S YOUR FAVORITE FOOD?
CRABMEAT.
HUH?
I'M NOT SURE I CAN FIND THAT ANYWHERE.
BUT I'LL SEE WHAT I CAN DO.

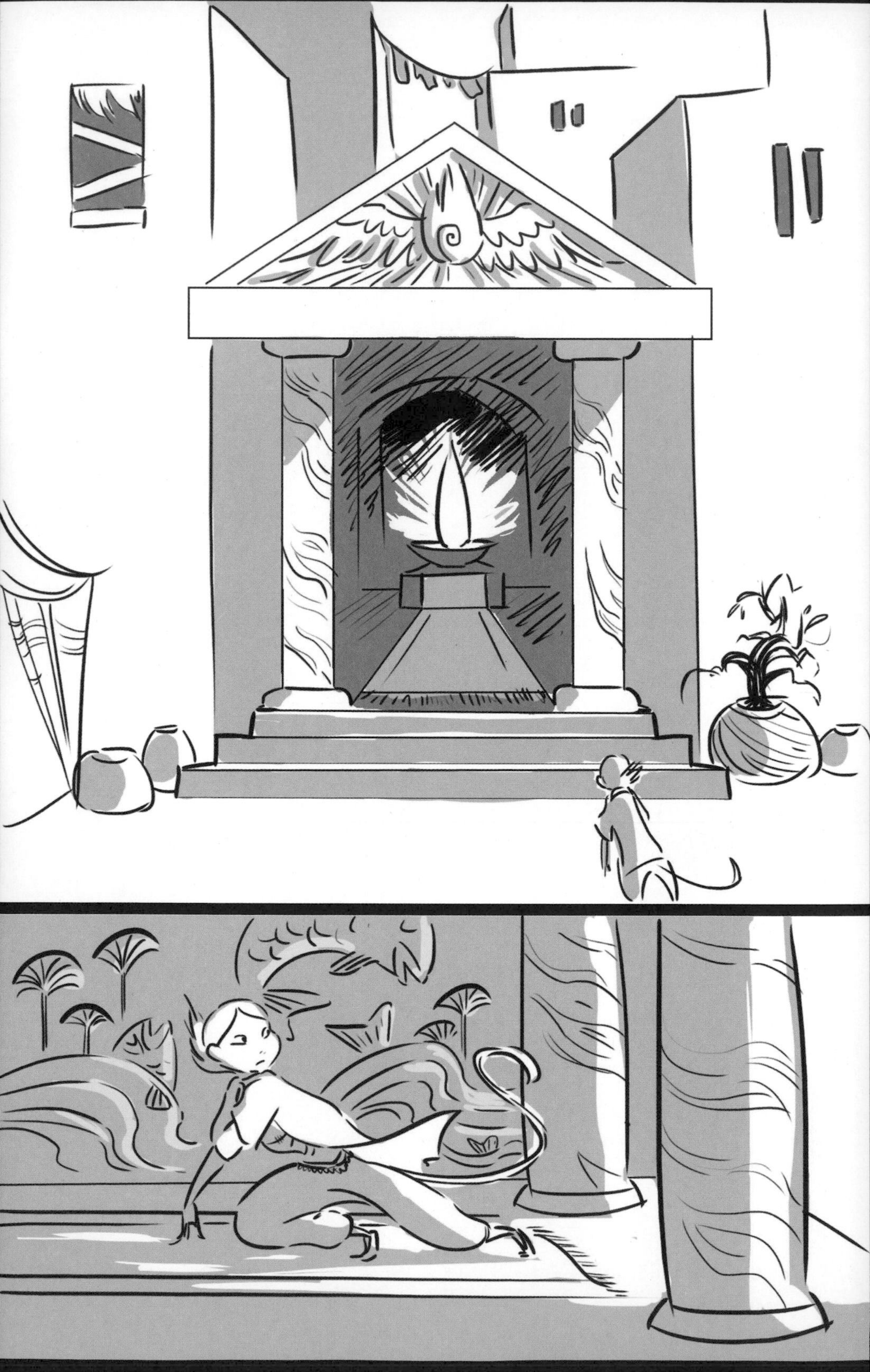

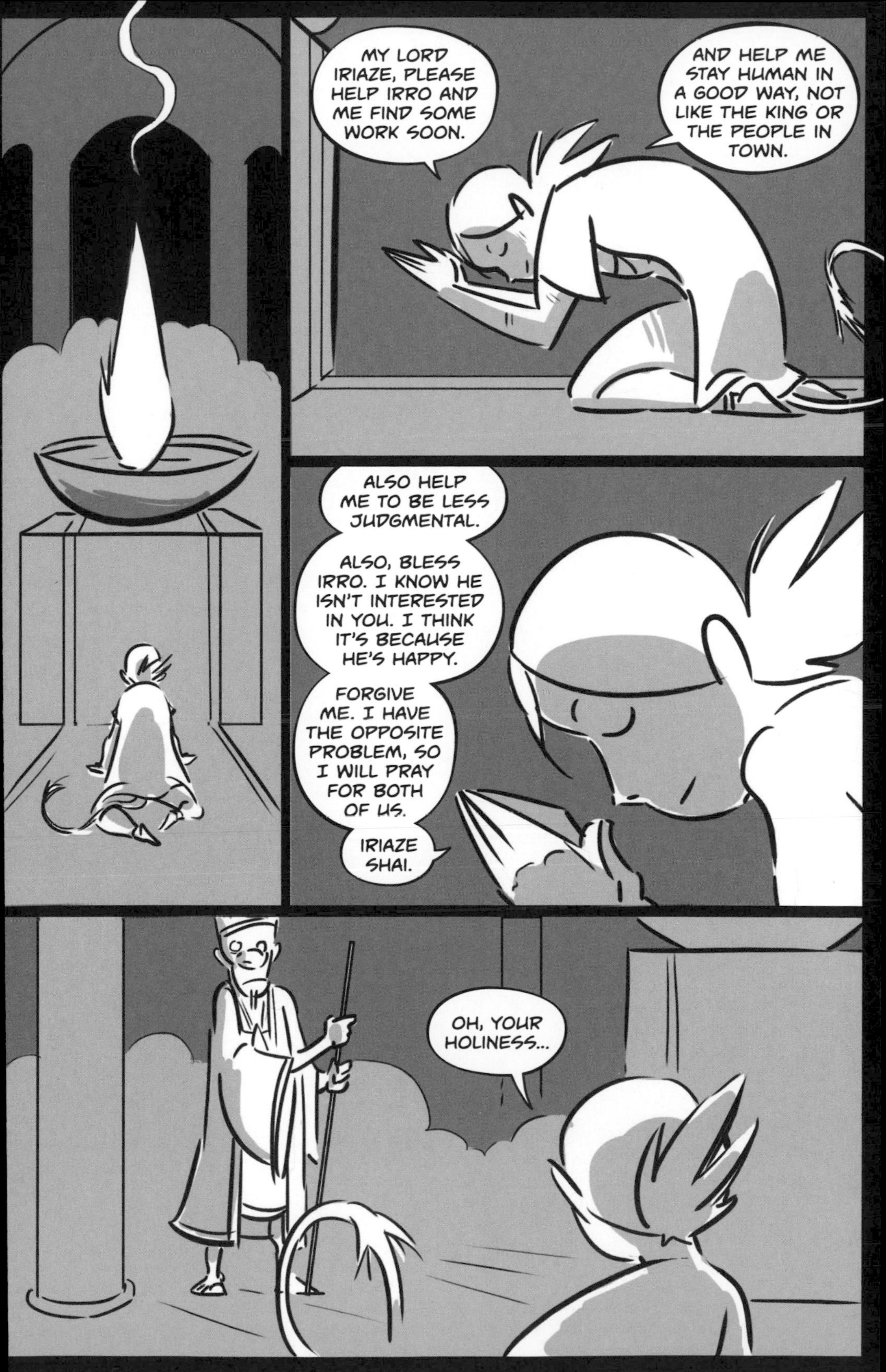
MY LORD IRIAZE, PLEASE HELP IRRO AND ME FIND SOME WORK SOON.
AND HELP ME STAY HUMAN IN A GOOD WAY, NOT LIKE THE KING OR THE PEOPLE IN TOWN.
ALSO HELP ME TO BE LESS JUDGMENTAL.
ALSO, BLESS IRRO. I KNOW HE ISN'T INTERESTED IN YOU. I THINK IT'S BECAUSE HE'S HAPPY.
FORGIVE ME. I HAVE THE OPPOSITE PROBLEM, SO I WILL PRAY FOR BOTH OF US.
IRIAZE SHAI.
OH, YOUR HOLINESS...

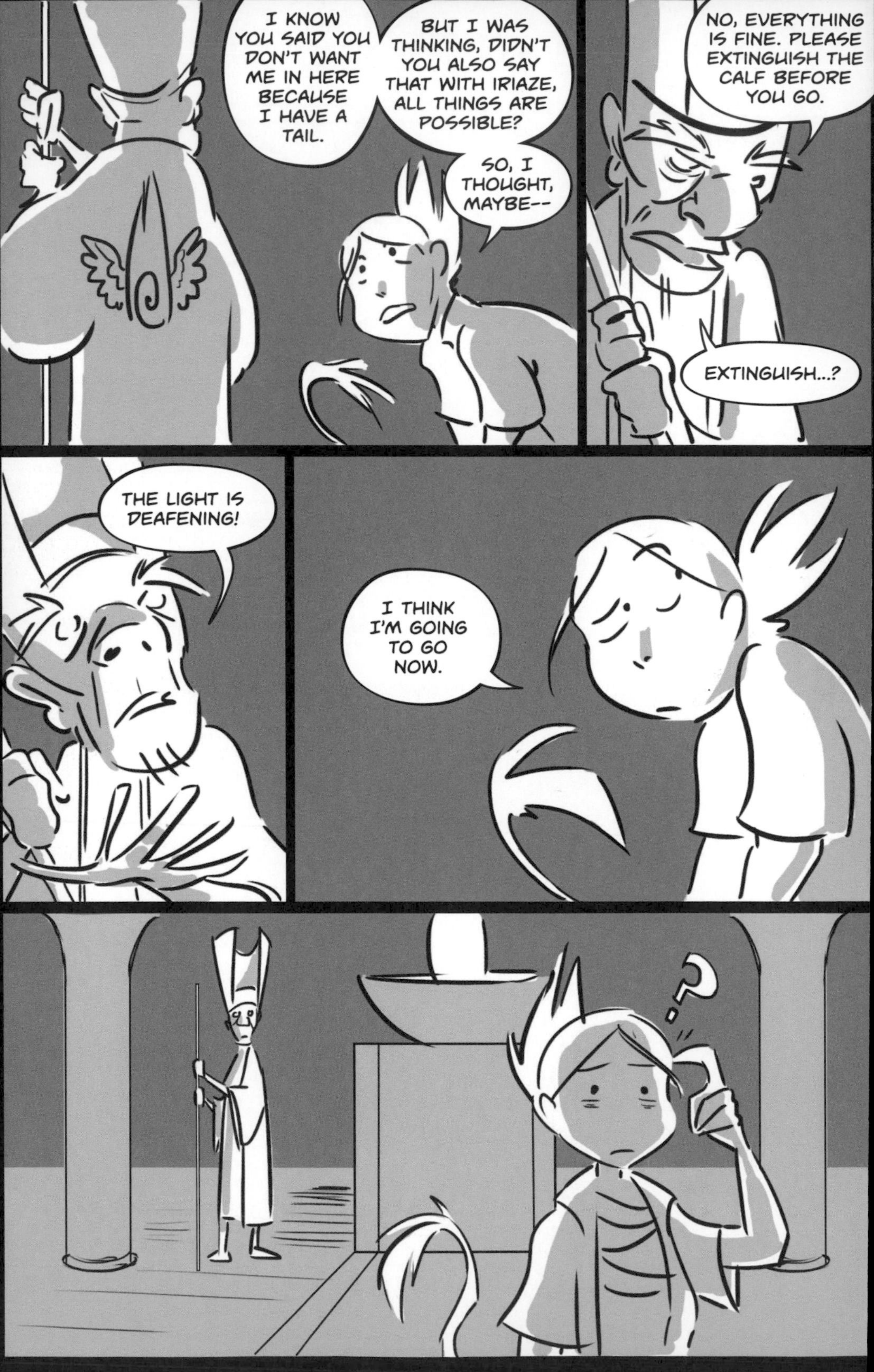
I KNOW YOU SAID YOU DON'T WANT ME IN HERE BECAUSE I HAVE A TAIL.
BUT I WAS THINKING, DIDN'T YOU ALSO SAY THAT WITH IRIAZE, ALL THINGS ARE POSSIBLE?
SO, I THOUGHT, MAYBE--
NO, EVERYTHING IS FINE. PLEASE EXTINGUISH THE CALF BEFORE YOU GO.
EXTINGUISH...?
THE LIGHT IS DEAFENING!
I THINK I'M GOING TO GO NOW.
?

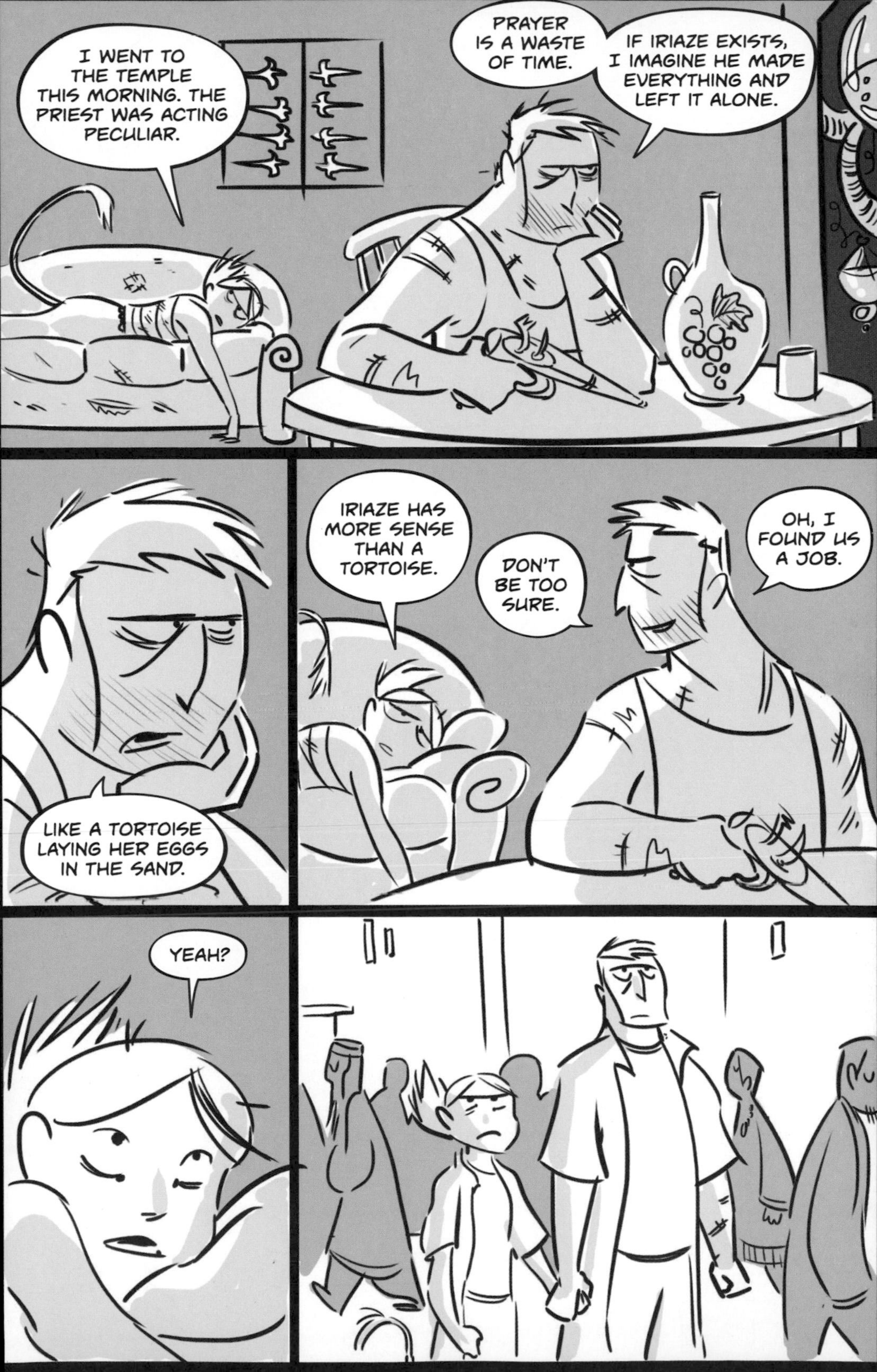
I WENT TO THE TEMPLE THIS MORNING. THE PRIEST WAS ACTING PECULIAR.
PRAYER IS A WASTE OF TIME.
IF IRIAZE EXISTS, I IMAGINE HE MADE EVERYTHING AND LEFT IT ALONE.
LIKE A TORTOISE LAYING HER EGGS IN THE SAND.
IRIAZE HAS MORE SENSE THAN A TORTOISE.
DON'T BE TOO SURE.
OH, I FOUND US A JOB.
YEAH?

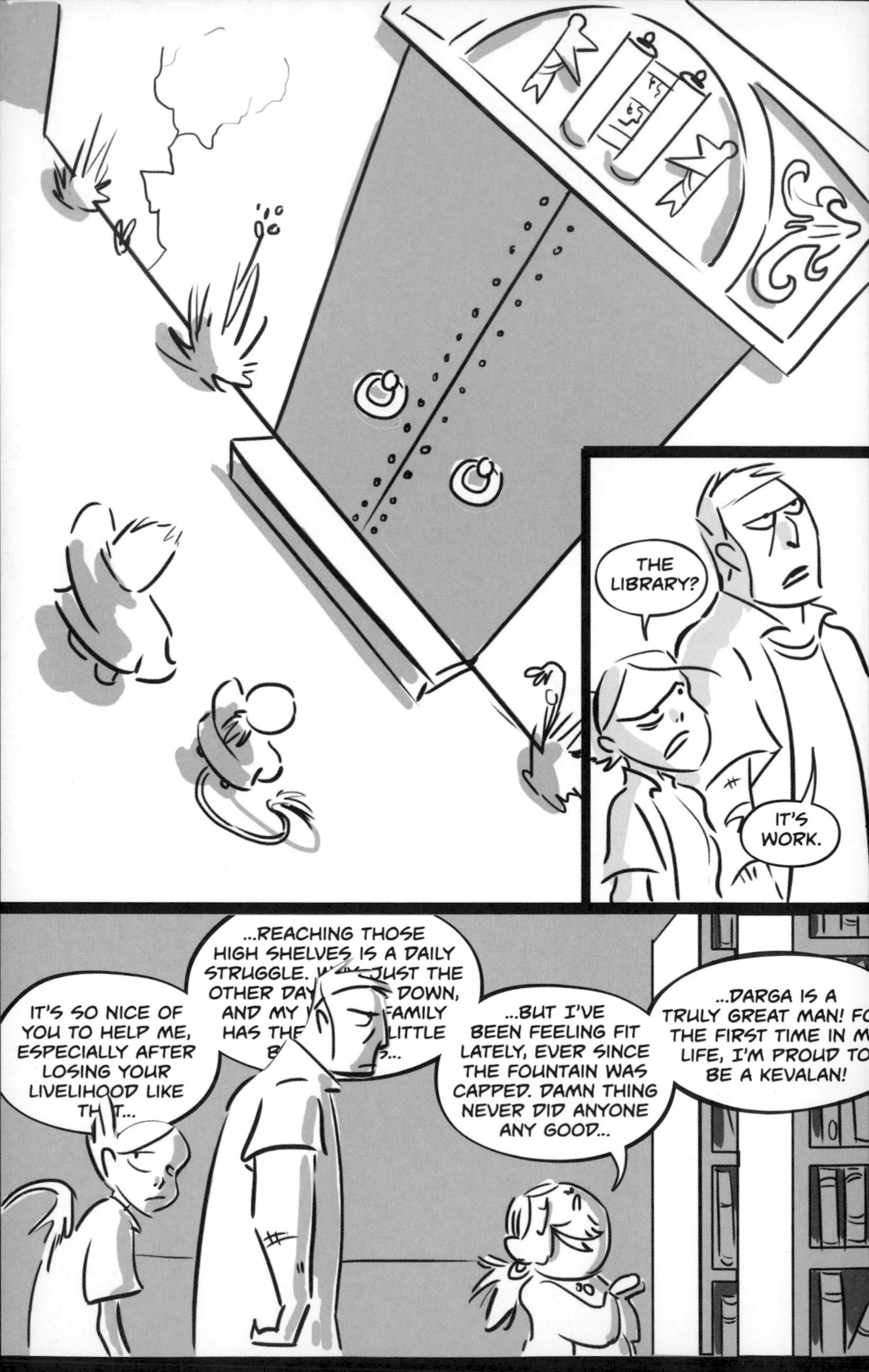
THE LIBRARY?
IT'S WORK.
IT'S SO NICE OF YOU TO HELP ME, ESPECIALLY AFTER LOSING YOUR LIVELIHOOD LIKE TH T...
...REACHING THOSE HIGH SHELVES IS A DAILY STRUGGLE. JUST THE OTHER DAY DOWN, AND MY FAMILY HAS THE LITTLE
...BUT I'VE BEEN FEELING FIT LATELY, EVER SINCE THE FOUNTAIN WAS CAPPED. DAMN THING NEVER DID ANYONE ANY GOOD...
...DARGA IS A TRULY GREAT MAN! FO THE FIRST TIME IN M LIFE, I'M PROUD TO BE A KEVALAN!

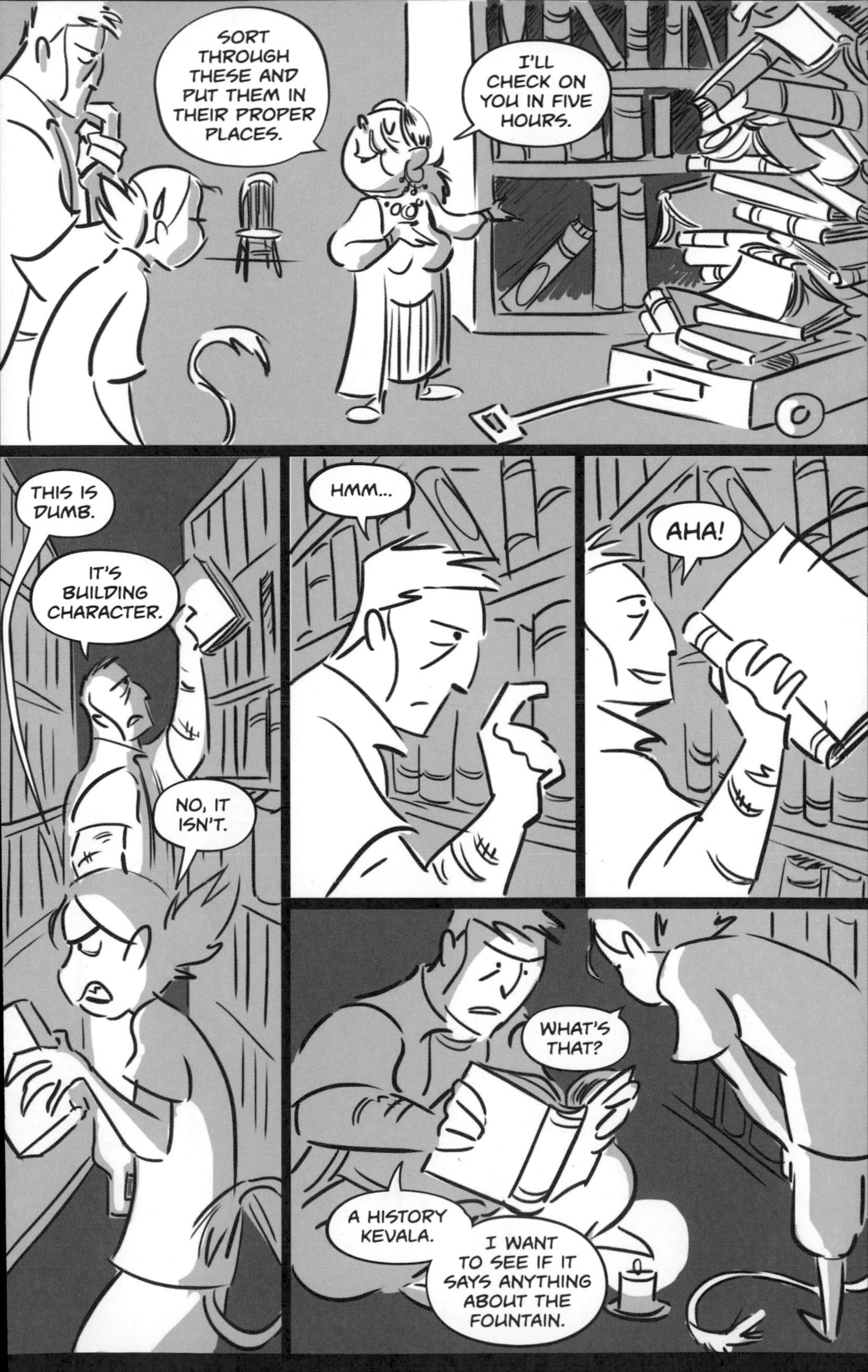
SORT THROUGH THESE AND PUT THEM IN THEIR PROPER PLACES.
I'LL CHECK ON YOU IN FIVE HOURS.
THIS IS DUMB.
IT'S BUILDING CHARACTER.
NO, IT ISN'T.
HMM...
AHA!
WHAT'S THAT?
A HISTORY KEVALA.
I WANT TO SEE IF IT SAYS ANYTHING ABOUT THE FOUNTAIN.

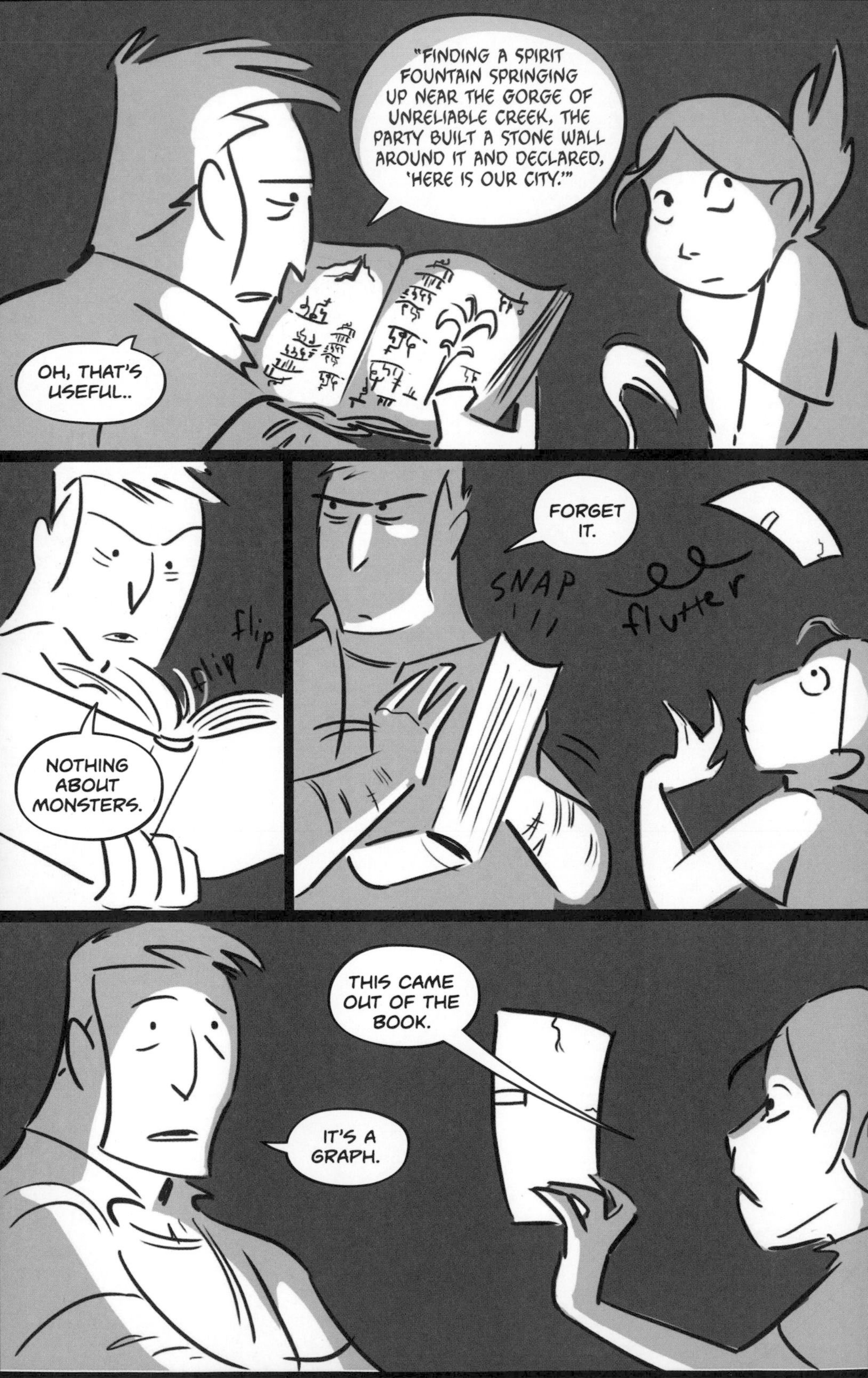
"FINDING A SPIRIT FOUNTAIN SPRINGING UP NEAR THE GORGE OF UNRELIABLE CREEK, THE PARTY BUILT A STONE WALL AROUND IT AND DECLARED, 'HERE IS OUR CITY.'"
OH, THAT'S USEFUL..
flip flip
NOTHING ABOUT MONSTERS.
FORGET IT.
SNAP
flutter
THIS CAME OUT OF THE BOOK.
IT'S A GRAPH.

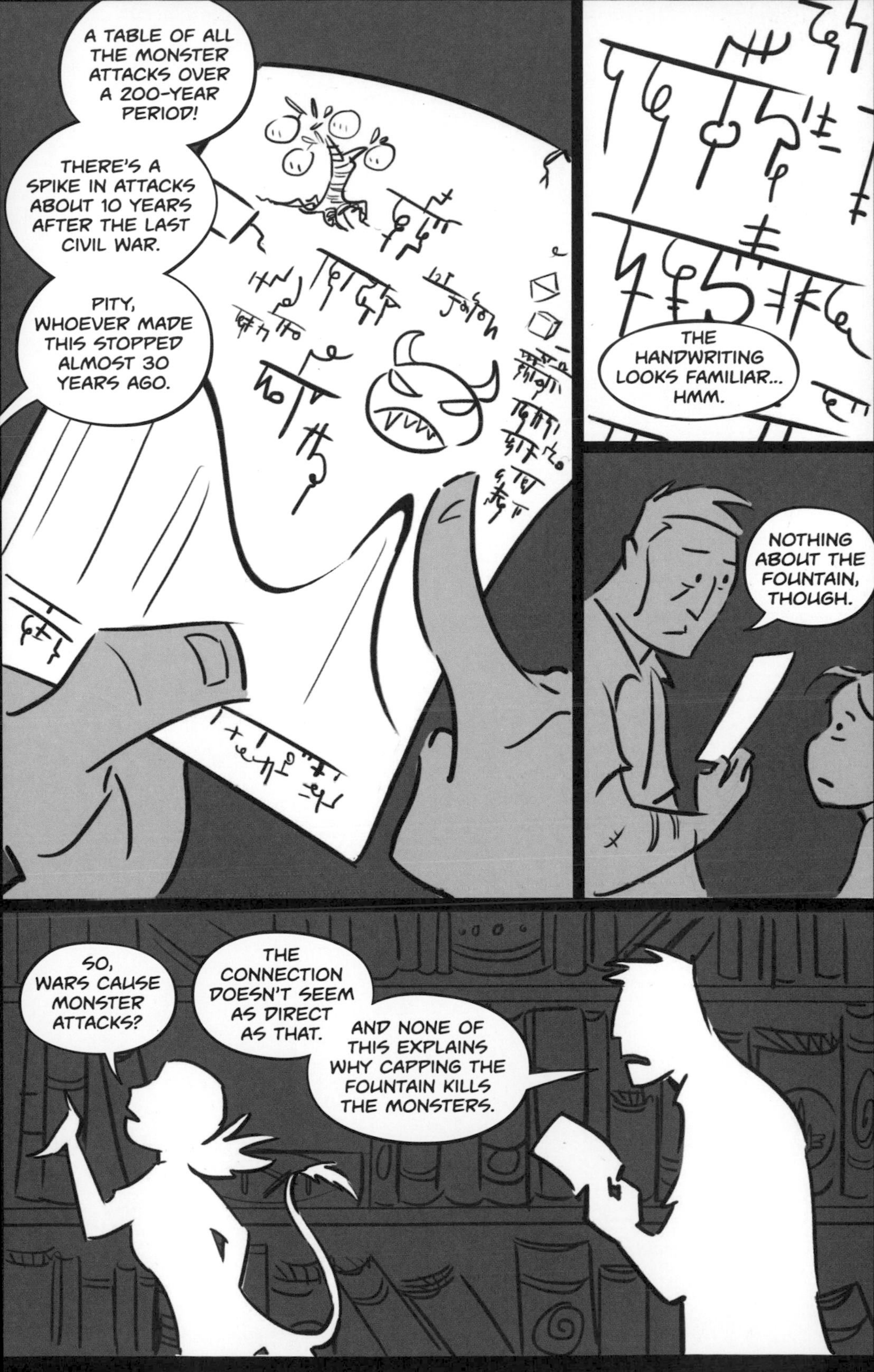
A TABLE OF ALL THE MONSTER ATTACKS OVER A 200-YEAR PERIOD!
THERE'S A SPIKE IN ATTACKS ABOUT 10 YEARS AFTER THE LAST CIVIL WAR.
PITY, WHOEVER MADE THIS STOPPED ALMOST 30 YEARS AGO.
THE HANDWRITING LOOKS FAMILIAR... HMM.
NOTHING ABOUT THE FOUNTAIN, THOUGH.
SO, WARS CAUSE MONSTER ATTACKS?
THE CONNECTION DOESN'T SEEM AS DIRECT AS THAT.
AND NONE OF THIS EXPLAINS WHY CAPPING THE FOUNTAIN KILLS THE MONSTERS.

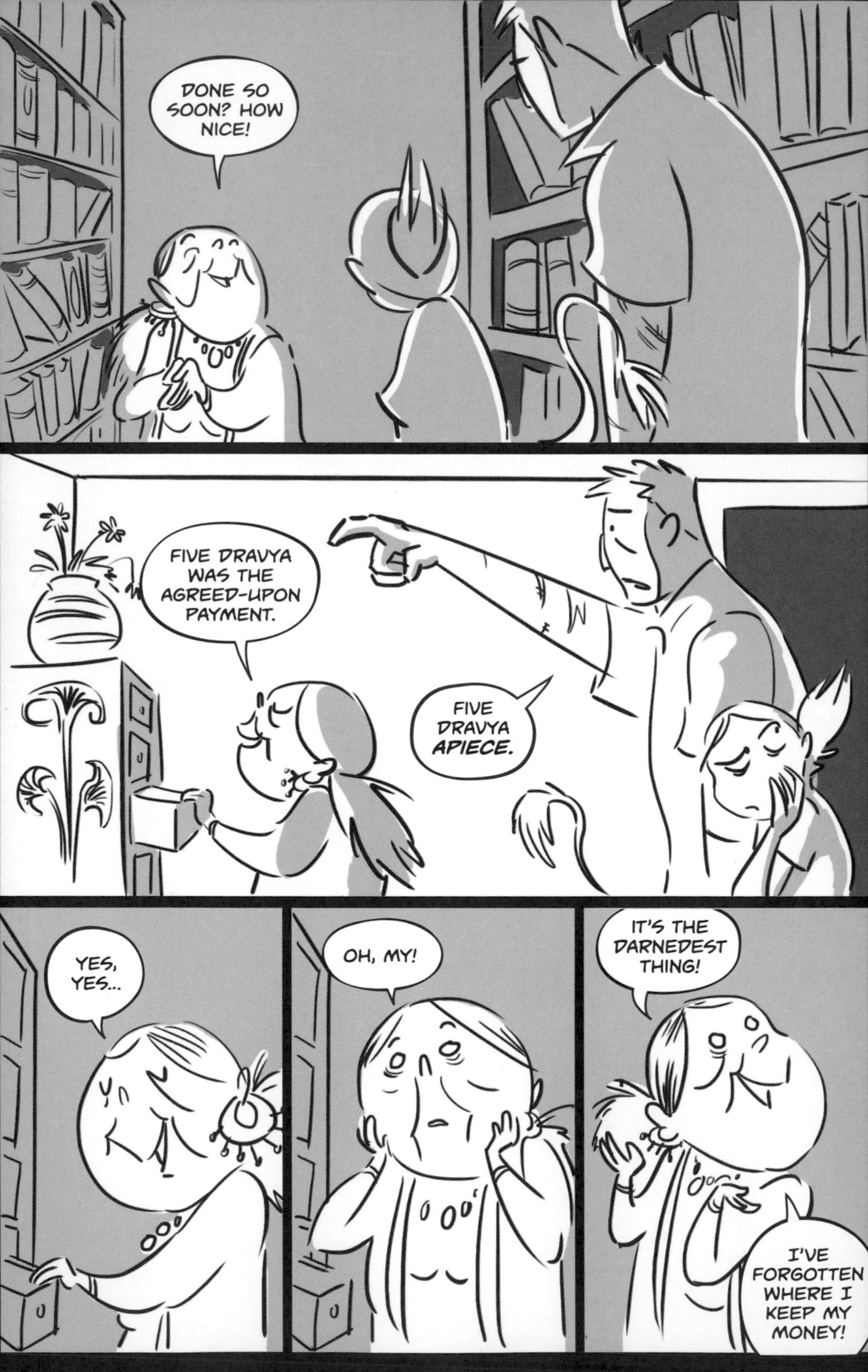
DONE SO SOON? HOW NICE!
FIVE DRAVYA WAS THE AGREED-UPON PAYMENT.
FIVE DRAVYA *APIECE.*
YES, YES...
OH, MY!
IT'S THE DARNEDEST THING!
I'VE FORGOTTEN WHERE I KEEP MY MONEY!

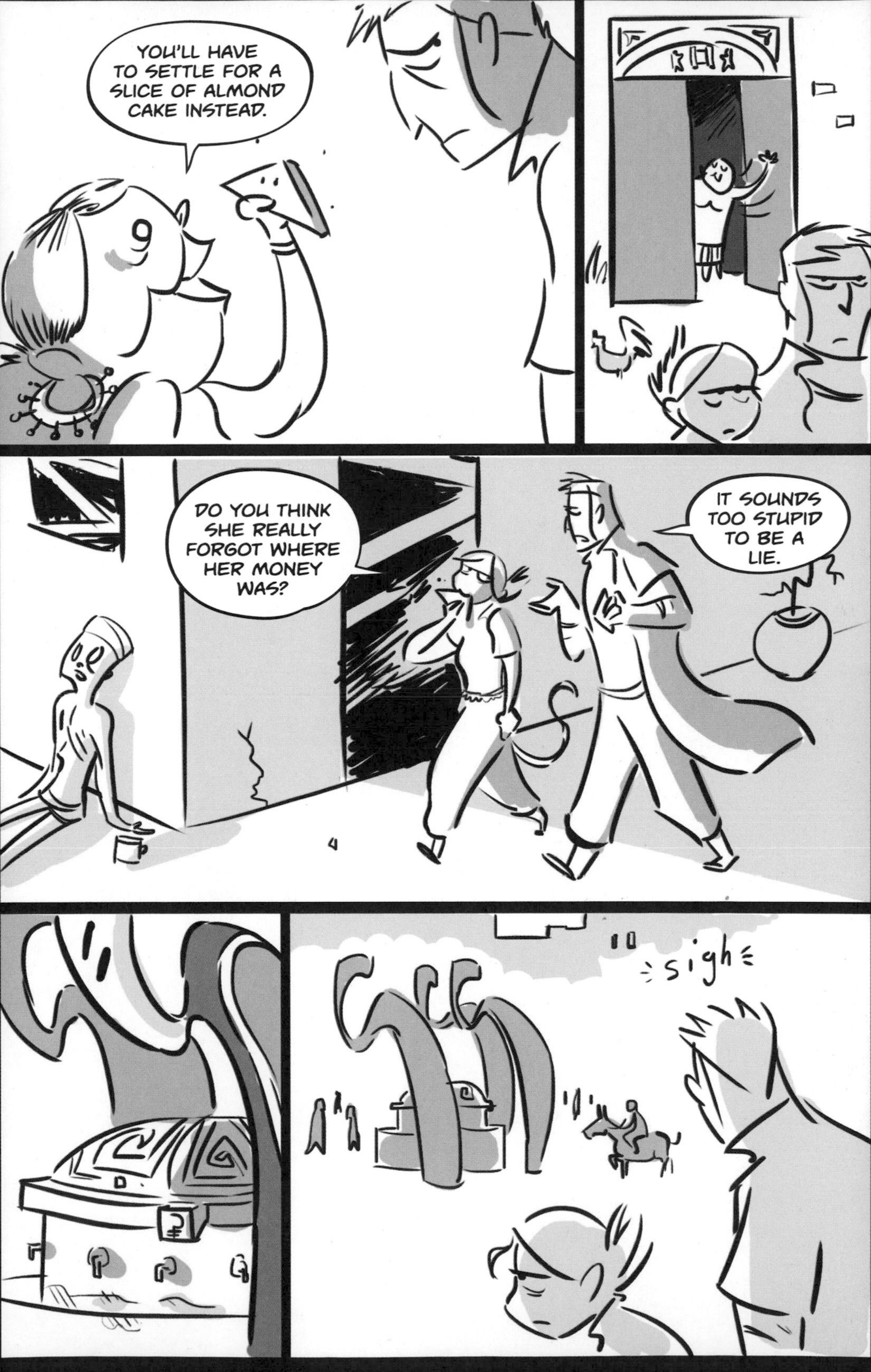
YOU'LL HAVE TO SETTLE FOR A SLICE OF ALMOND CAKE INSTEAD.
DO YOU THINK SHE REALLY FORGOT WHERE HER MONEY WAS?
IT SOUNDS TOO STUPID TO BE A LIE.
sigh

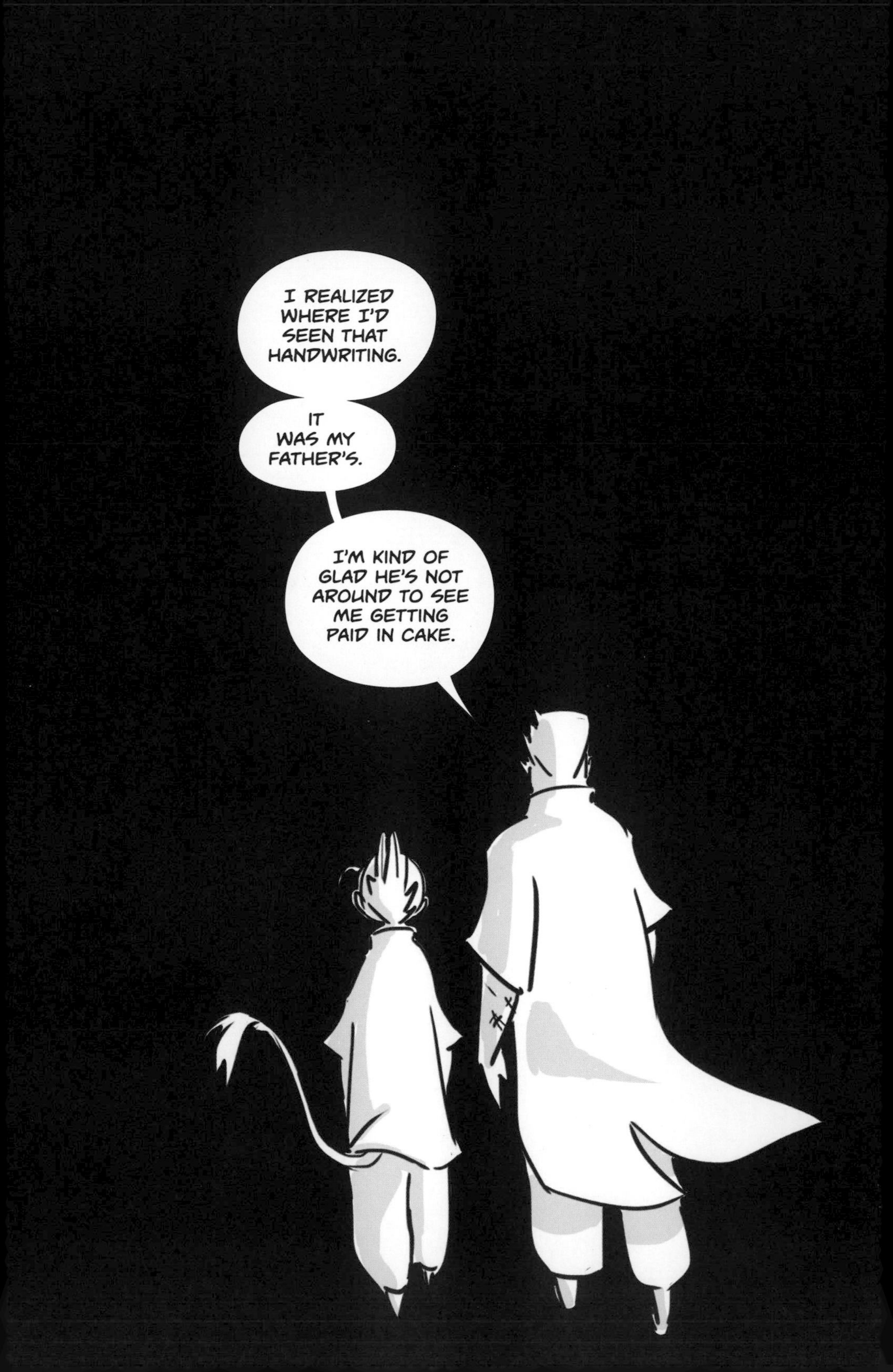
I REALIZED WHERE I'D SEEN THAT HANDWRITING.
IT WAS MY FATHER'S.
I'M KIND OF GLAD HE'S NOT AROUND TO SEE ME GETTING PAID IN CAKE.

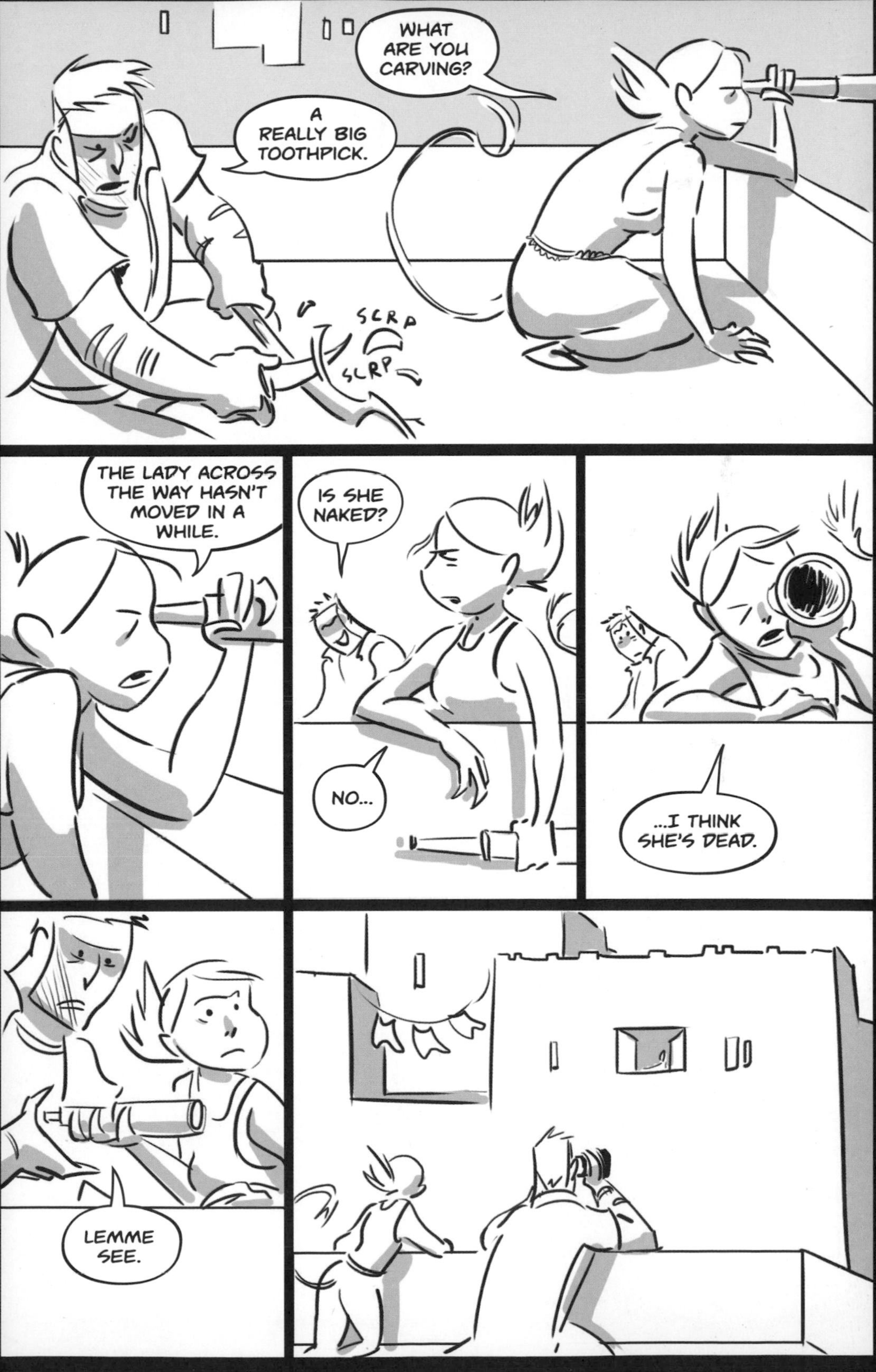
WHAT ARE YOU CARVING?
A REALLY BIG TOOTHPICK.
SCRP
SCRP
THE LADY ACROSS THE WAY HASN'T MOVED IN A WHILE.
IS SHE NAKED?
NO...
...I THINK SHE'S DEAD.
LEMME SEE.

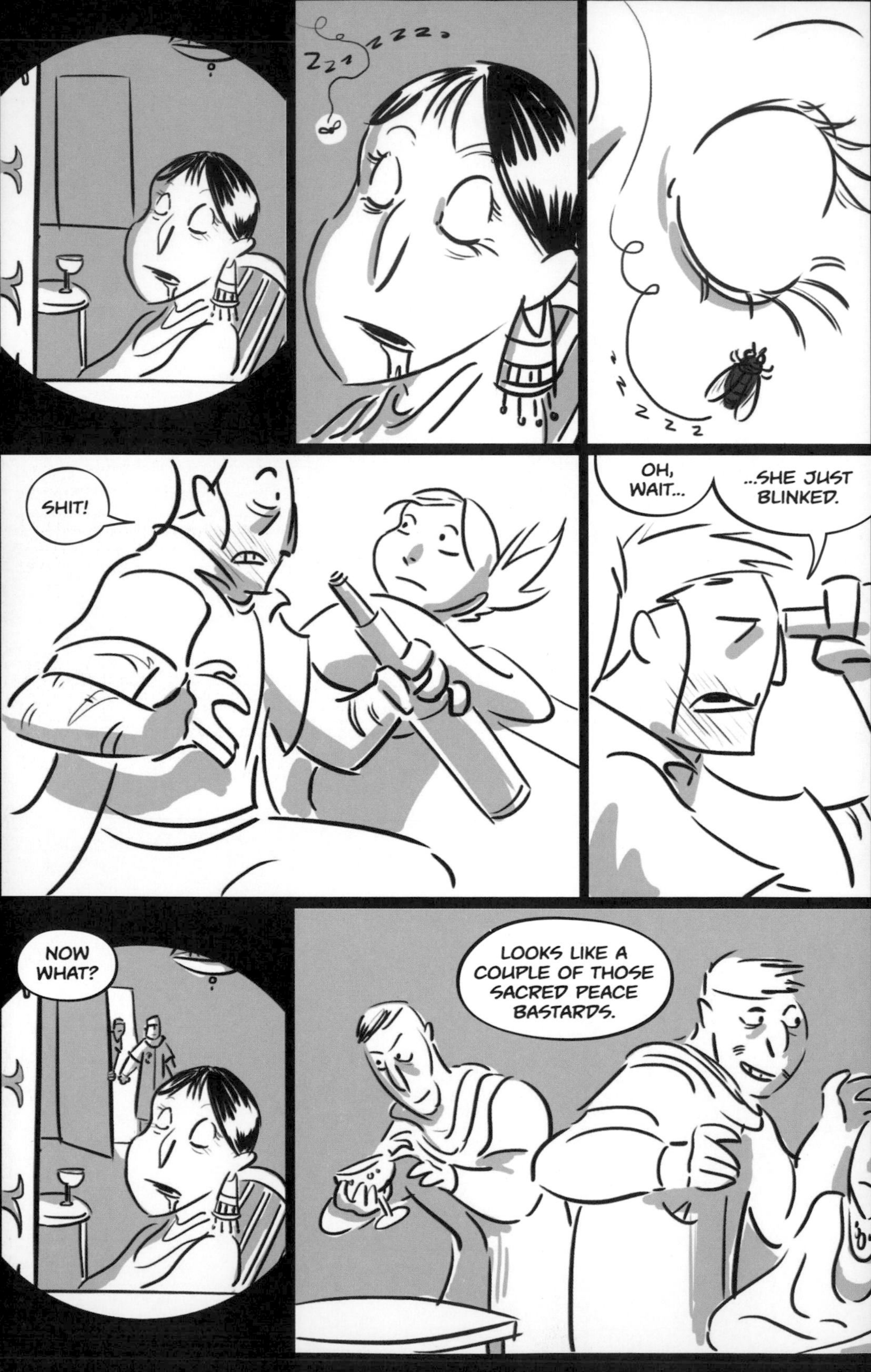
ZZZ
ZZZZ
SHIT!
OH, WAIT...
...SHE JUST BLINKED.
NOW WHAT?
LOOKS LIKE A COUPLE OF THOSE SACRED PEACE BASTARDS.

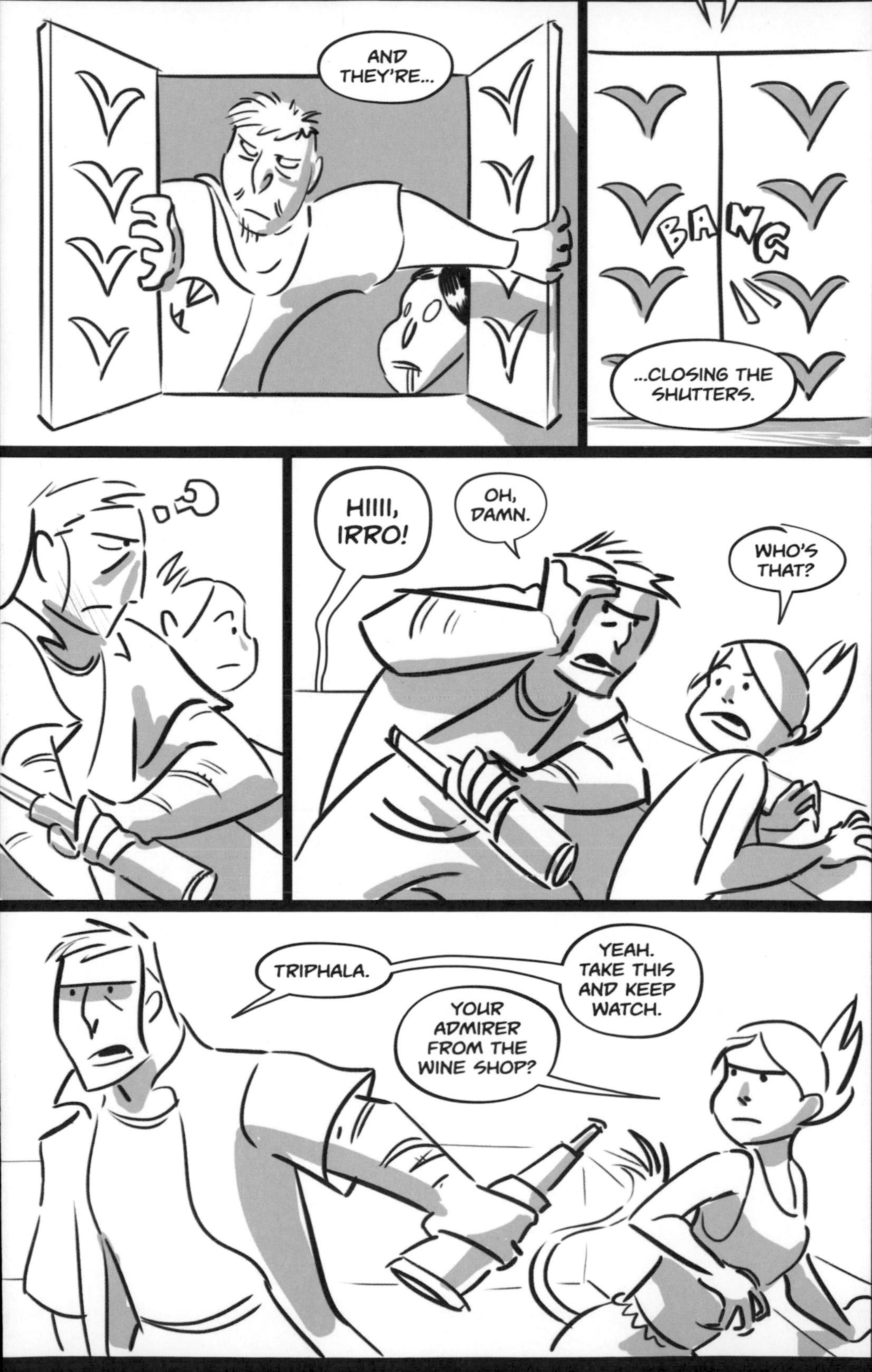
AND THEY'RE...
BANG
...CLOSING THE SHUTTERS.
HIIII, IRRO!
OH, DAMN.
WHO'S THAT?
TRIPHALA.
YOUR ADMIRER FROM THE WINE SHOP?
YEAH. TAKE THIS AND KEEP WATCH.

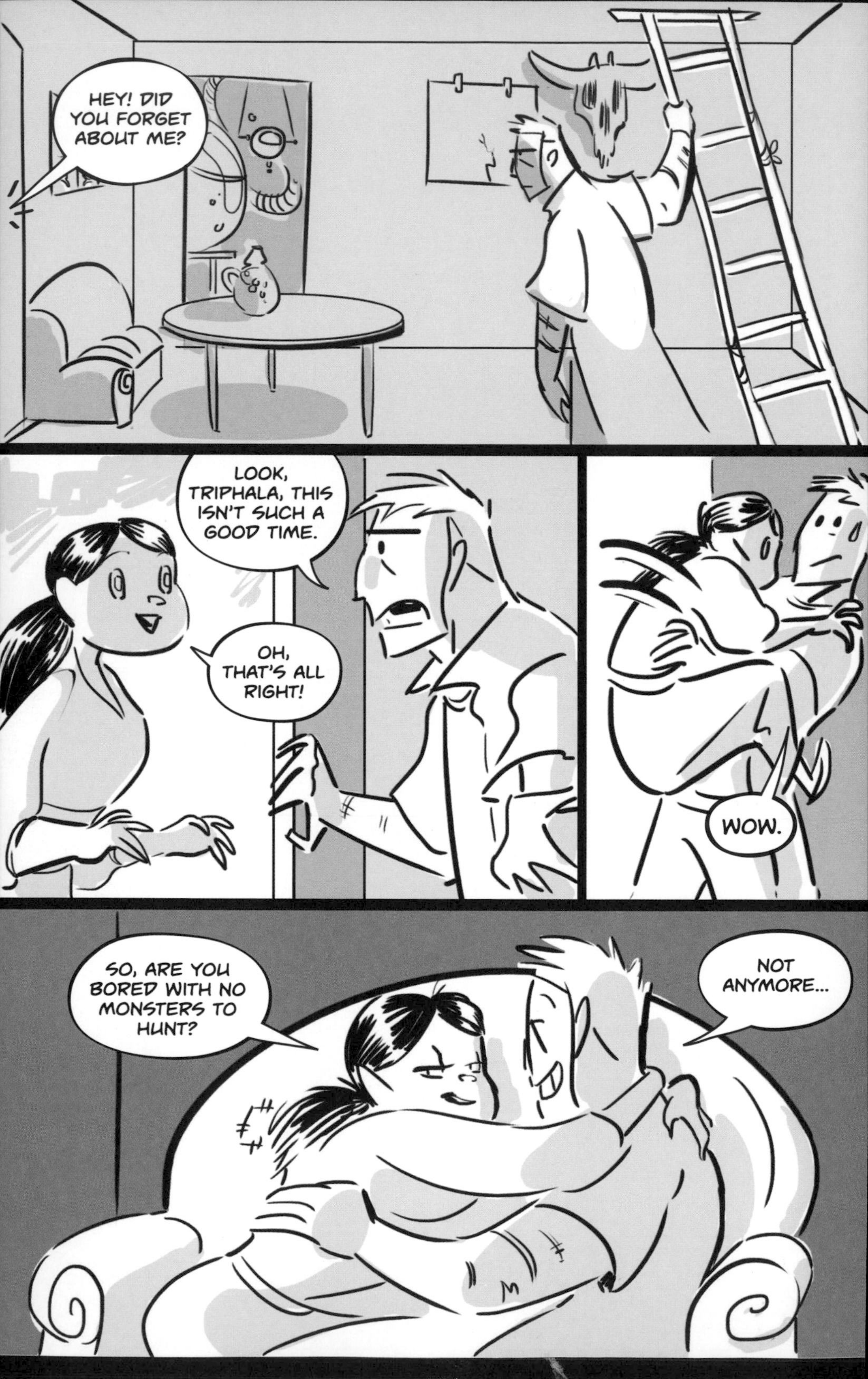
HEY! DID YOU FORGET ABOUT ME?
LOOK, TRIPHALA, THIS ISN'T SUCH A GOOD TIME.
OH, THAT'S ALL RIGHT!
WOW.
SO, ARE YOU BORED WITH NO MONSTERS TO HUNT?
NOT ANYMORE...

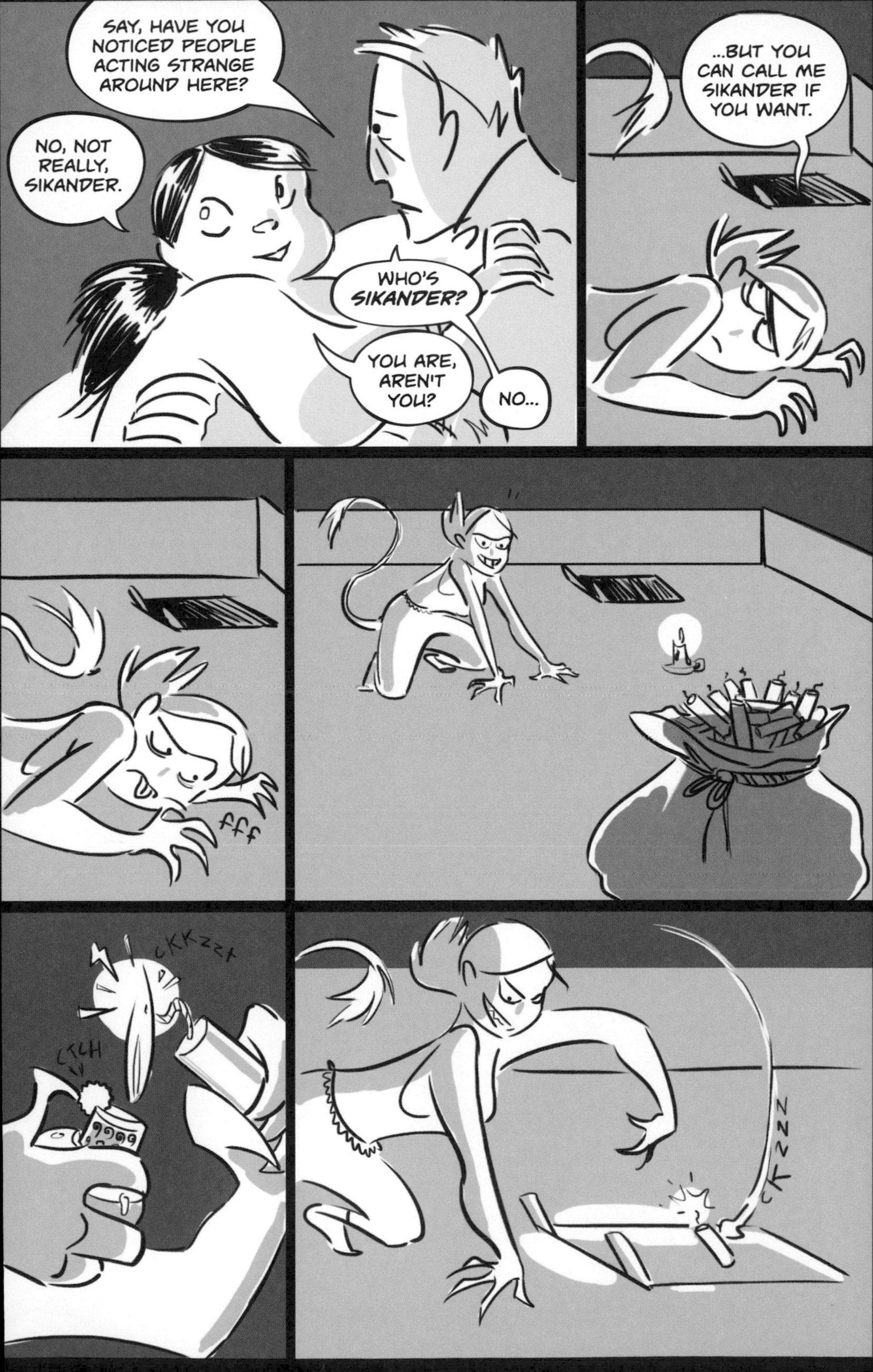
SAY, HAVE YOU NOTICED PEOPLE ACTING STRANGE AROUND HERE?
NO, NOT REALLY, SIKANDER.
WHO'S SIKANDER?
YOU ARE, AREN'T YOU?
NO...
...BUT YOU CAN CALL ME SIKANDER IF YOU WANT.
fff
cKKzzt
CTCH
cKZZZ

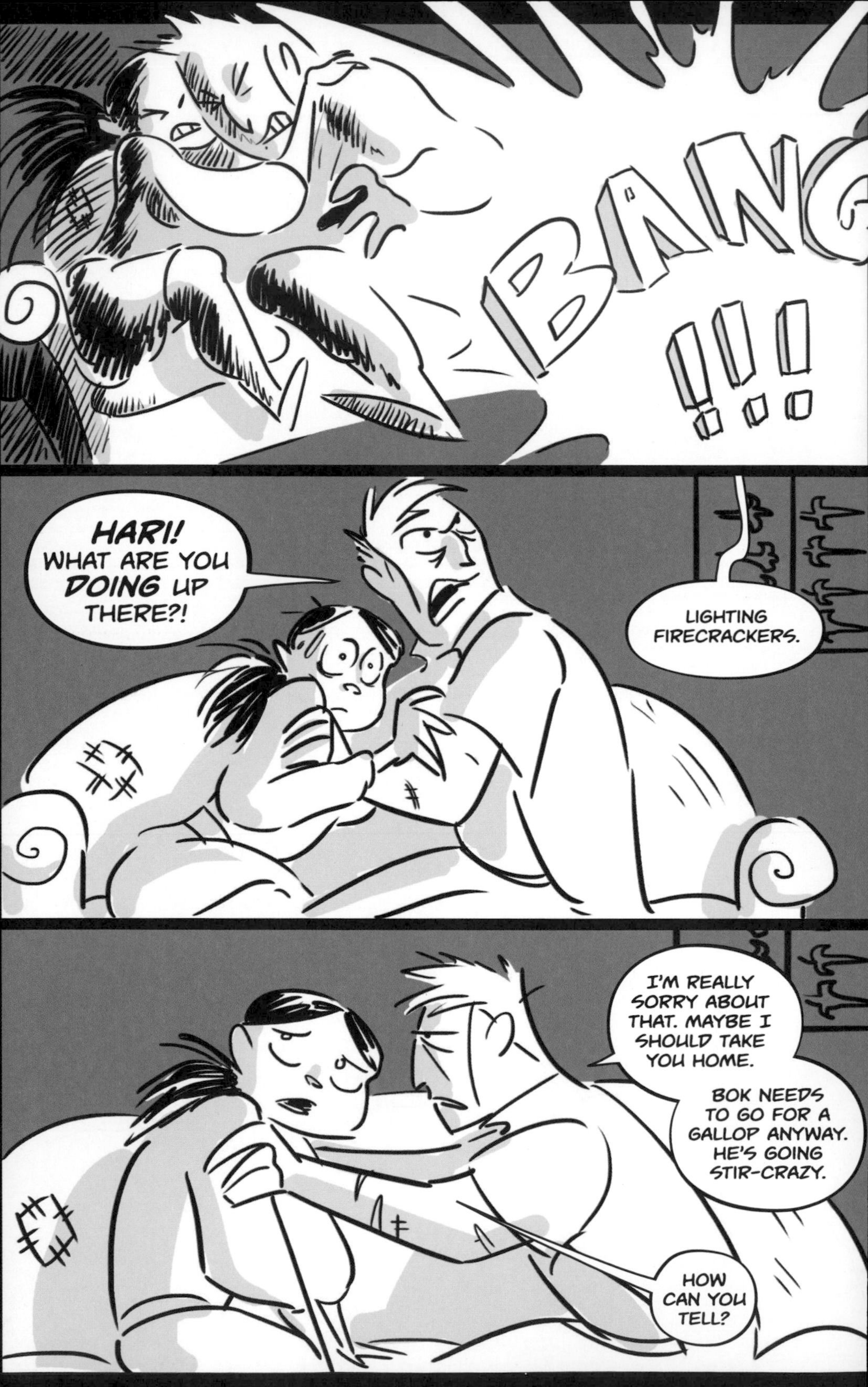
BANG!!!!
HARI! WHAT ARE YOU DOING UP THERE?!
LIGHTING FIRECRACKERS.
I'M REALLY SORRY ABOUT THAT. MAYBE I SHOULD TAKE YOU HOME.
BOK NEEDS TO GO FOR A GALLOP ANYWAY. HE'S GOING STIR-CRAZY.
HOW CAN YOU TELL?

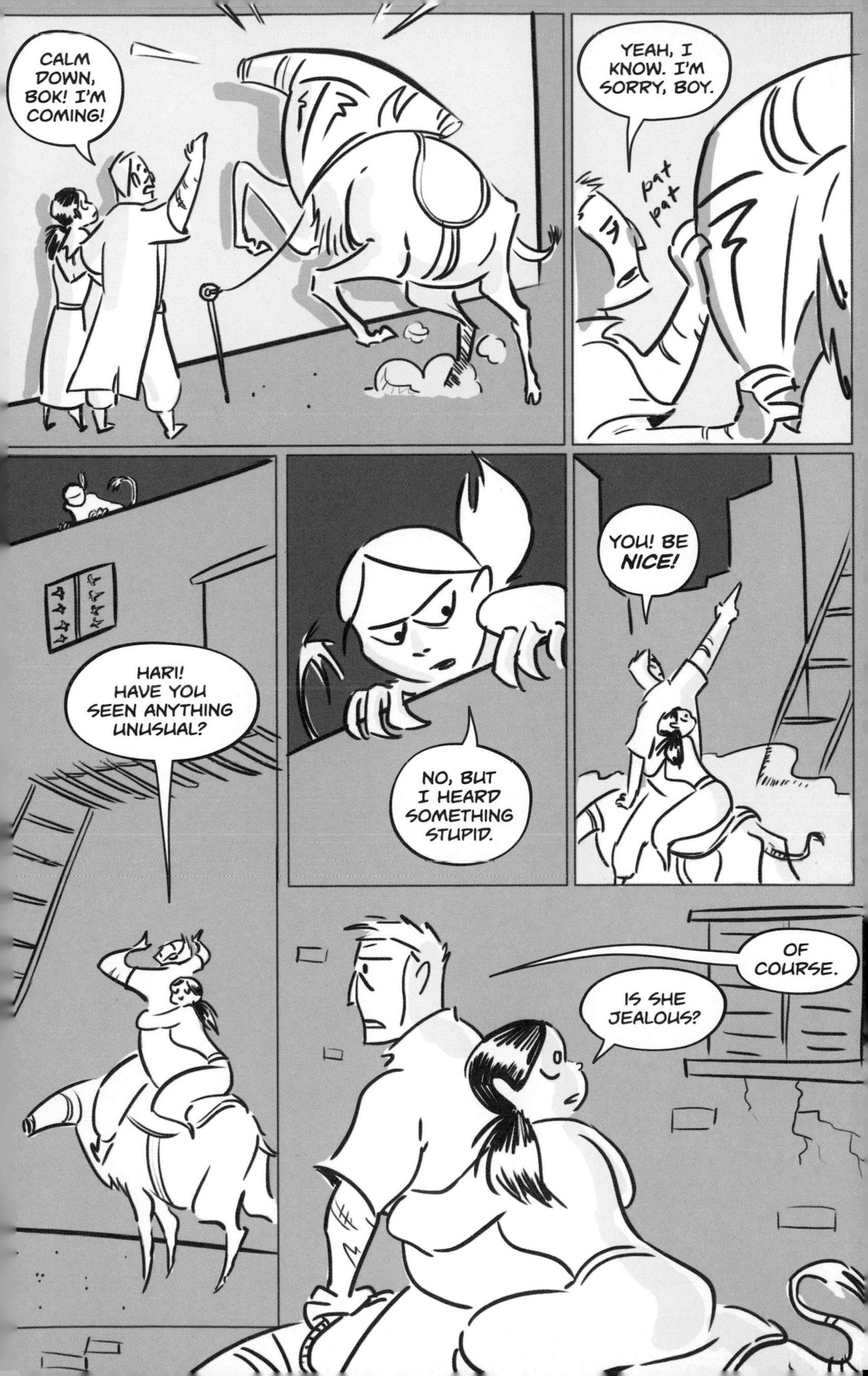
CALM DOWN, BOK! I'M COMING!
YEAH, I KNOW. I'M SORRY, BOY.
pat pat
HARI! HAVE YOU SEEN ANYTHING UNUSUAL?
NO, BUT I HEARD SOMETHING STUPID.
YOU! BE NICE!
IS SHE JEALOUS?
OF COURSE.

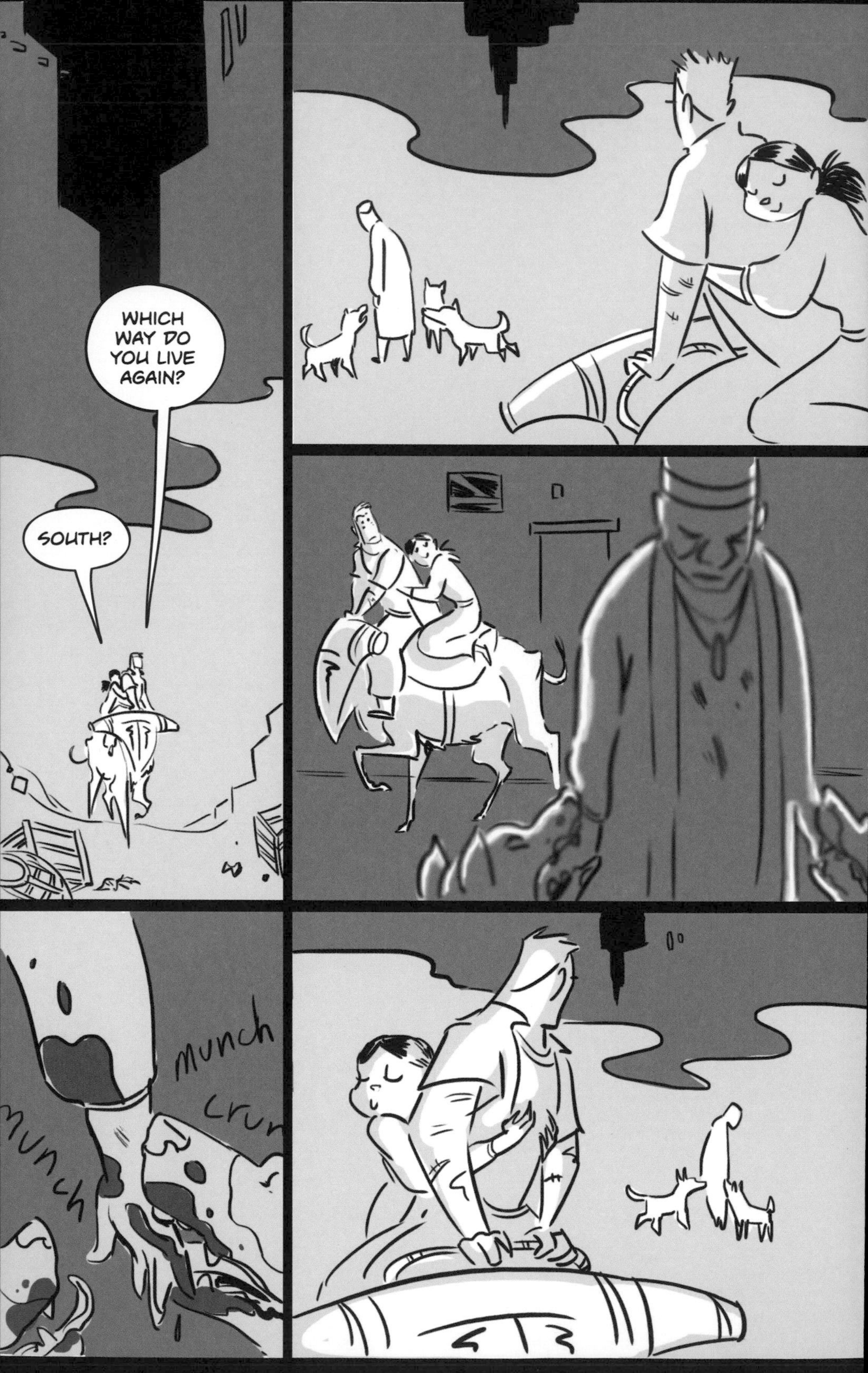
WHICH WAY DO YOU LIVE AGAIN?
SOUTH?
munch
crun
munch

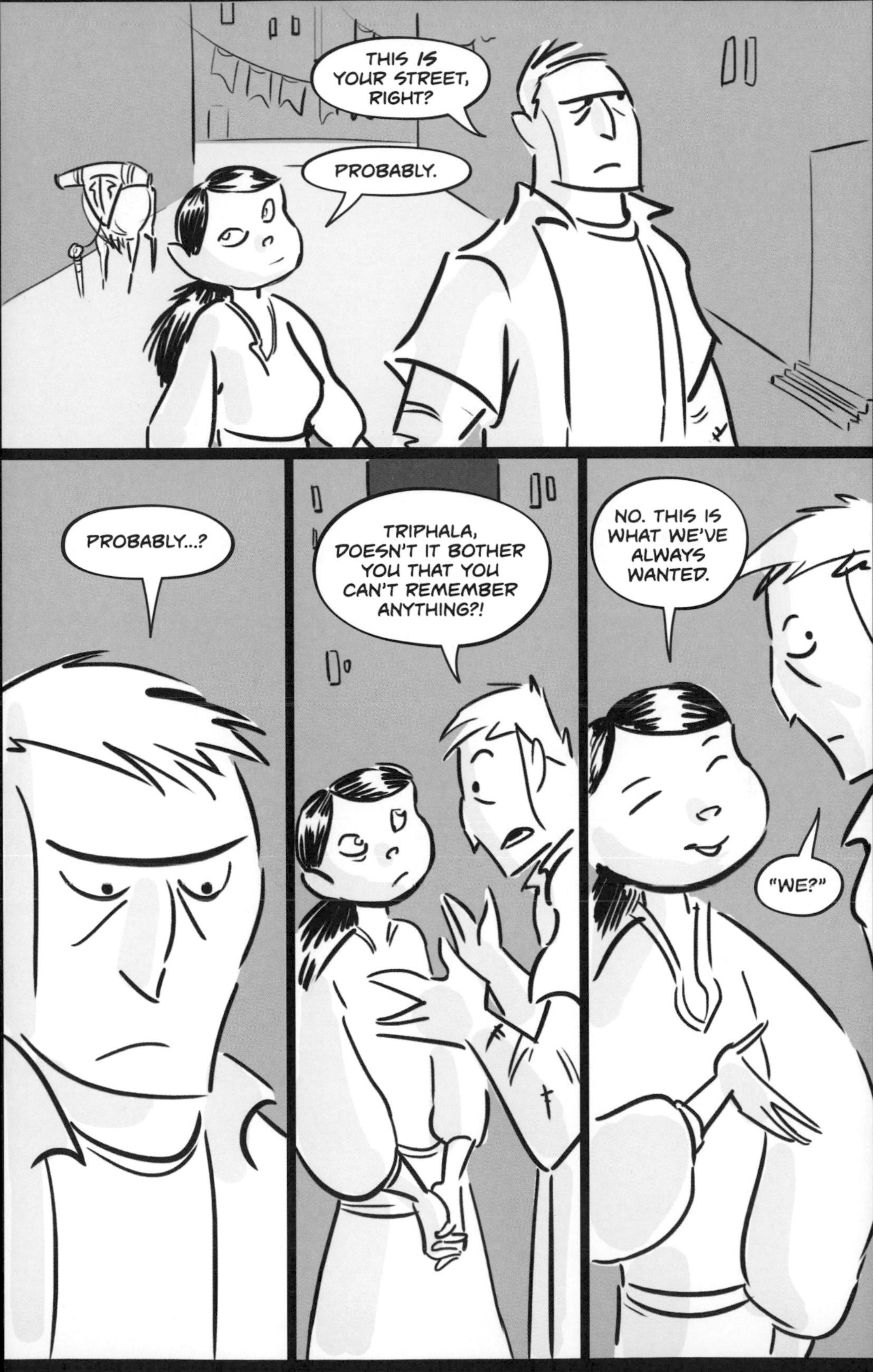
THIS IS YOUR STREET, RIGHT?
PROBABLY.
PROBABLY...?
TRIPHALA, DOESN'T IT BOTHER YOU THAT YOU CAN'T REMEMBER ANYTHING?!
NO. THIS IS WHAT WE'VE ALWAYS WANTED.
"WE?"

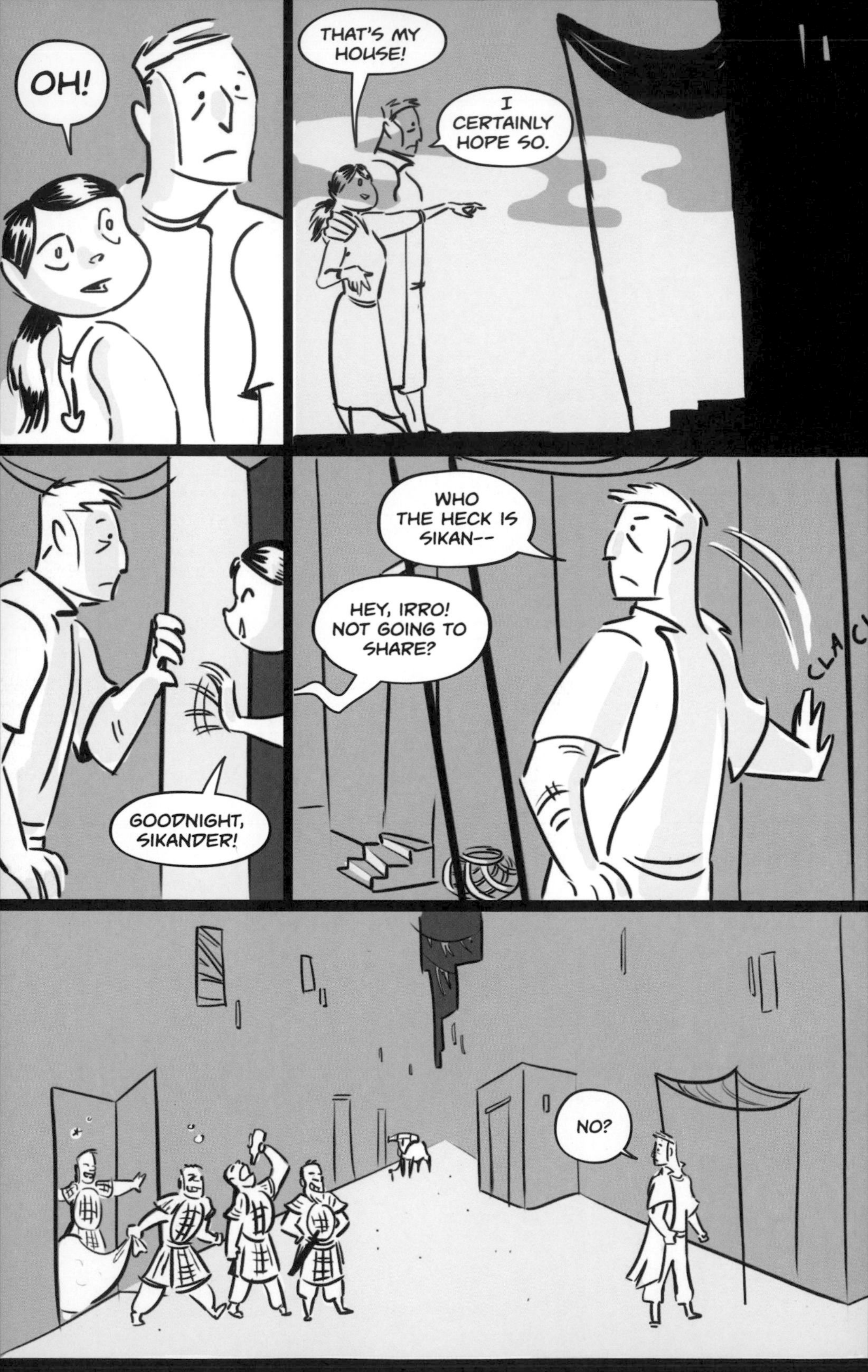
OH!
THAT'S MY HOUSE!
I CERTAINLY HOPE SO.
GOODNIGHT, SIKANDER!
WHO THE HECK IS SIKAN--
HEY, IRRO! NOT GOING TO SHARE?
NO?

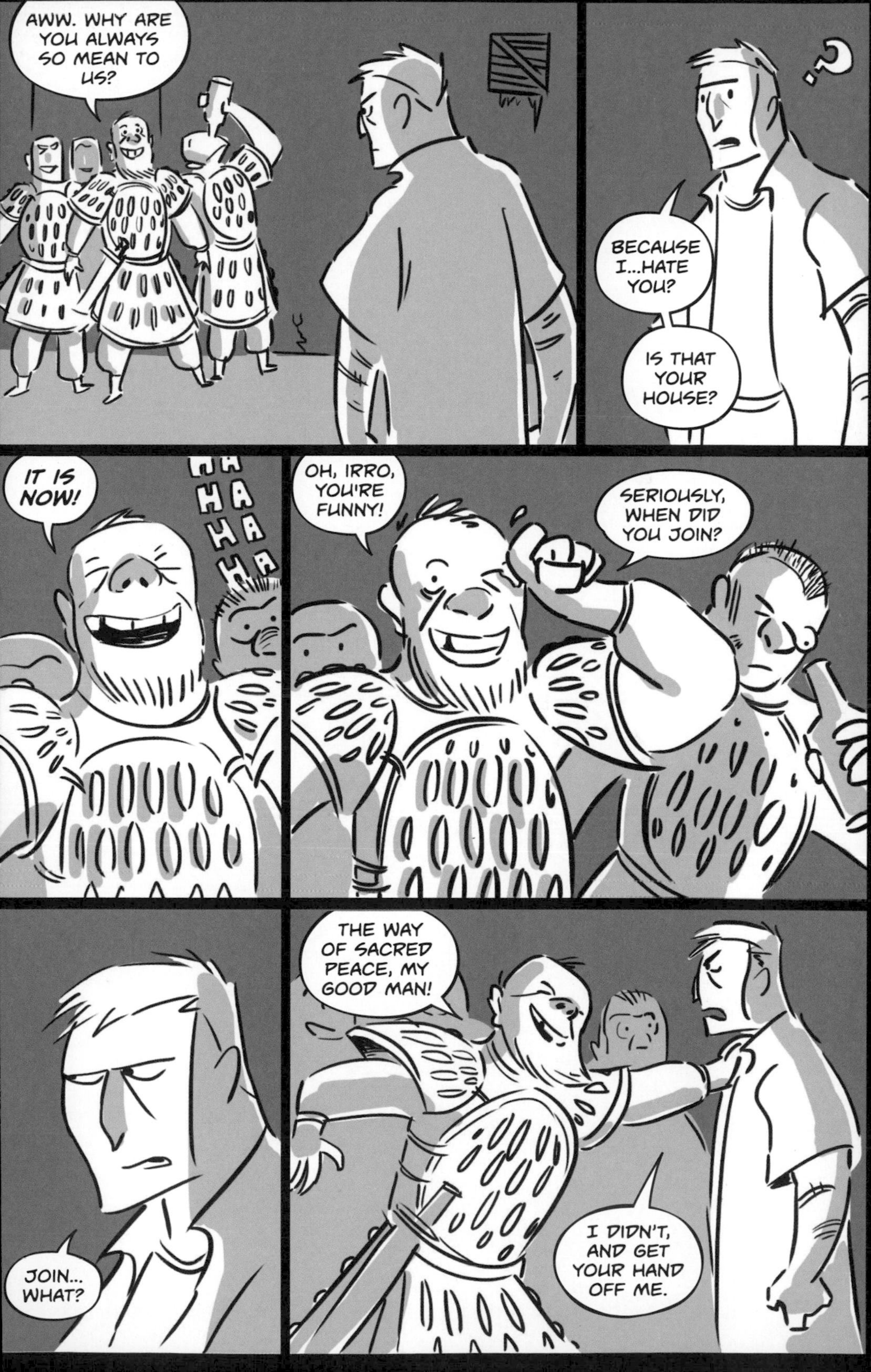
AWW. WHY ARE YOU ALWAYS SO MEAN TO US?
BECAUSE I...HATE YOU?
IS THAT YOUR HOUSE?
IT IS NOW!
HA HA HA HA HA HA HA
OH, IRRO, YOU'RE FUNNY!
SERIOUSLY, WHEN DID YOU JOIN?
JOIN... WHAT?
THE WAY OF SACRED PEACE, MY GOOD MAN!
I DIDN'T, AND GET YOUR HAND OFF ME.

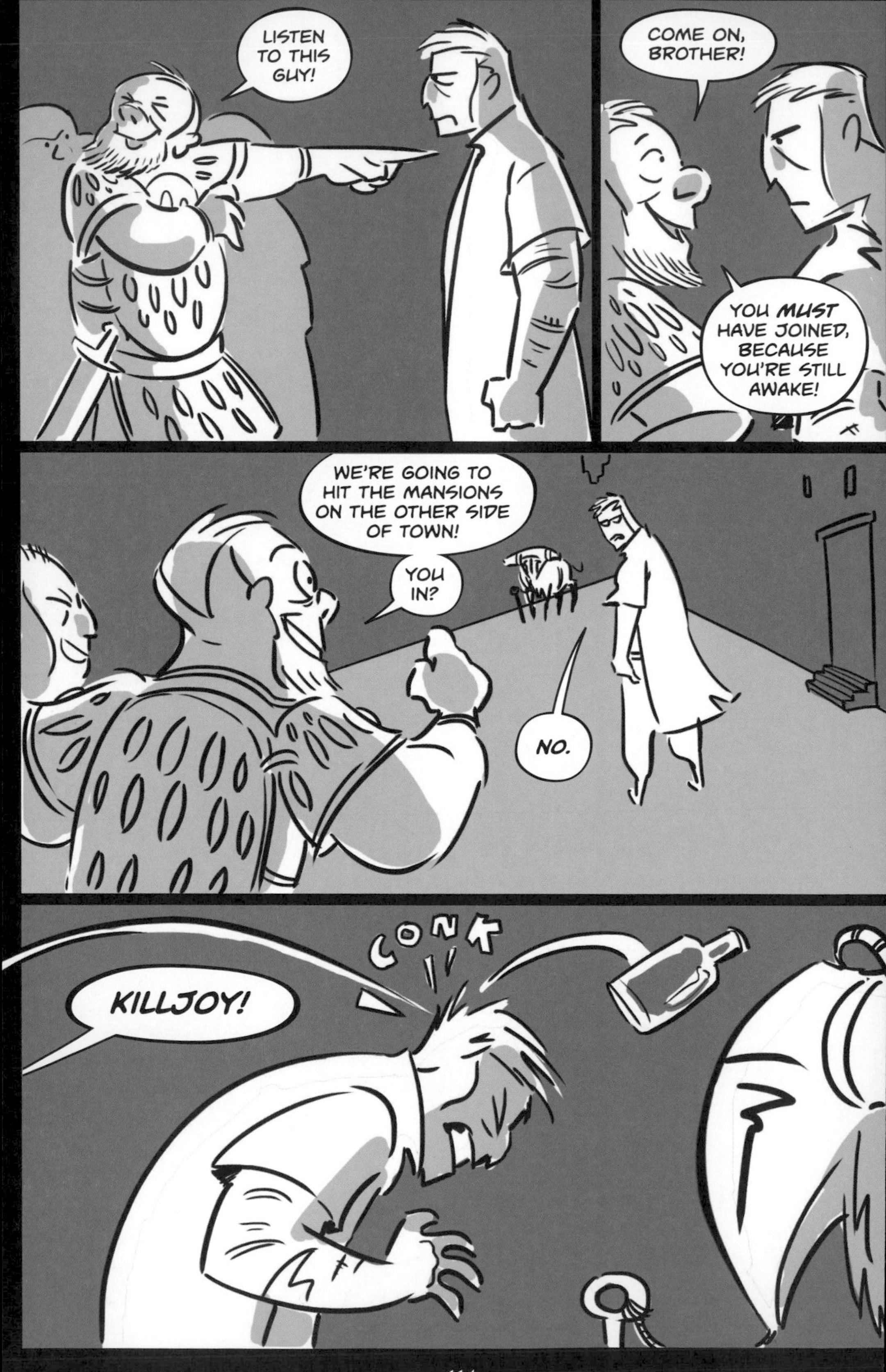
LISTEN TO THIS GUY!
COME ON, BROTHER!
YOU *MUST* HAVE JOINED, BECAUSE YOU'RE STILL AWAKE!
WE'RE GOING TO HIT THE MANSIONS ON THE OTHER SIDE OF TOWN!
YOU IN?
NO.
CONK
KILLJOY!

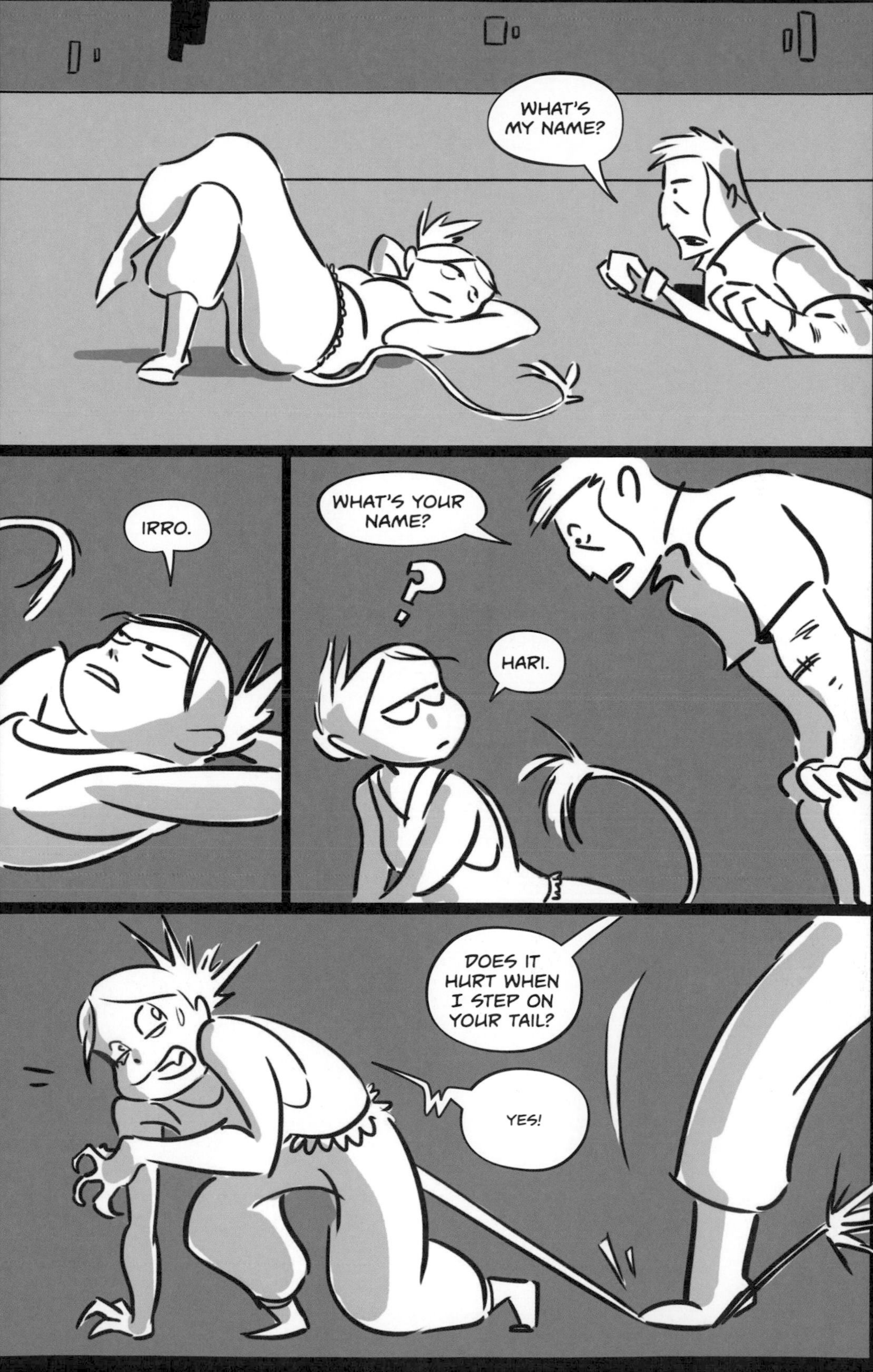
WHAT'S MY NAME?
IRRO.
WHAT'S YOUR NAME?
?
HARI.
DOES IT HURT WHEN I STEP ON YOUR TAIL?
YES!

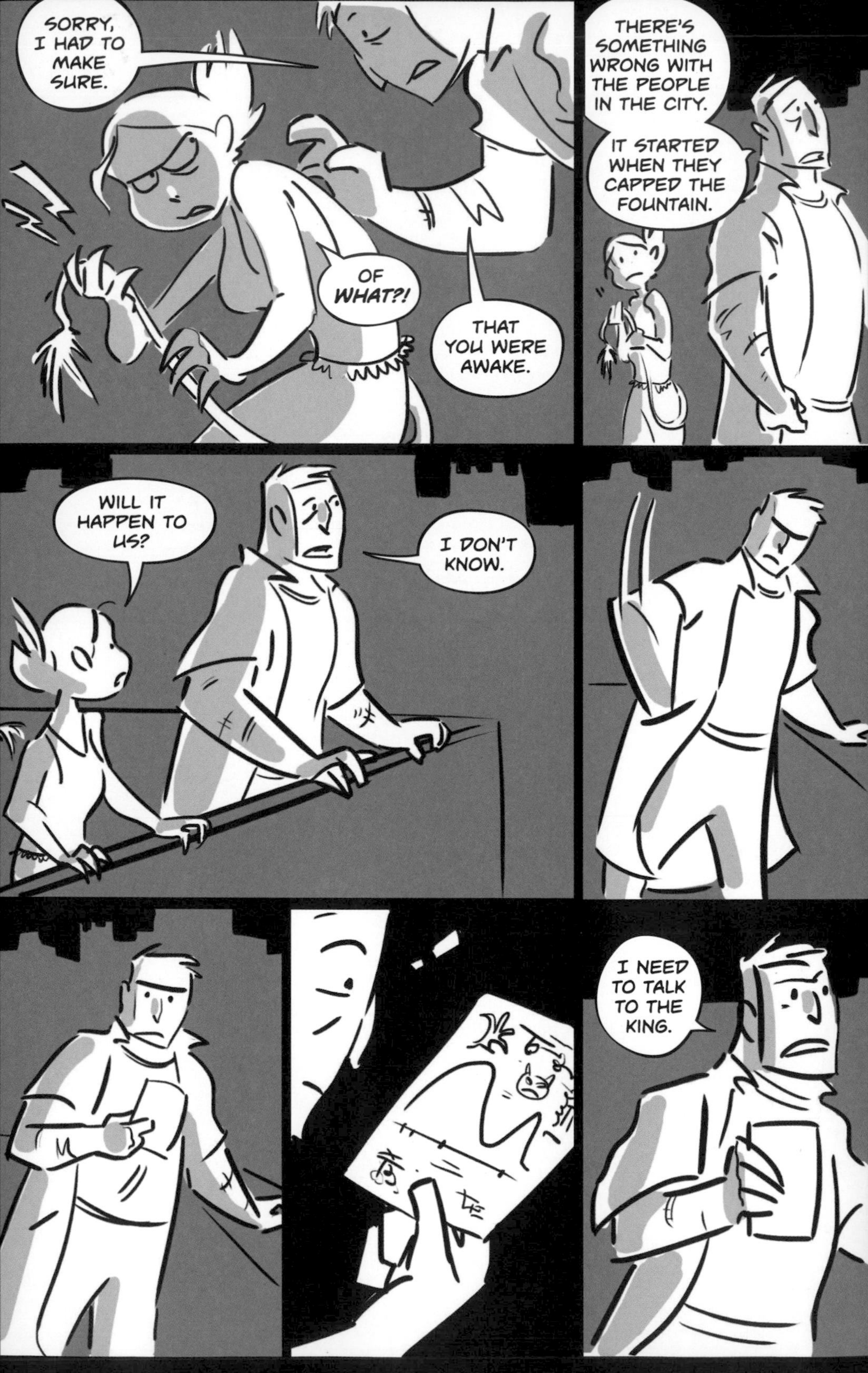
SORRY, I HAD TO MAKE SURE.
OF WHAT?!
THAT YOU WERE AWAKE.
THERE'S SOMETHING WRONG WITH THE PEOPLE IN THE CITY.
IT STARTED WHEN THEY CAPPED THE FOUNTAIN.
WILL IT HAPPEN TO US?
I DON'T KNOW.
I NEED TO TALK TO THE KING.

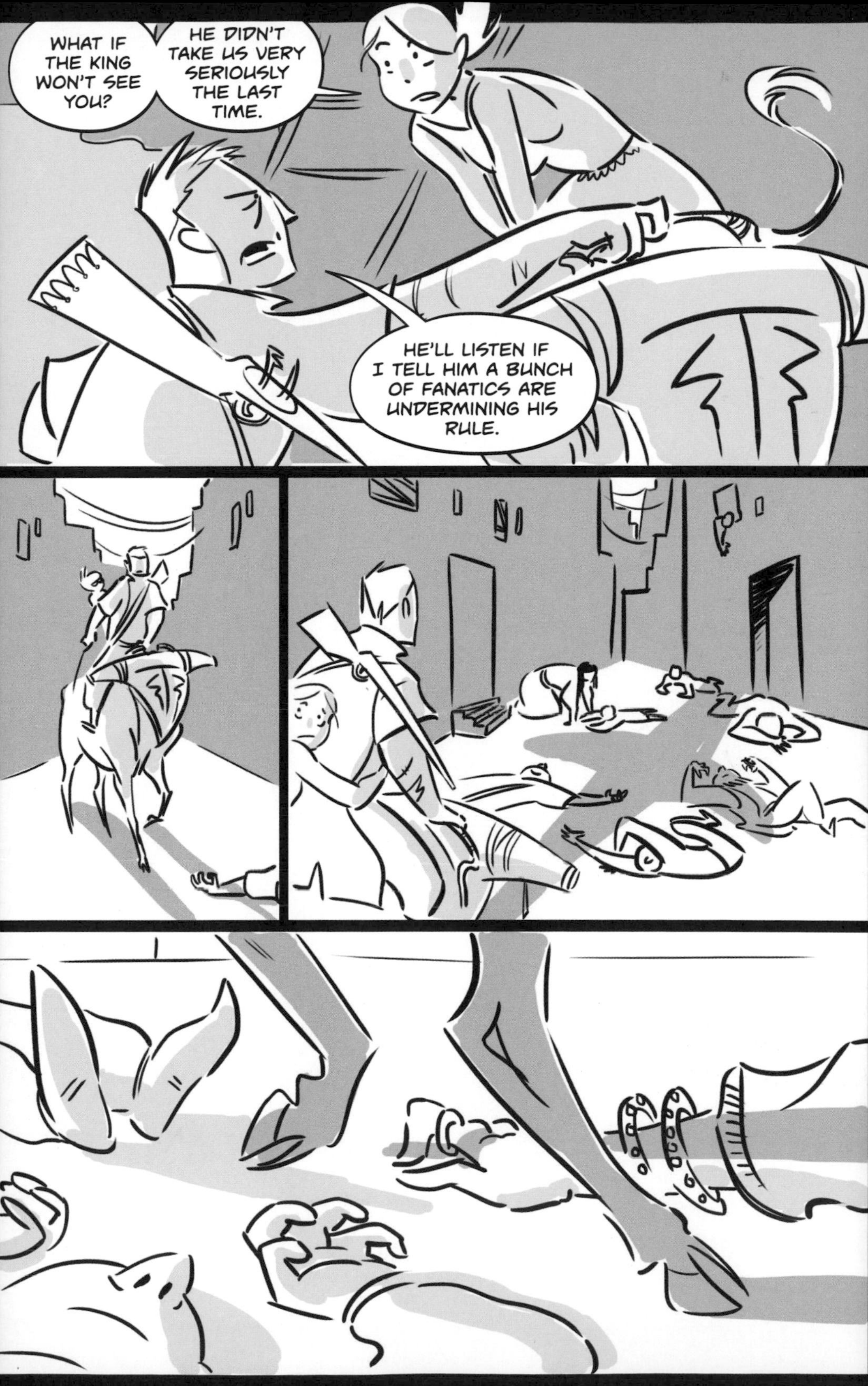
WHAT IF THE KING WON'T SEE YOU?
HE DIDN'T TAKE US VERY SERIOUSLY THE LAST TIME.
HE'LL LISTEN IF I TELL HIM A BUNCH OF FANATICS ARE UNDERMINING HIS RULE.

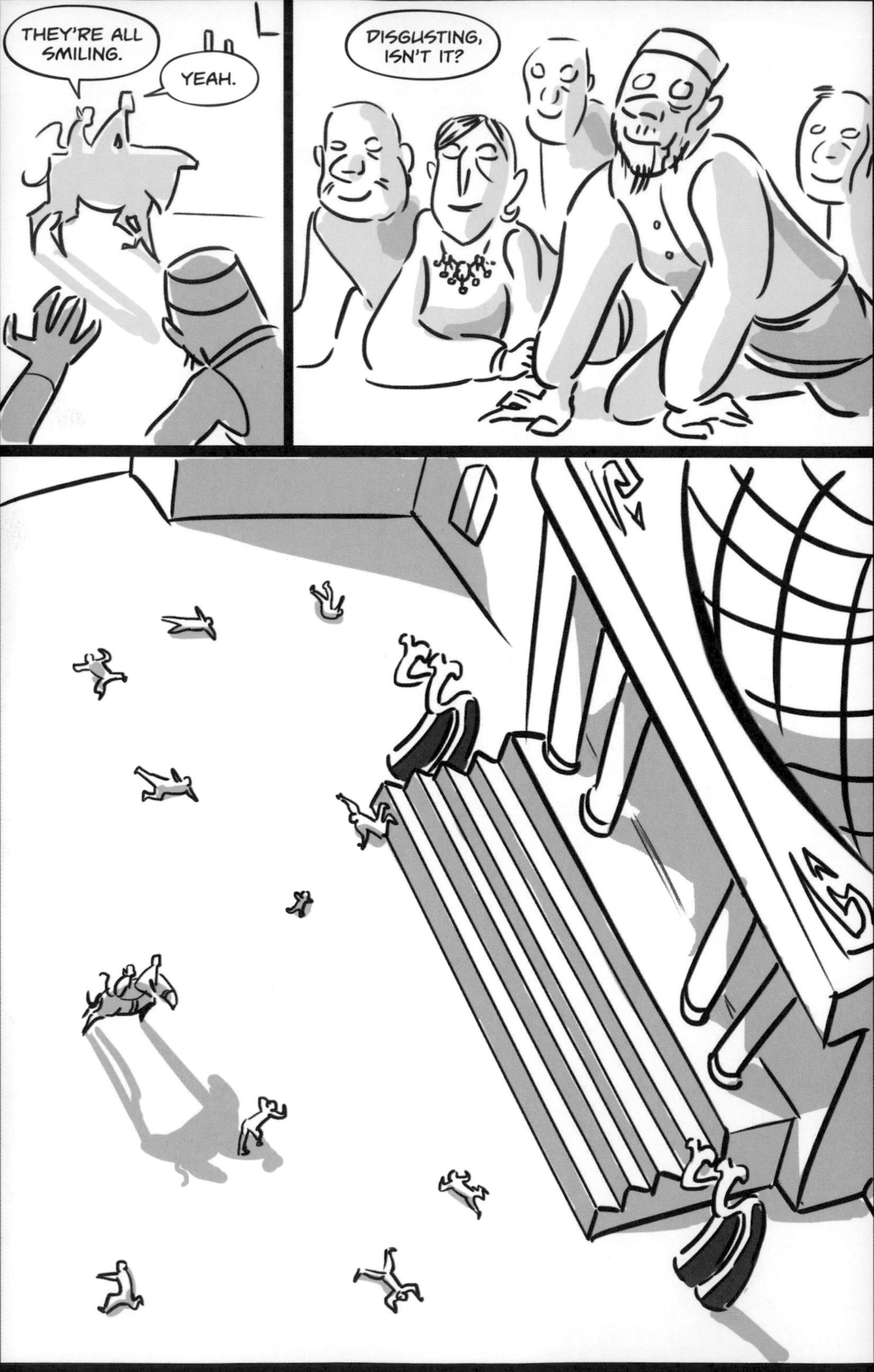
THEY'RE ALL SMILING.
YEAH.
DISGUSTING, ISN'T IT?

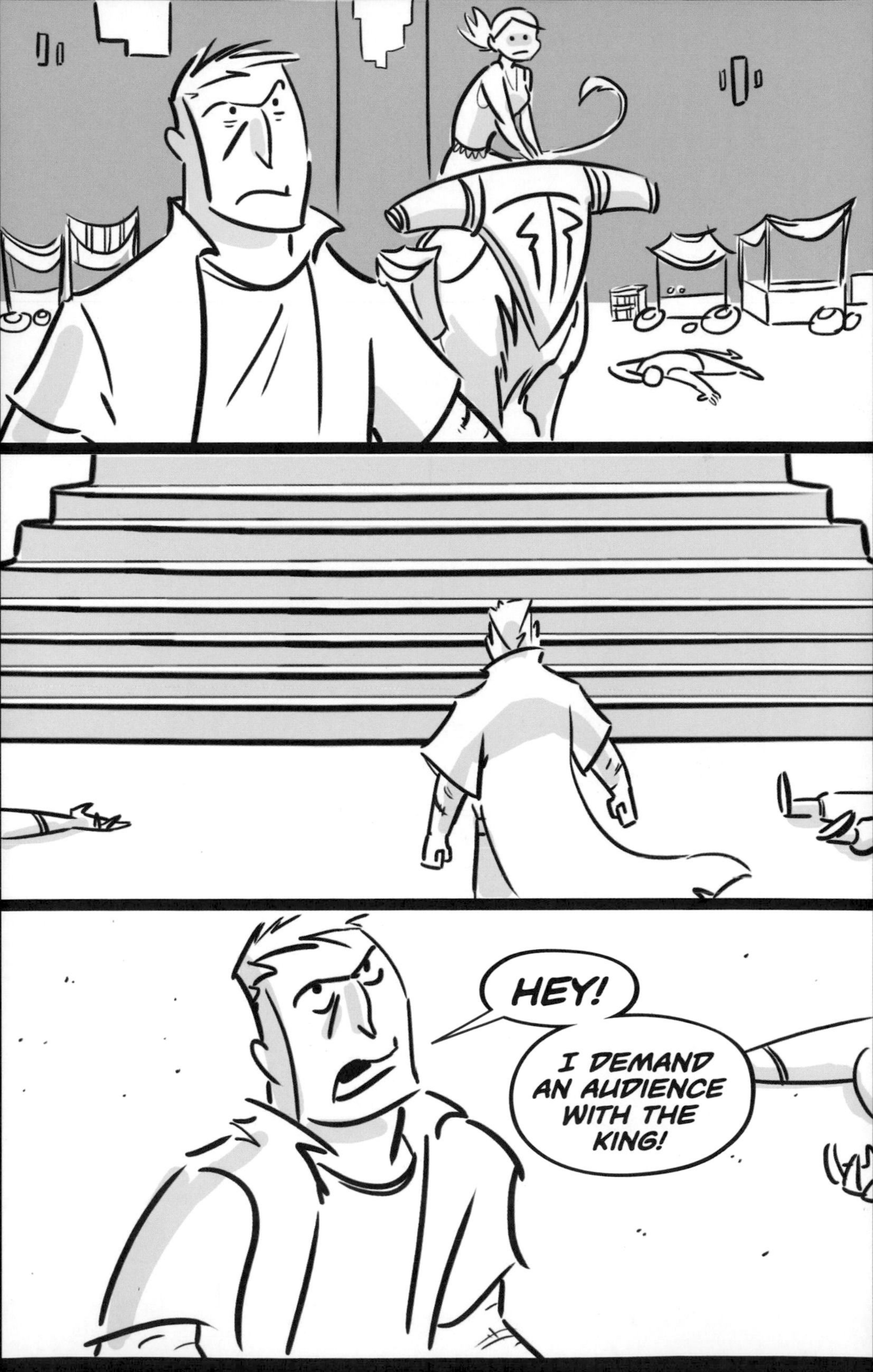
HEY!
I DEMAND AN AUDIENCE WITH THE KING!

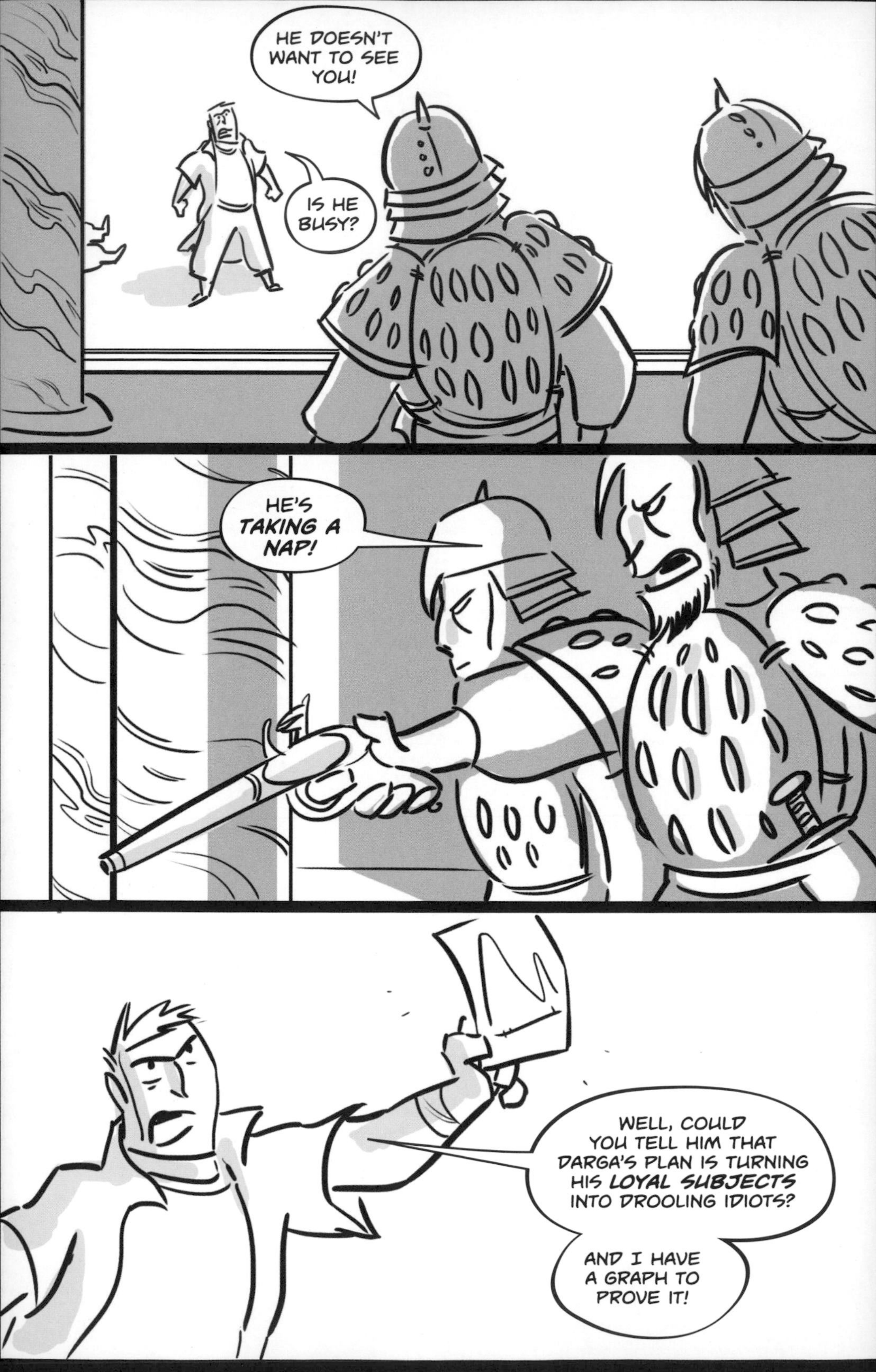
HE DOESN'T WANT TO SEE YOU!
IS HE BUSY?
HE'S *TAKING A NAP!*
WELL, COULD YOU TELL HIM THAT DARGA'S PLAN IS TURNING HIS *LOYAL SUBJECTS* INTO DROOLING IDIOTS?
AND I HAVE A GRAPH TO PROVE IT!

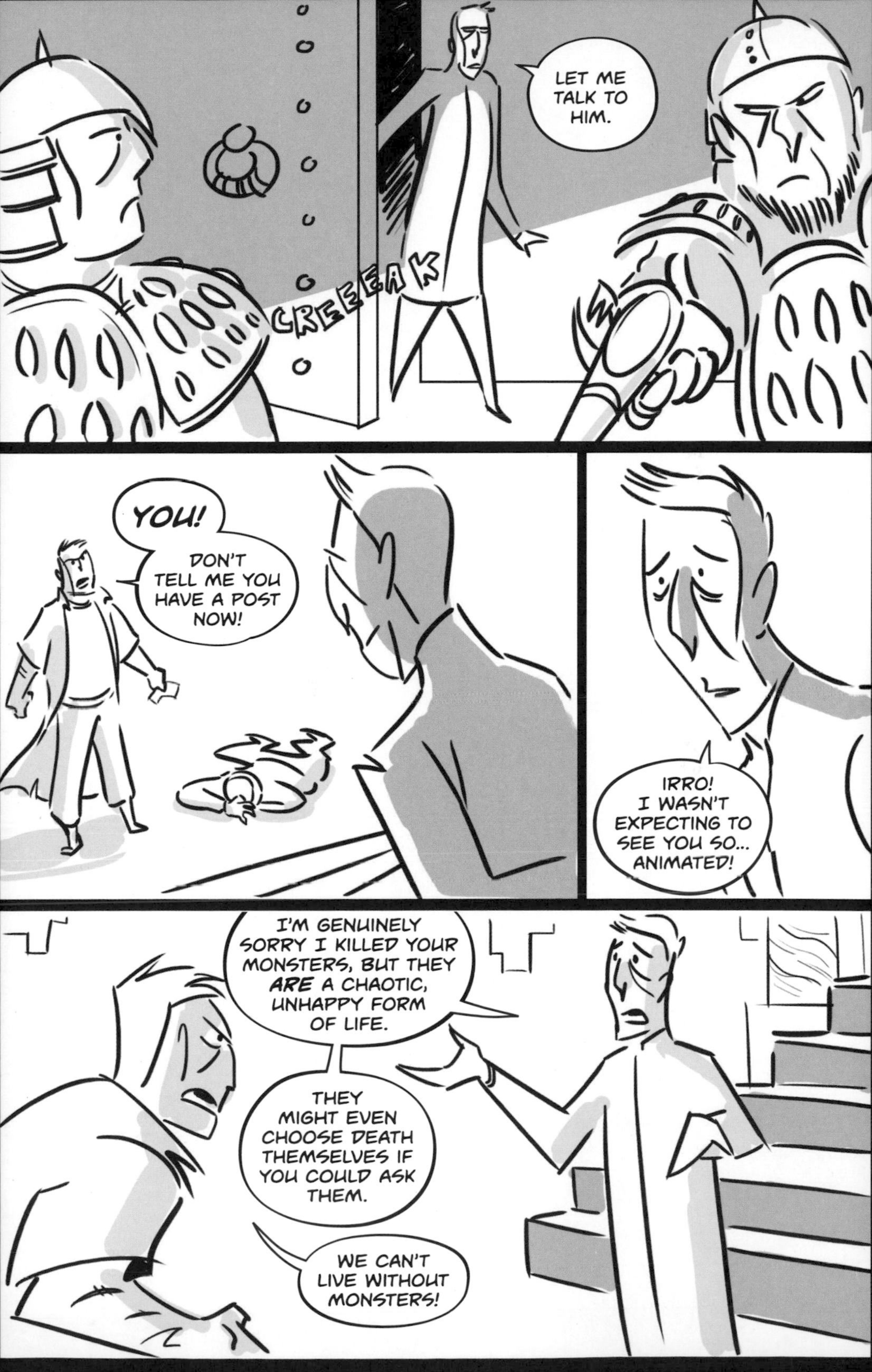

CREEEAK
LET ME TALK TO HIM.
YOU!
DON'T TELL ME YOU HAVE A POST NOW!
IRRO! I WASN'T EXPECTING TO SEE YOU SO... ANIMATED!
I'M GENUINELY SORRY I KILLED YOUR MONSTERS, BUT THEY ARE A CHAOTIC, UNHAPPY FORM OF LIFE.
THEY MIGHT EVEN CHOOSE DEATH THEMSELVES IF YOU COULD ASK THEM.
WE CAN'T LIVE WITHOUT MONSTERS!

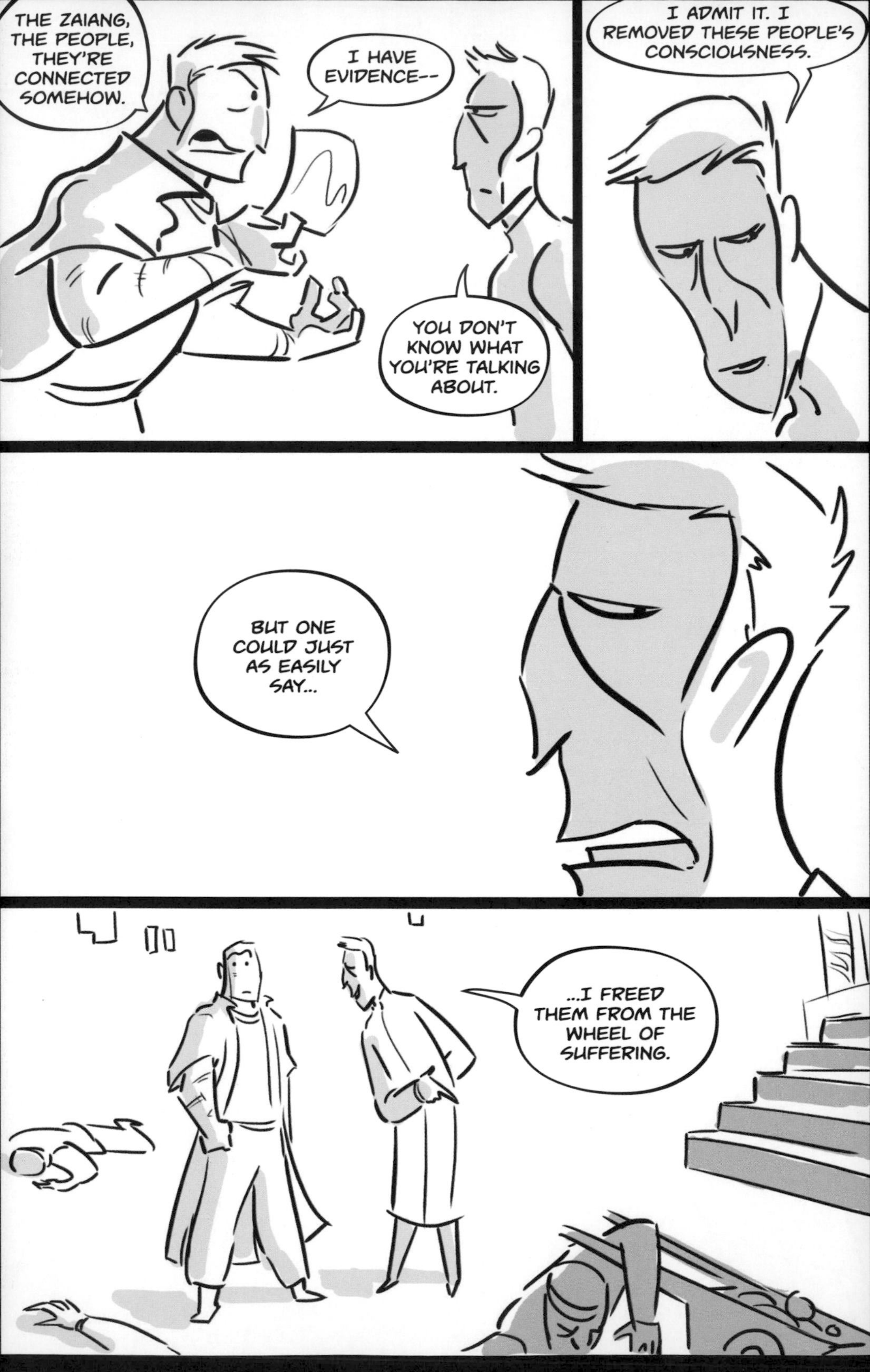
THE ZAIANG, THE PEOPLE, THEY'RE CONNECTED SOMEHOW.
I HAVE EVIDENCE--
YOU DON'T KNOW WHAT YOU'RE TALKING ABOUT.
I ADMIT IT. I REMOVED THESE PEOPLE'S CONSCIOUSNESS.
BUT ONE COULD JUST AS EASILY SAY...
...I FREED THEM FROM THE WHEEL OF SUFFERING.

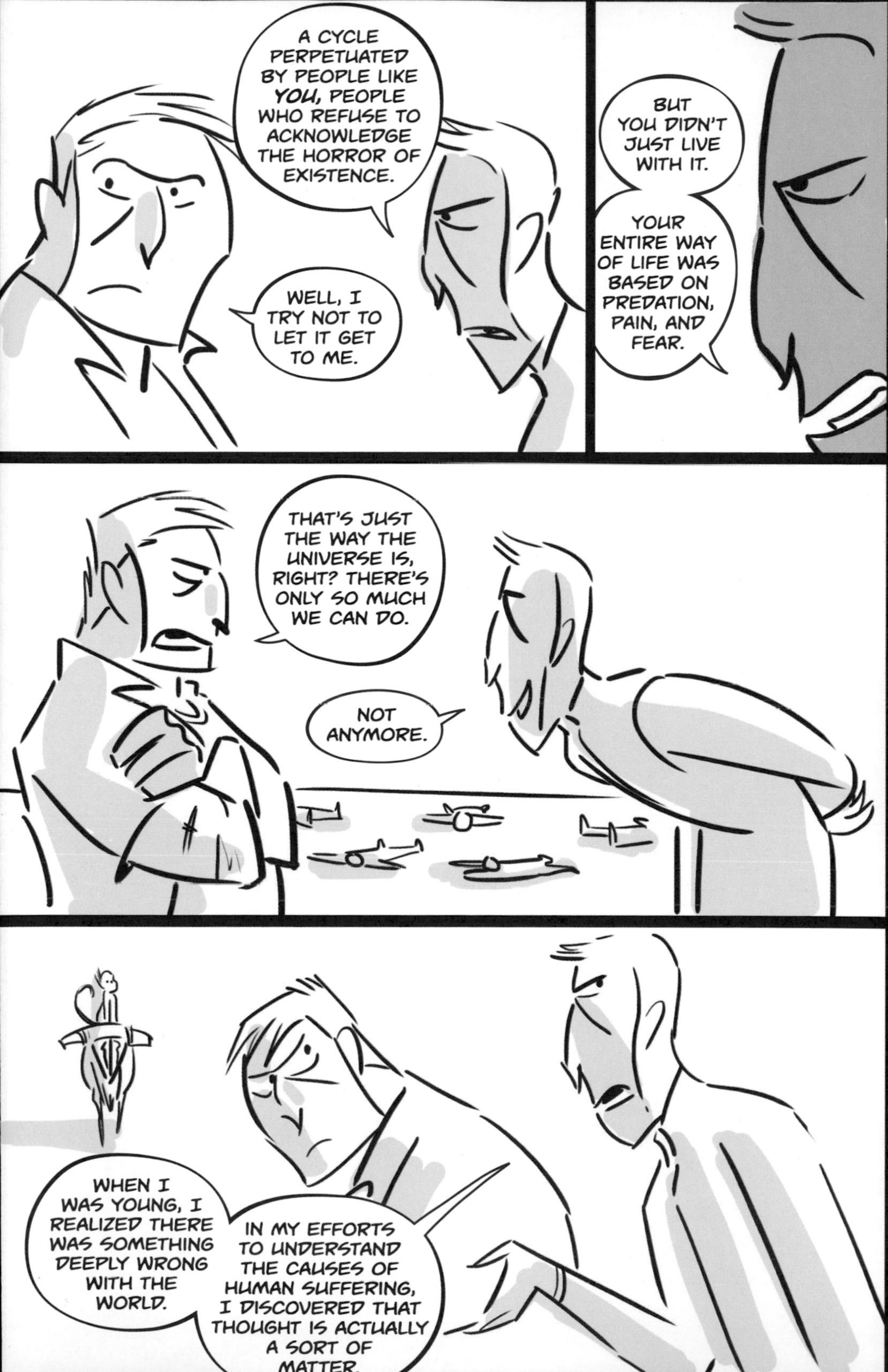
A CYCLE PERPETUATED BY PEOPLE LIKE *YOU*, PEOPLE WHO REFUSE TO ACKNOWLEDGE THE HORROR OF EXISTENCE.
WELL, I TRY NOT TO LET IT GET TO ME.
BUT YOU DIDN'T JUST LIVE WITH IT.
YOUR ENTIRE WAY OF LIFE WAS BASED ON PREDATION, PAIN, AND FEAR.
THAT'S JUST THE WAY THE UNIVERSE IS, RIGHT? THERE'S ONLY SO MUCH WE CAN DO.
NOT ANYMORE.
WHEN I WAS YOUNG, I REALIZED THERE WAS SOMETHING DEEPLY WRONG WITH THE WORLD.
IN MY EFFORTS TO UNDERSTAND THE CAUSES OF HUMAN SUFFERING, I DISCOVERED THAT THOUGHT IS ACTUALLY A SORT OF MATTER.

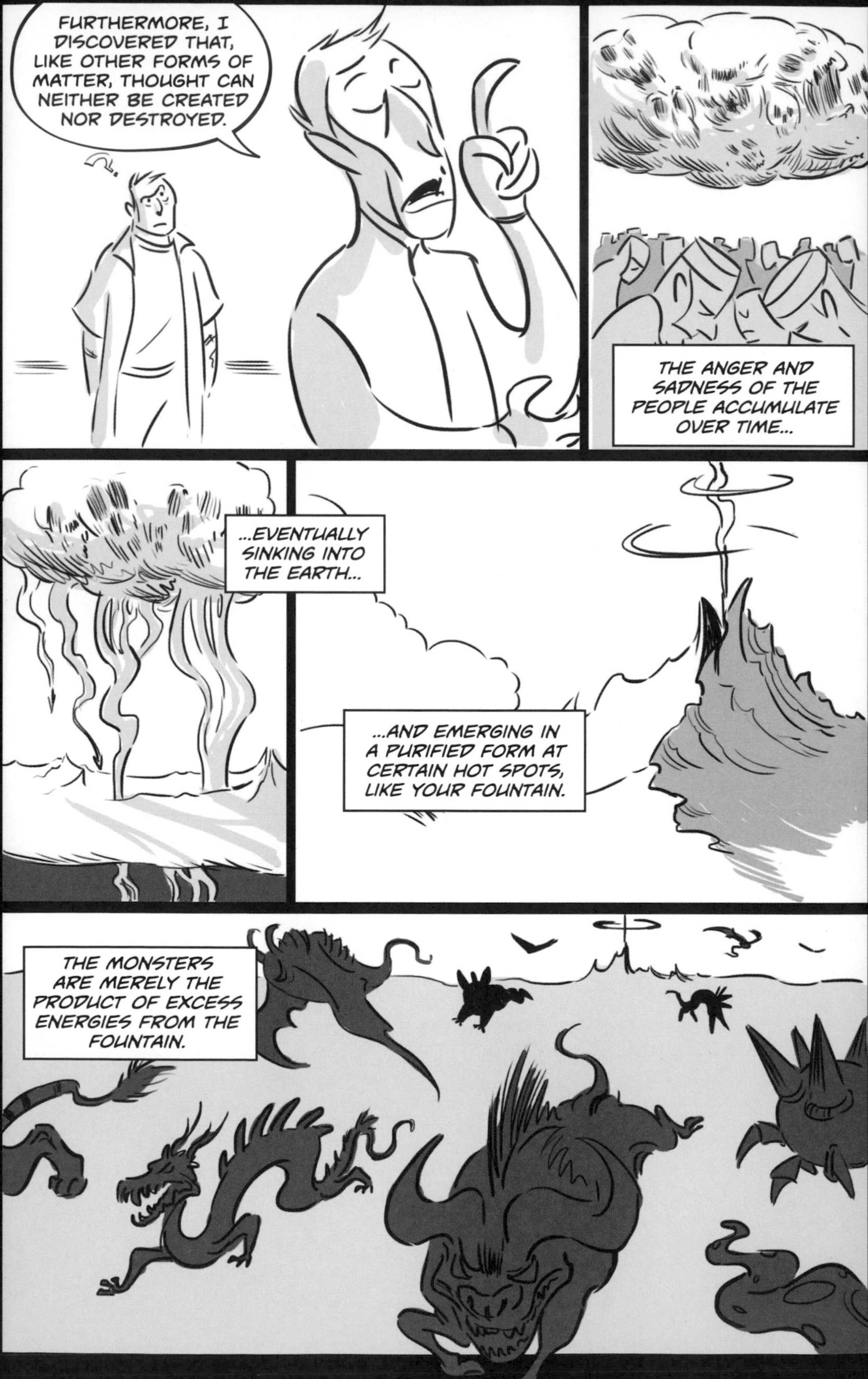
FURTHERMORE, I DISCOVERED THAT, LIKE OTHER FORMS OF MATTER, THOUGHT CAN NEITHER BE CREATED NOR DESTROYED.
?
THE ANGER AND SADNESS OF THE PEOPLE ACCUMULATE OVER TIME...
...EVENTUALLY SINKING INTO THE EARTH...
...AND EMERGING IN A PURIFIED FORM AT CERTAIN HOT SPOTS, LIKE YOUR FOUNTAIN.
THE MONSTERS ARE MERELY THE PRODUCT OF EXCESS ENERGIES FROM THE FOUNTAIN.

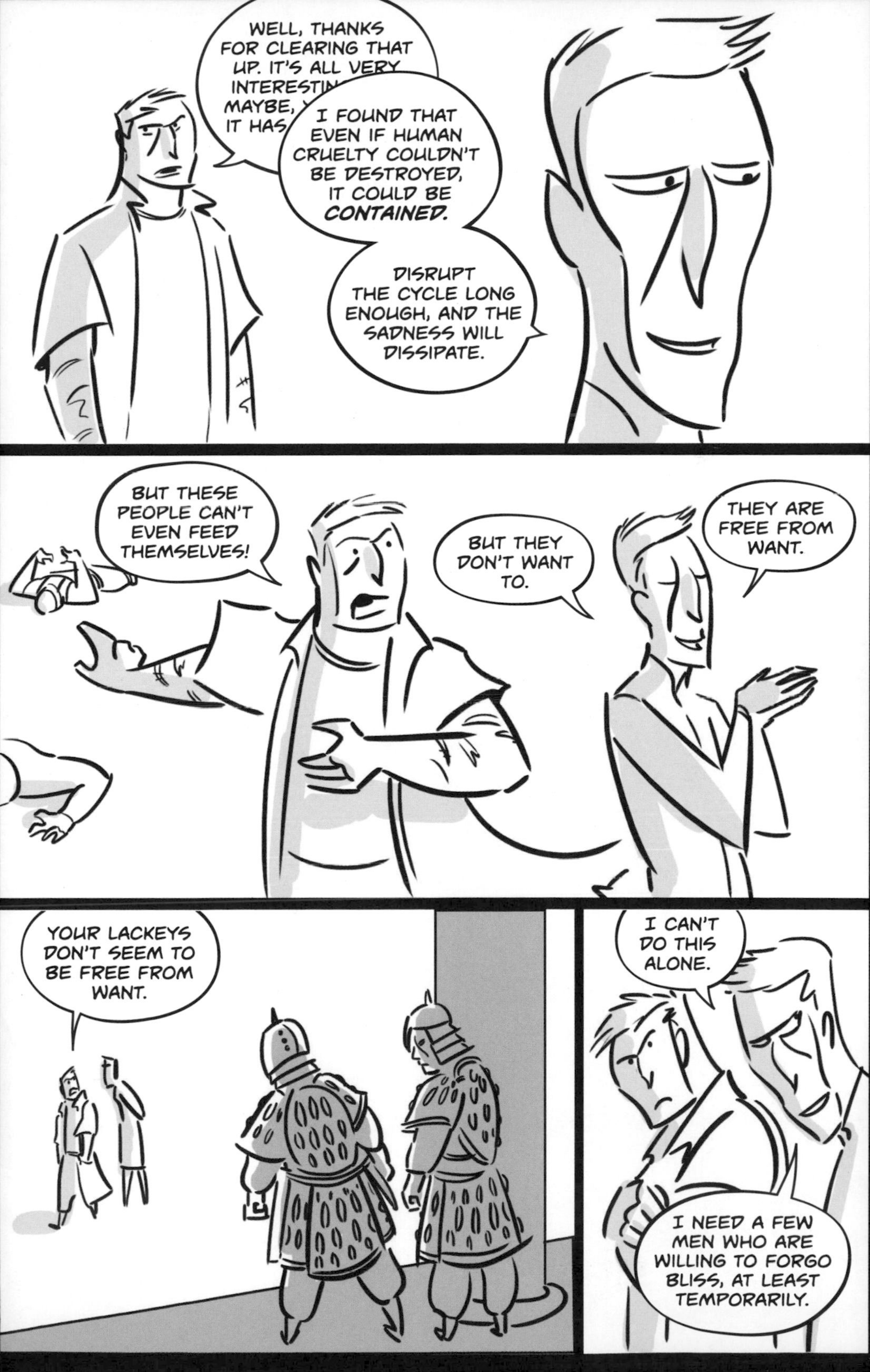

WELL, THANKS FOR CLEARING THAT UP. IT'S ALL VERY
I FOUND THAT EVEN IF HUMAN CRUELTY COULDN'T BE DESTROYED, IT COULD BE **CONTAINED.**
DISRUPT THE CYCLE LONG ENOUGH, AND THE SADNESS WILL DISSIPATE.
BUT THESE PEOPLE CAN'T EVEN FEED THEMSELVES!
BUT THEY DON'T WANT TO.
THEY ARE FREE FROM WANT.
YOUR LACKEYS DON'T SEEM TO BE FREE FROM WANT.
I CAN'T DO THIS ALONE.
I NEED A FEW MEN WHO ARE WILLING TO FORGO BLISS, AT LEAST TEMPORARILY.

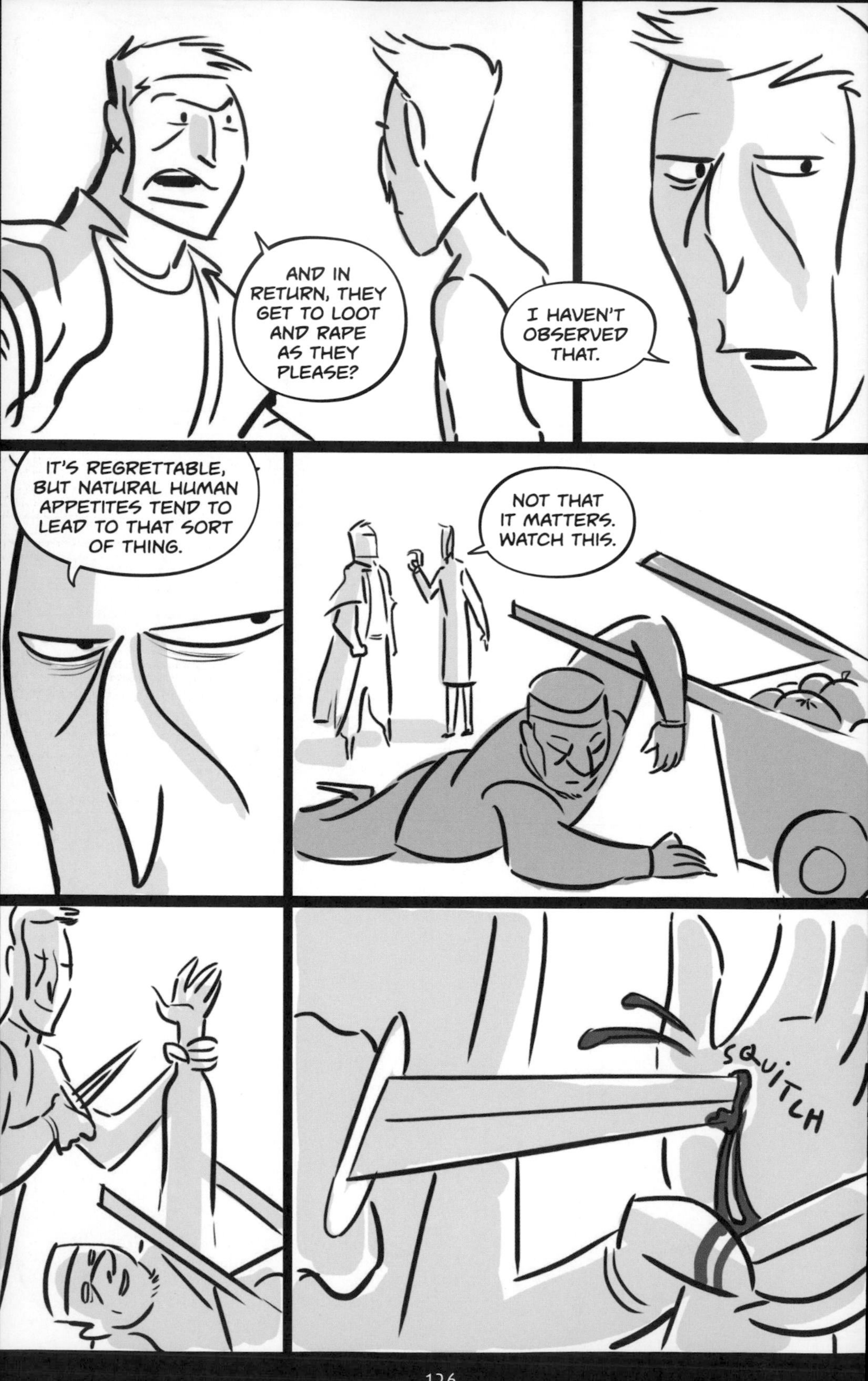
AND IN RETURN, THEY GET TO LOOT AND RAPE AS THEY PLEASE?
I HAVEN'T OBSERVED THAT.
IT'S REGRETTABLE, BUT NATURAL HUMAN APPETITES TEND TO LEAD TO THAT SORT OF THING.
NOT THAT IT MATTERS. WATCH THIS.
SQUITCH

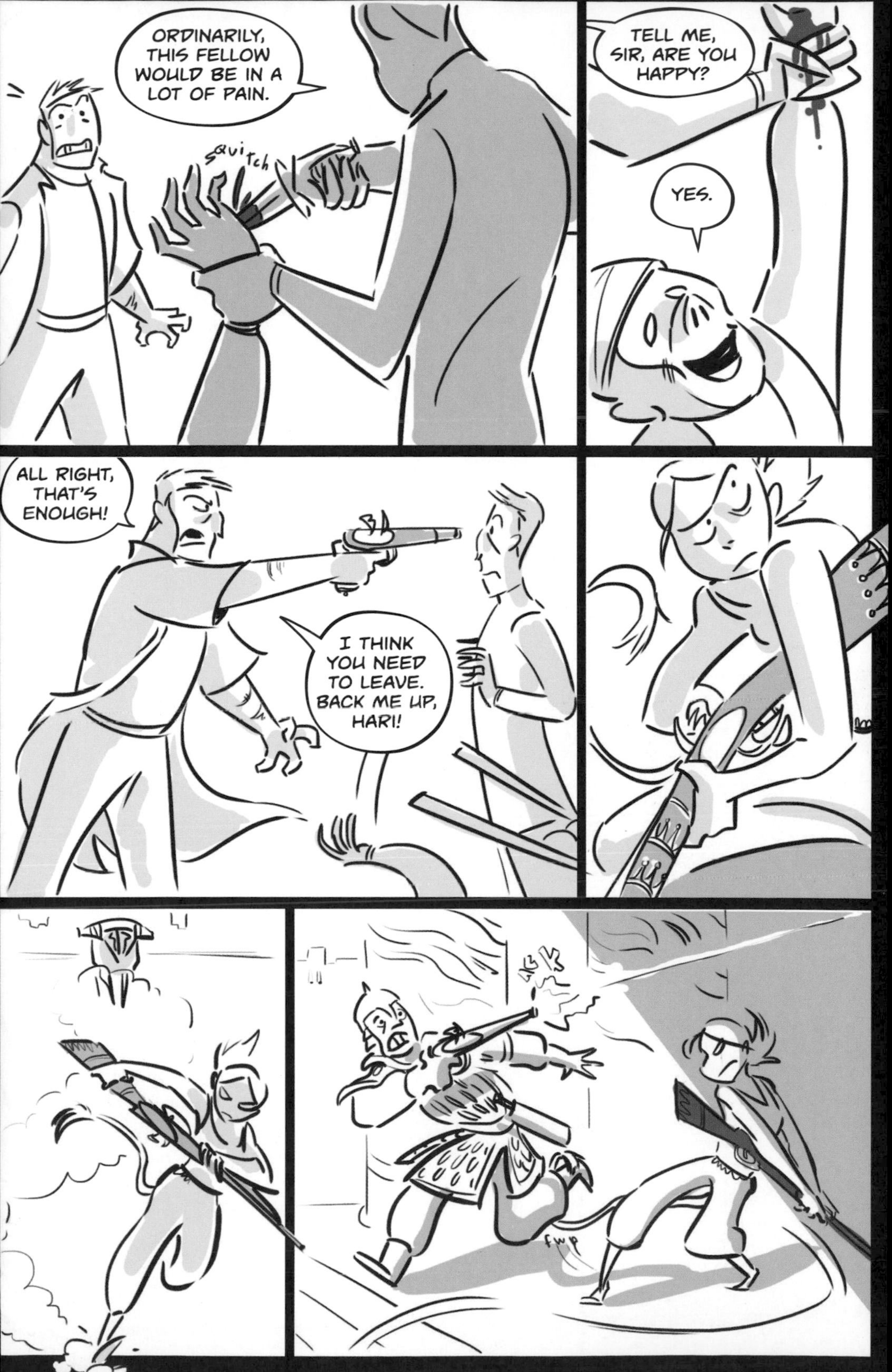
ORDINARILY, THIS FELLOW WOULD BE IN A LOT OF PAIN.
squitch
TELL ME, SIR, ARE YOU HAPPY?
YES.
ALL RIGHT, THAT'S ENOUGH!
I THINK YOU NEED TO LEAVE. BACK ME UP, HARI!
fwp

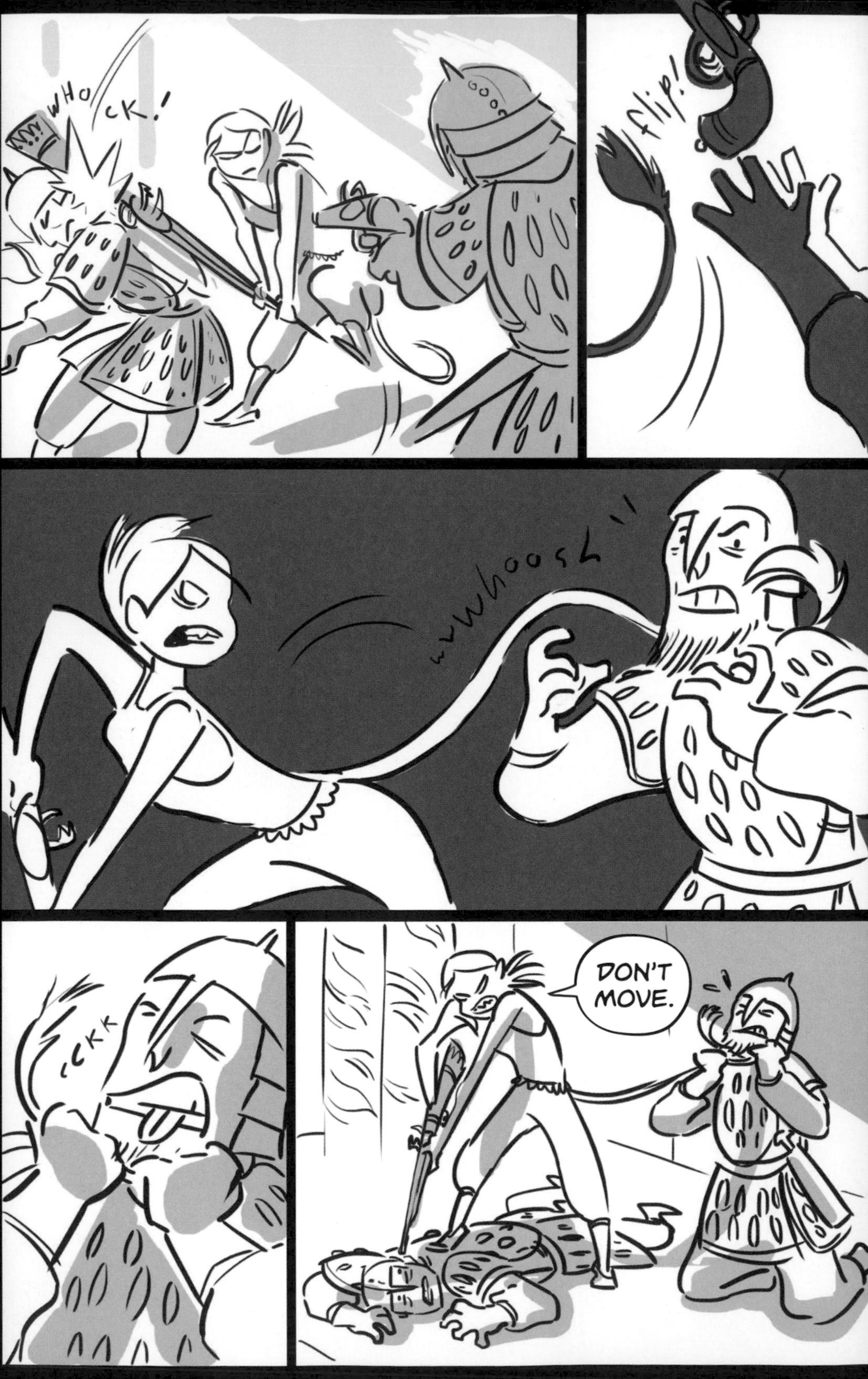
WHOCK!
flip!
wwwhoosh
CKK
DON'T MOVE.

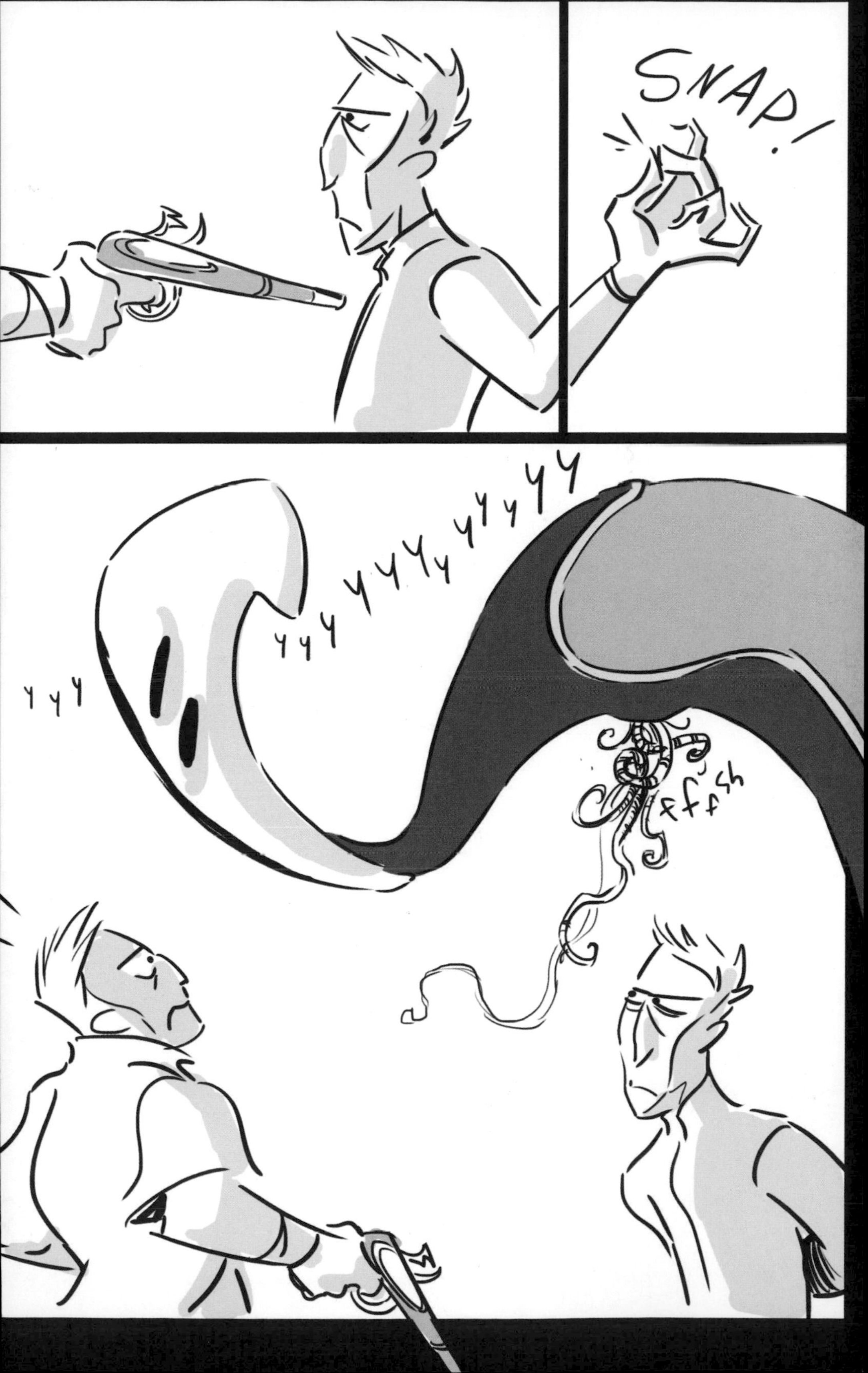
SNAP!
yyy
yyyyyyyyyyyyyyyyy
ffsh

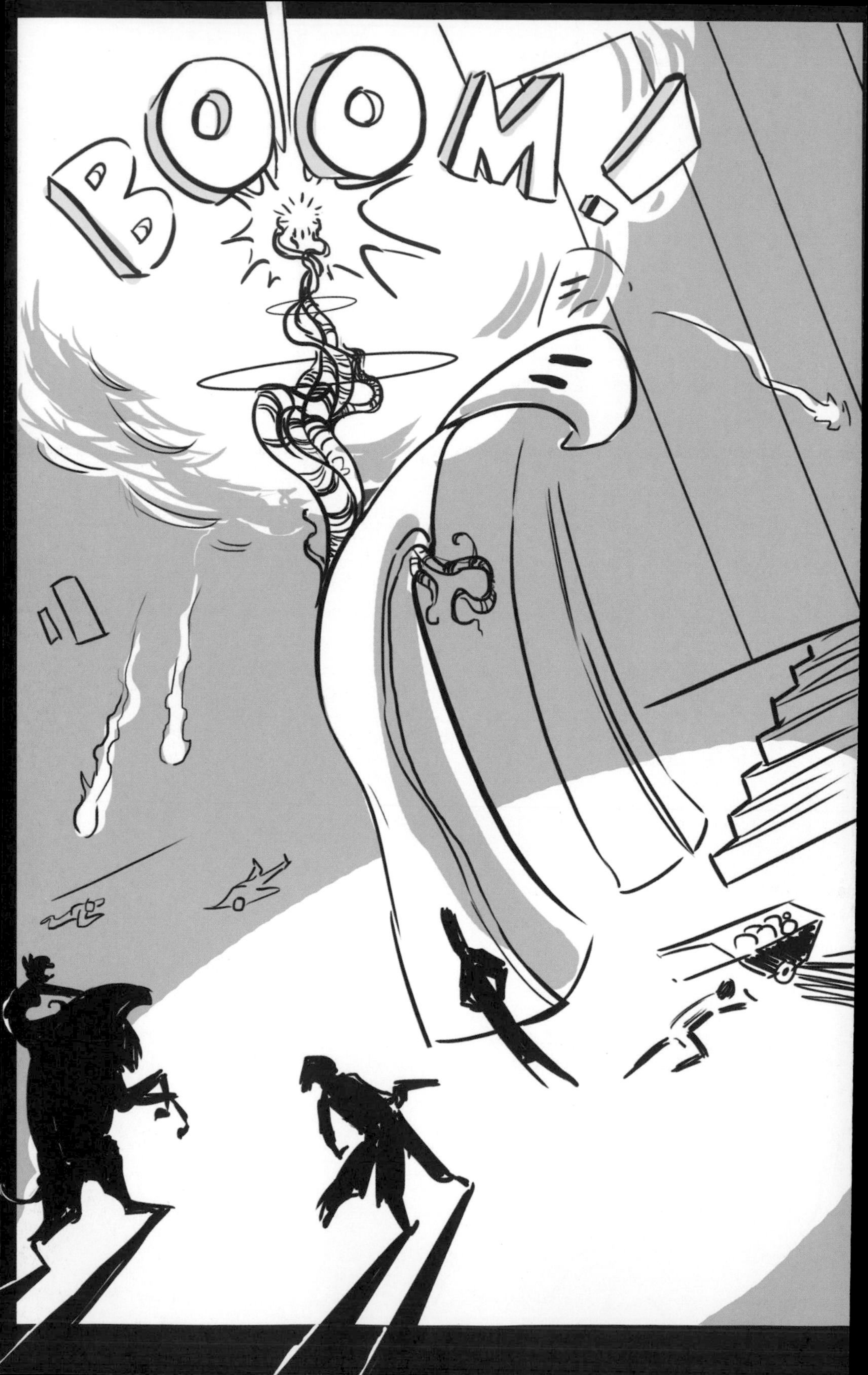
BOOM!

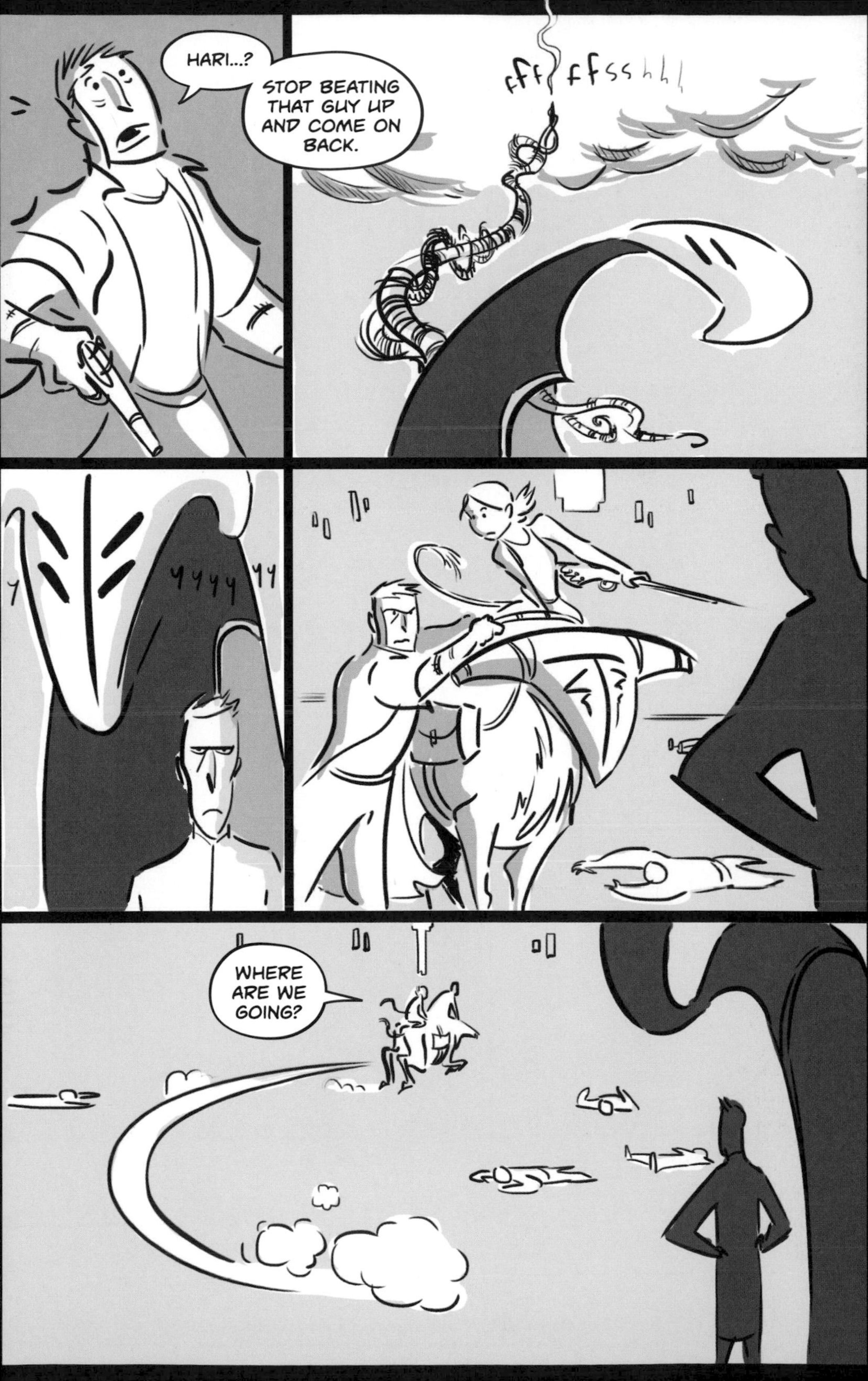
HARI...?
STOP BEATING THAT GUY UP AND COME ON BACK.
fff ffsshhh
yyyy yy
WHERE ARE WE GOING?

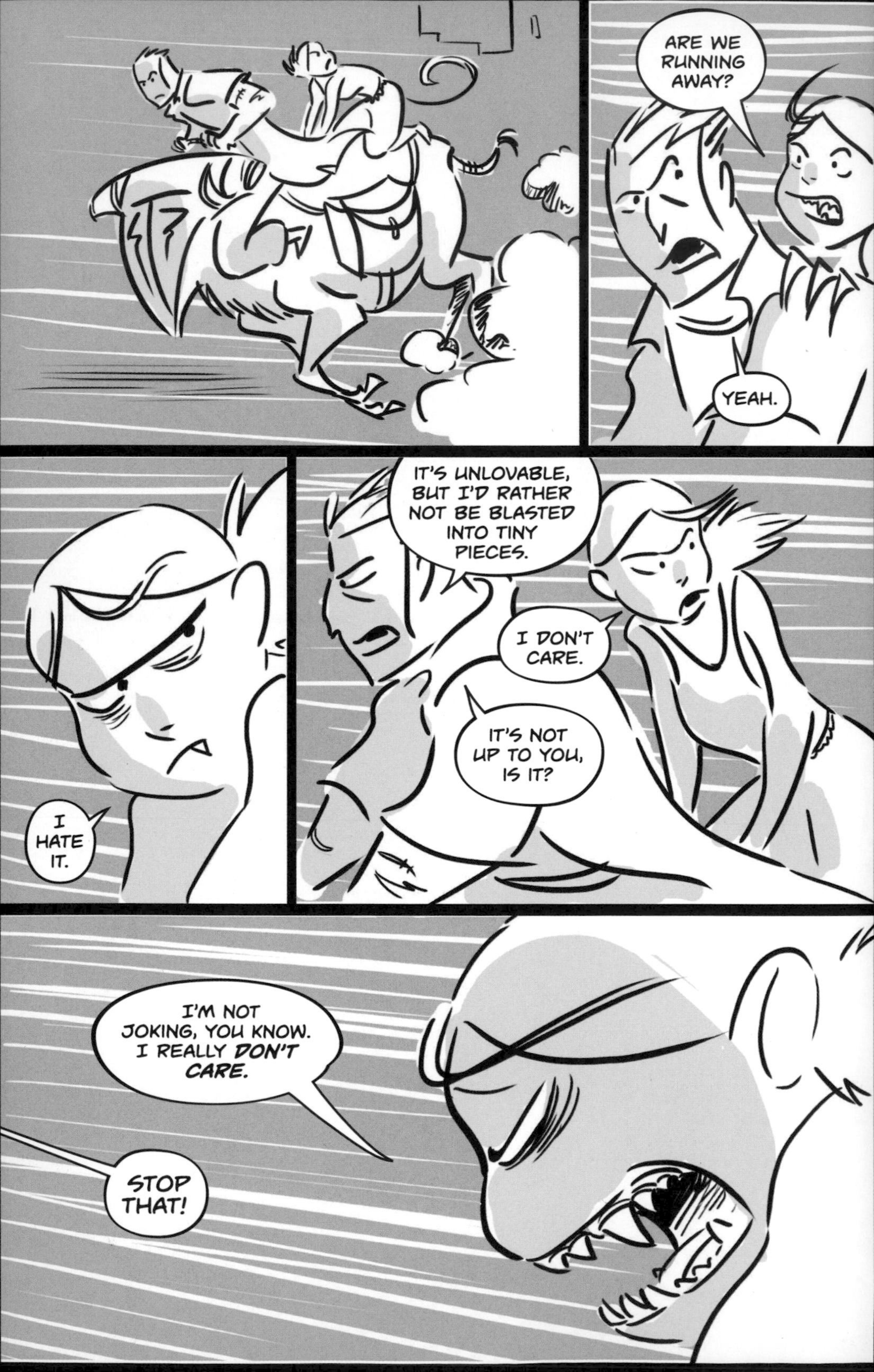
ARE WE RUNNING AWAY?
YEAH.
I HATE IT.
IT'S UNLOVABLE, BUT I'D RATHER NOT BE BLASTED INTO TINY PIECES.
I DON'T CARE.
IT'S NOT UP TO YOU, IS IT?
I'M NOT JOKING, YOU KNOW. I REALLY *DON'T CARE.*
STOP THAT!

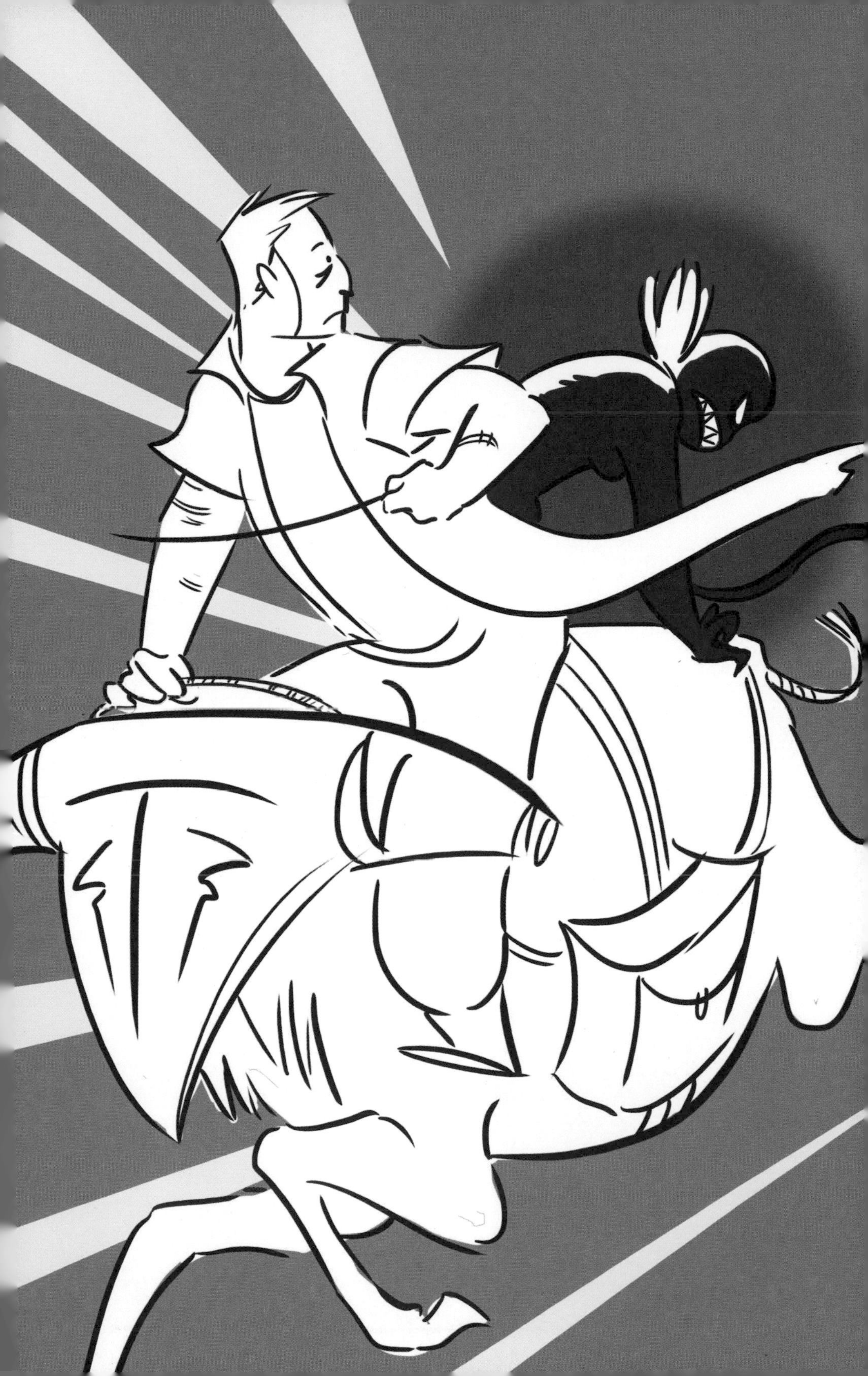

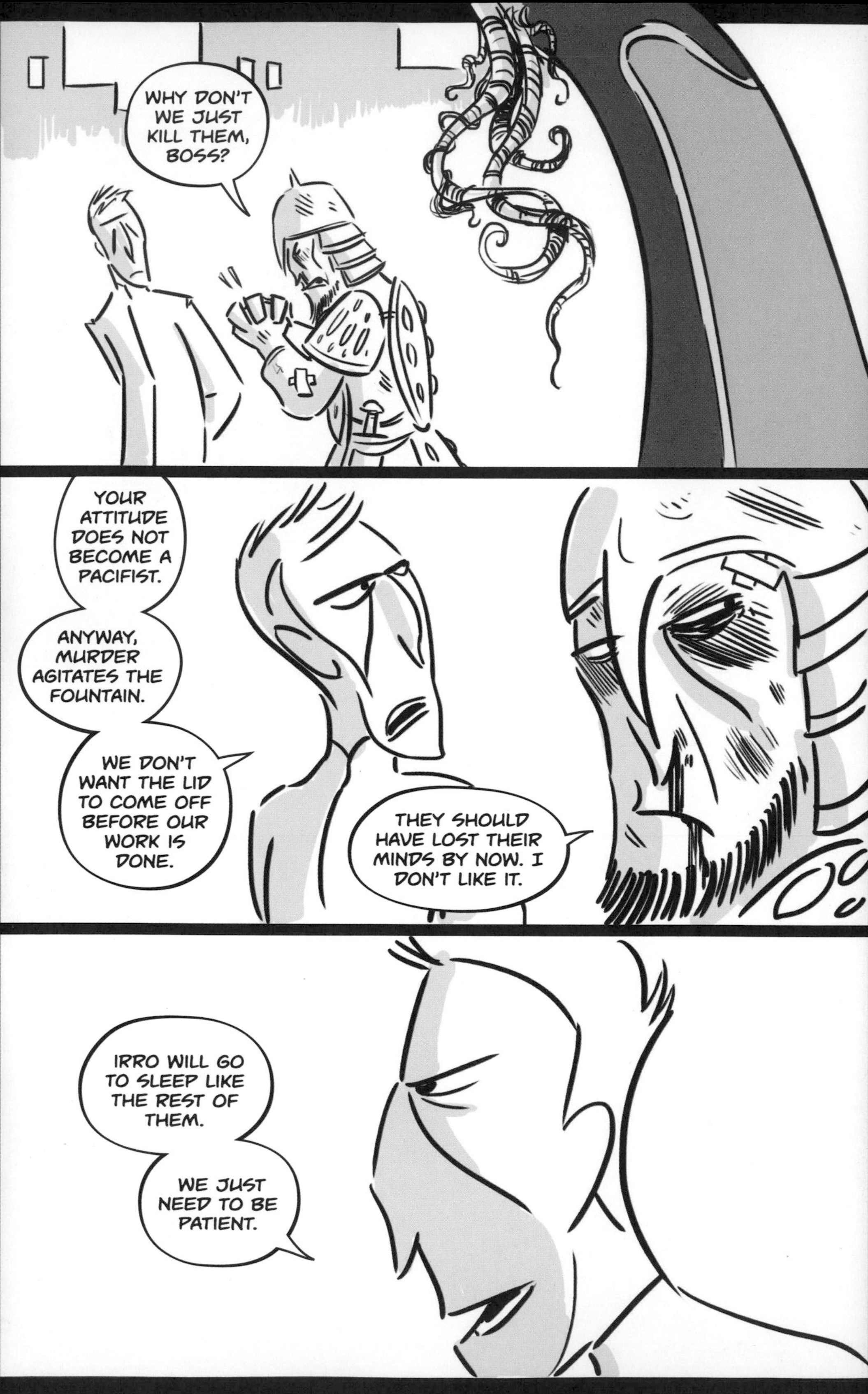
WHY DON'T WE JUST KILL THEM, BOSS?
YOUR ATTITUDE DOES NOT BECOME A PACIFIST.
ANYWAY, MURDER AGITATES THE FOUNTAIN.
WE DON'T WANT THE LID TO COME OFF BEFORE OUR WORK IS DONE.
THEY SHOULD HAVE LOST THEIR MINDS BY NOW. I DON'T LIKE IT.
IRRO WILL GO TO SLEEP LIKE THE REST OF THEM.
WE JUST NEED TO BE PATIENT.

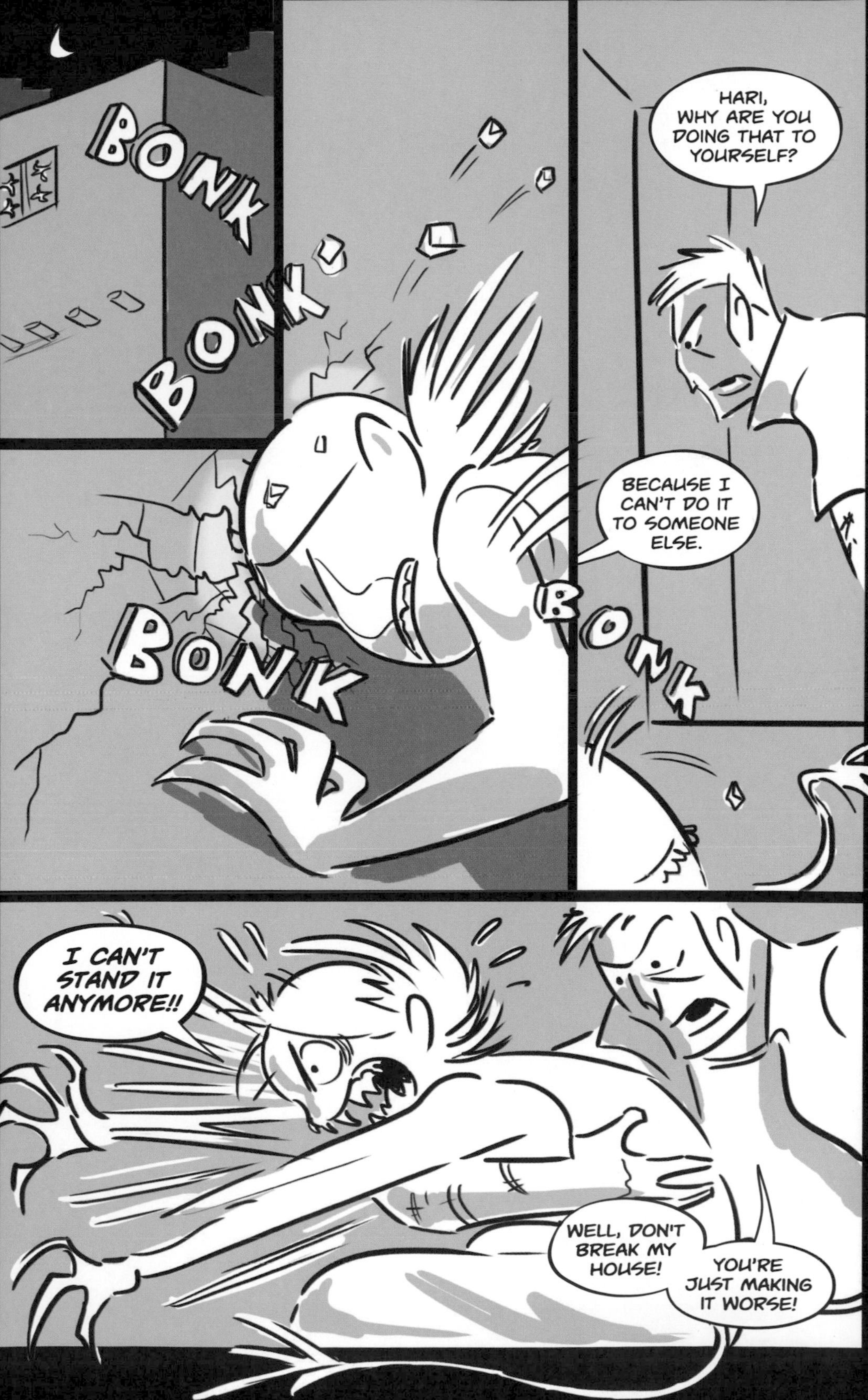
BONK
BONK
BONK
HARI, WHY ARE YOU DOING THAT TO YOURSELF?
BECAUSE I CAN'T DO IT TO SOMEONE ELSE.
BONK
I CAN'T STAND IT ANYMORE!!
WELL, DON'T BREAK MY HOUSE!
YOU'RE JUST MAKING IT WORSE!

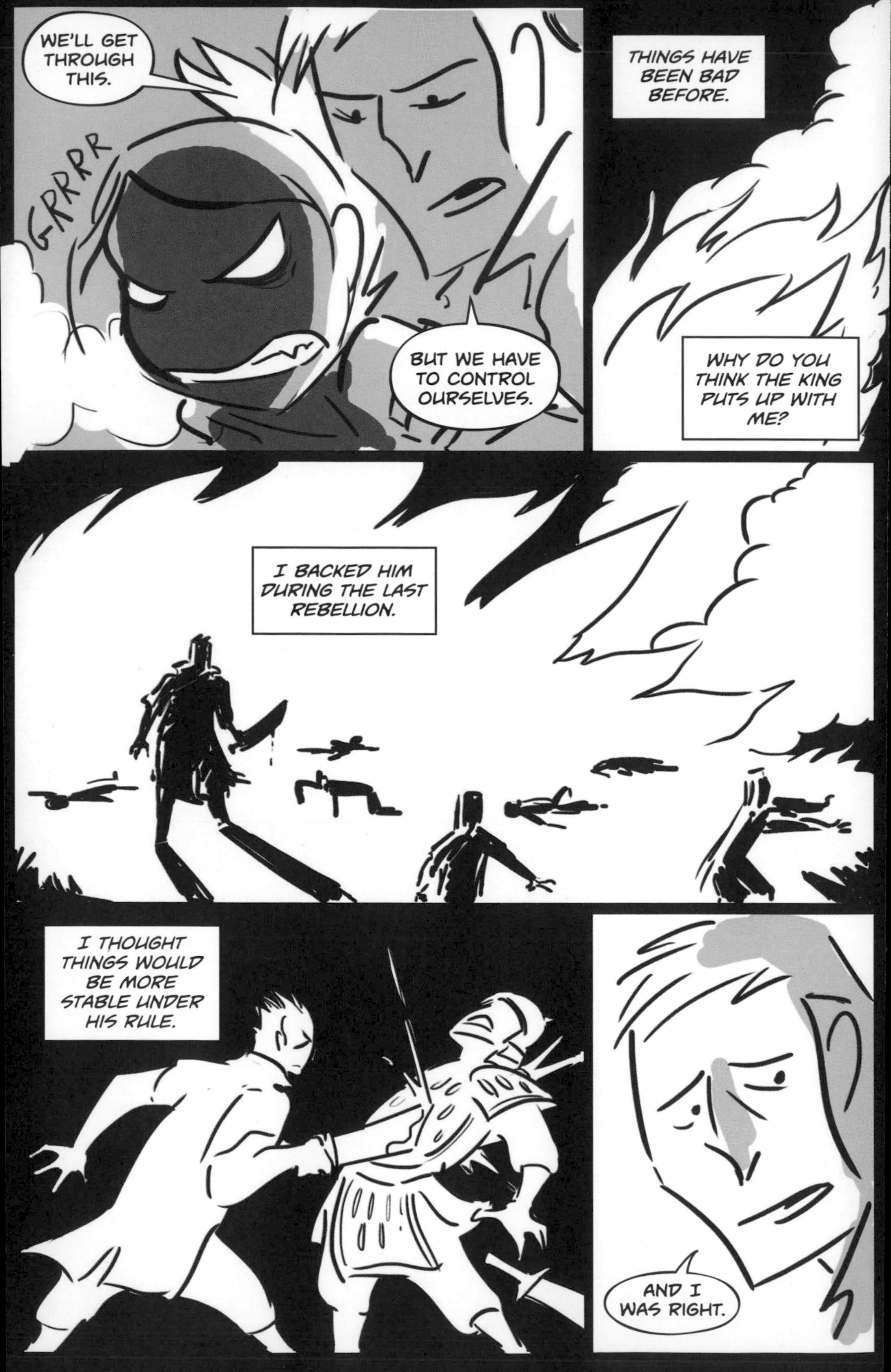
WE'LL GET THROUGH THIS.
GRRRR
BUT WE HAVE TO CONTROL OURSELVES.
THINGS HAVE BEEN BAD BEFORE.
WHY DO YOU THINK THE KING PUTS UP WITH ME?
I BACKED HIM DURING THE LAST REBELLION.
I THOUGHT THINGS WOULD BE MORE STABLE UNDER HIS RULE.
AND I WAS RIGHT.

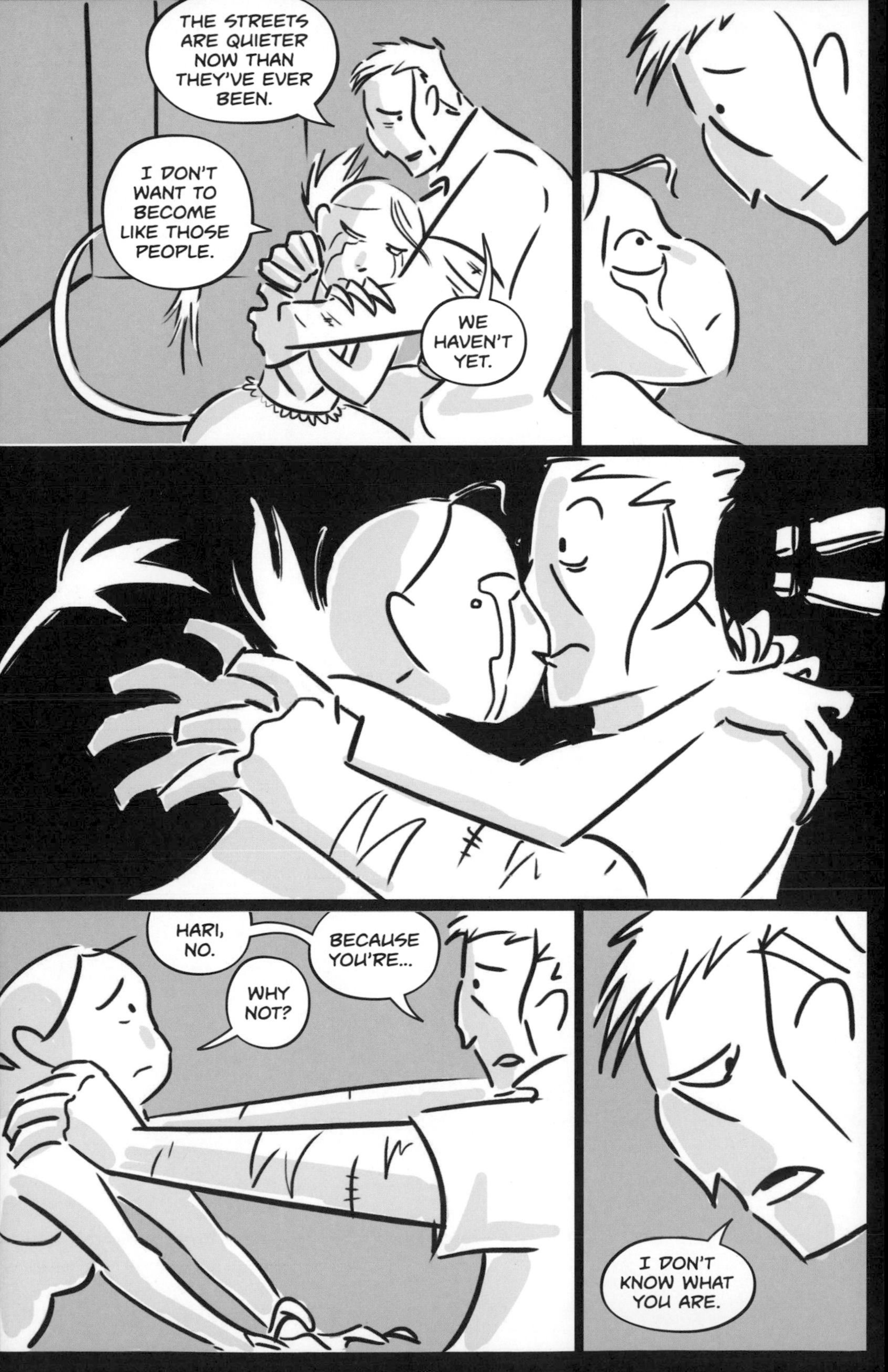
THE STREETS ARE QUIETER NOW THAN THEY'VE EVER BEEN.
I DON'T WANT TO BECOME LIKE THOSE PEOPLE.
WE HAVEN'T YET.
HARI, NO.
WHY NOT?
BECAUSE YOU'RE...
I DON'T KNOW WHAT YOU ARE.

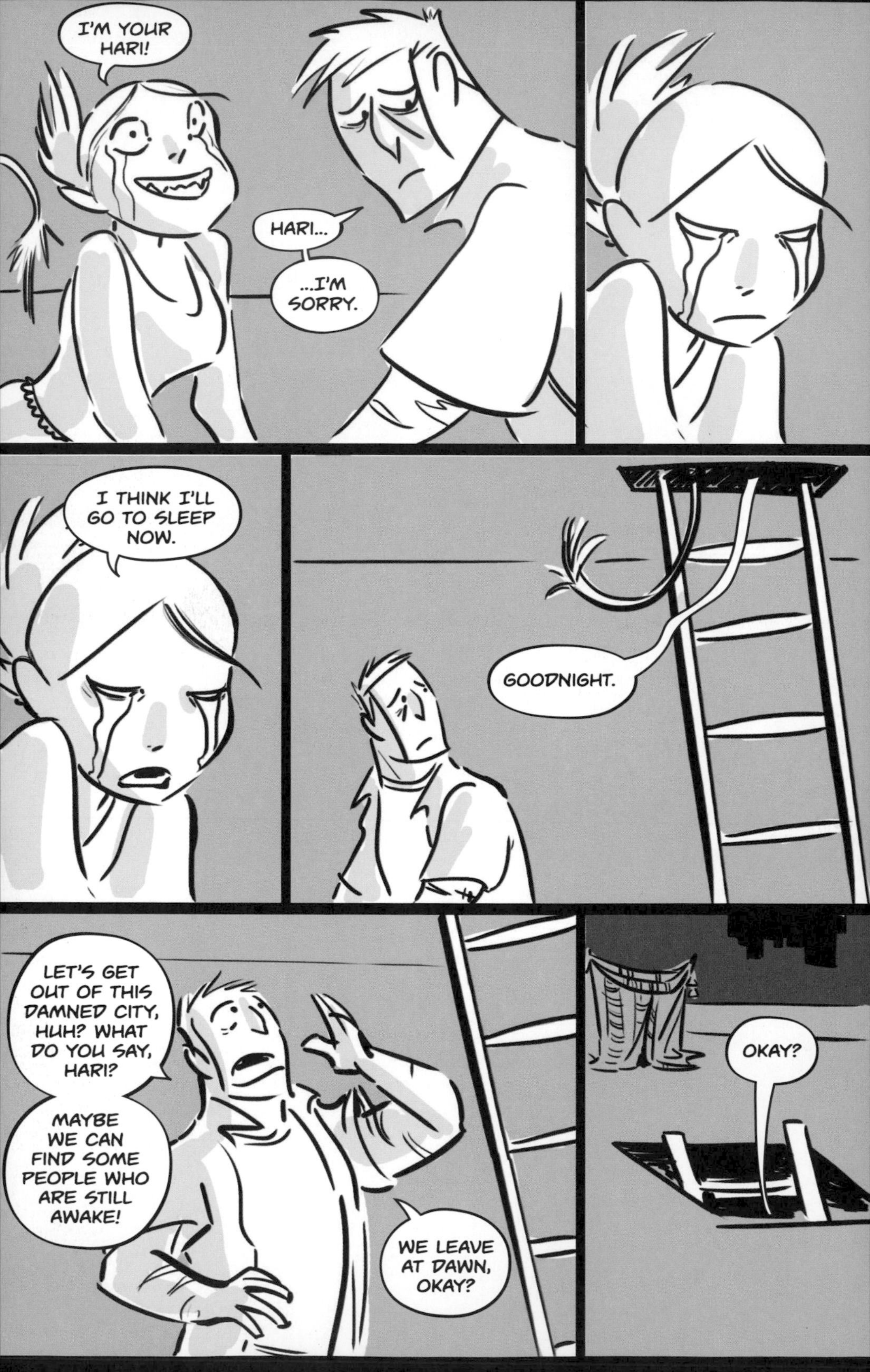
I'M YOUR HARI!
HARI...
...I'M SORRY.
I THINK I'LL GO TO SLEEP NOW.
GOODNIGHT.
LET'S GET OUT OF THIS DAMNED CITY, HUH? WHAT DO YOU SAY, HARI?
MAYBE WE CAN FIND SOME PEOPLE WHO ARE STILL AWAKE!
WE LEAVE AT DAWN, OKAY?
OKAY?

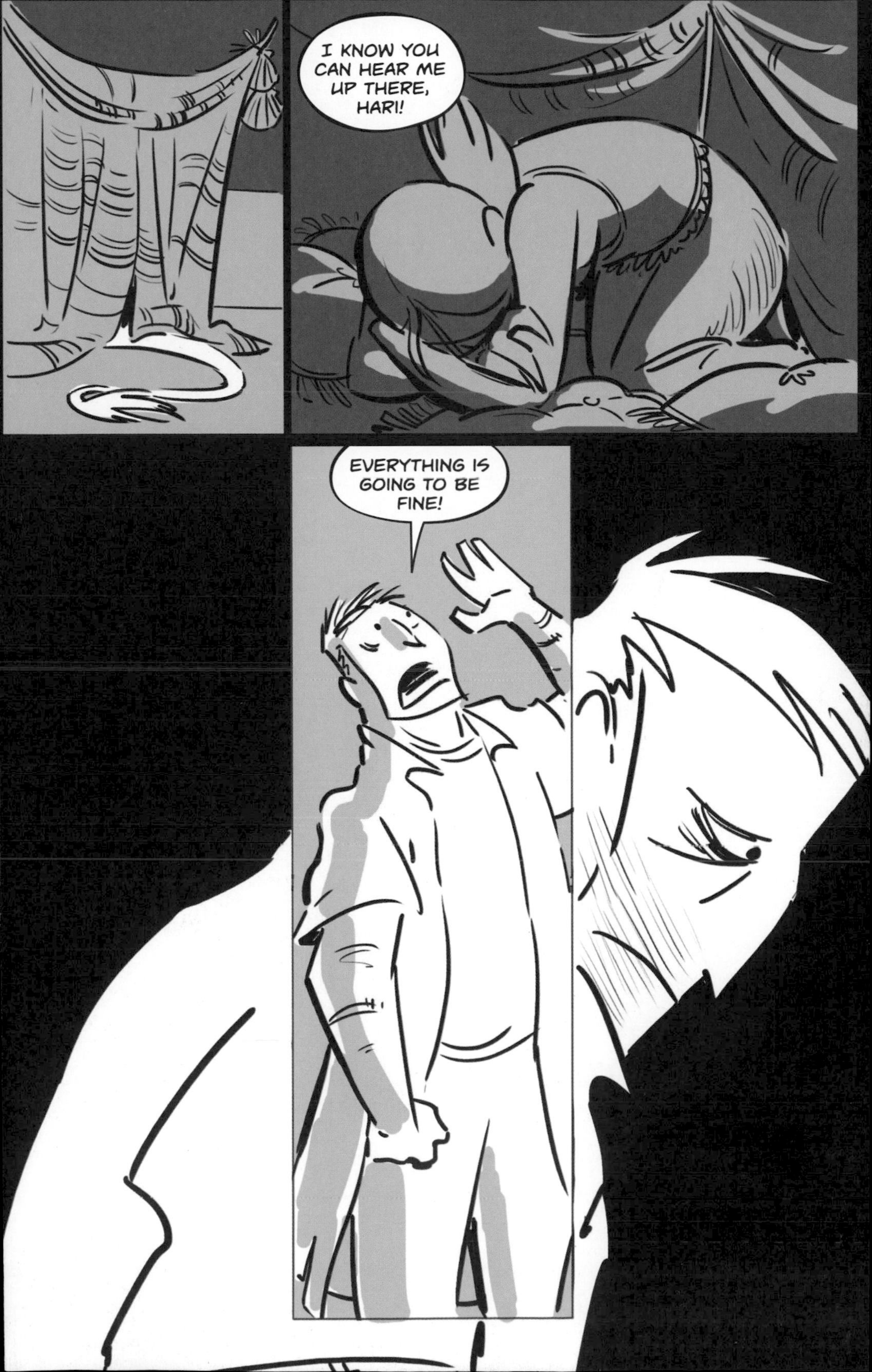
I KNOW YOU CAN HEAR ME UP THERE, HARI!
EVERYTHING IS GOING TO BE FINE!

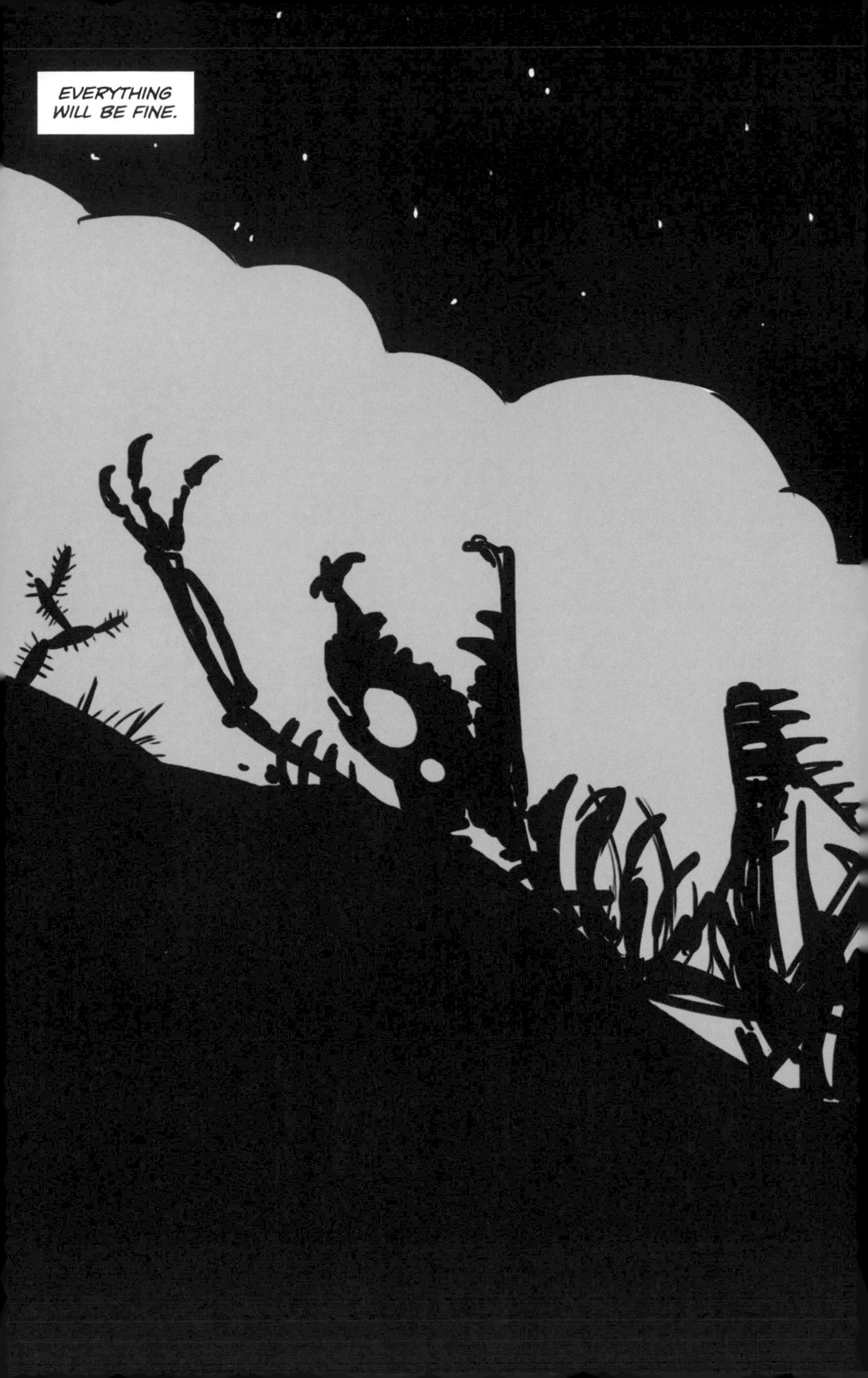
EVERYTHING WILL BE FINE.

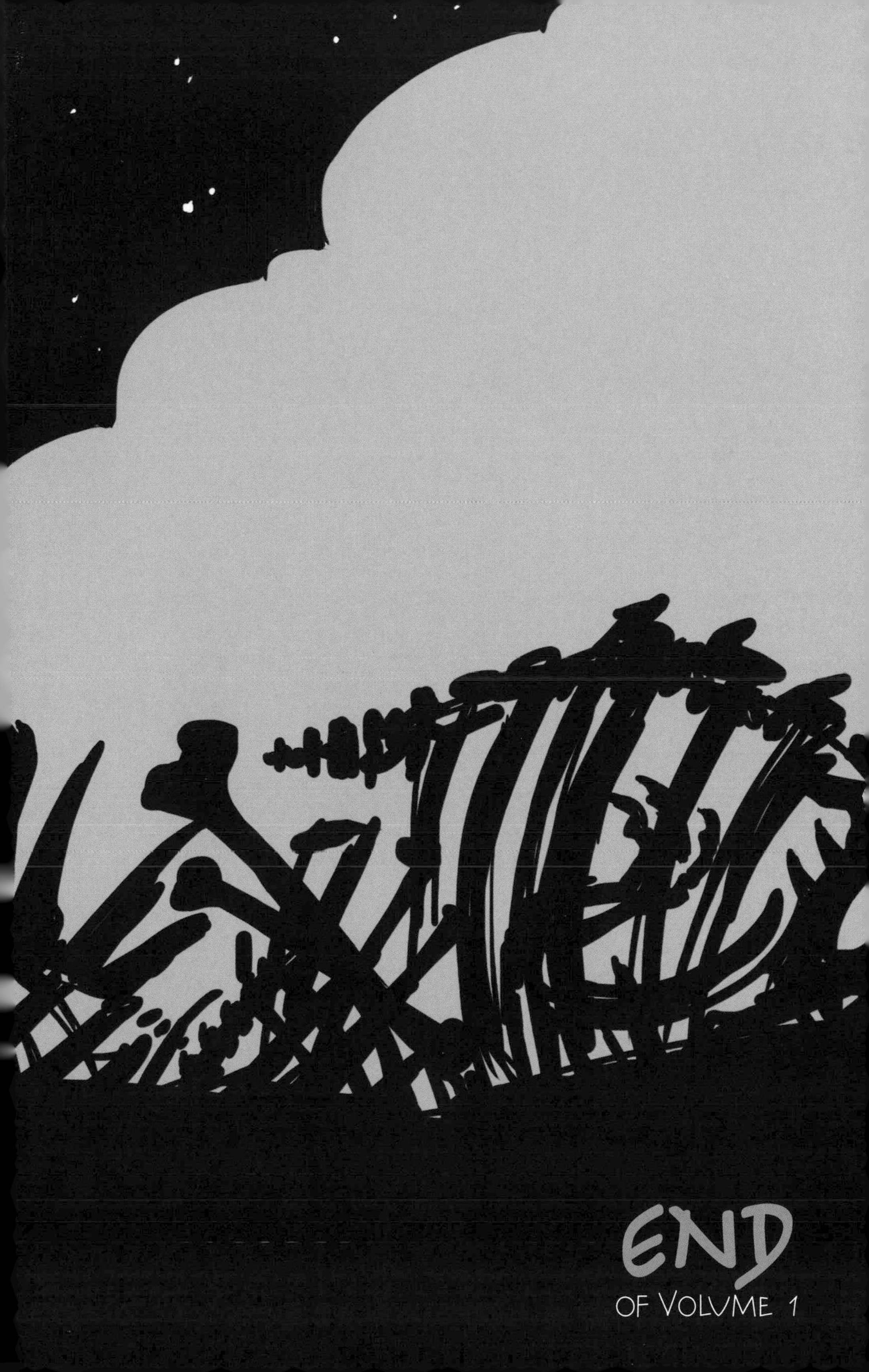
END
OF VOLUME 1

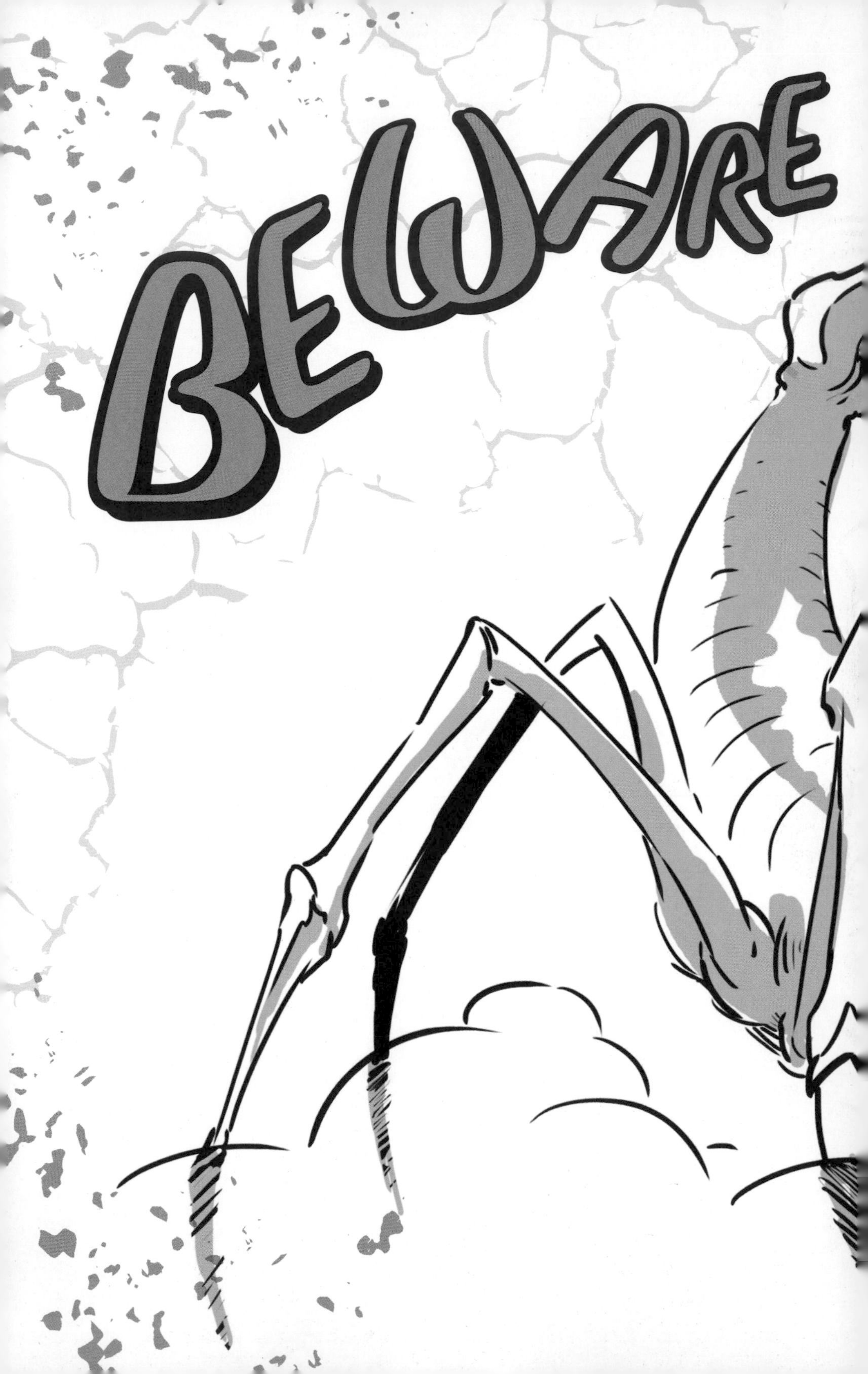
BEWARE

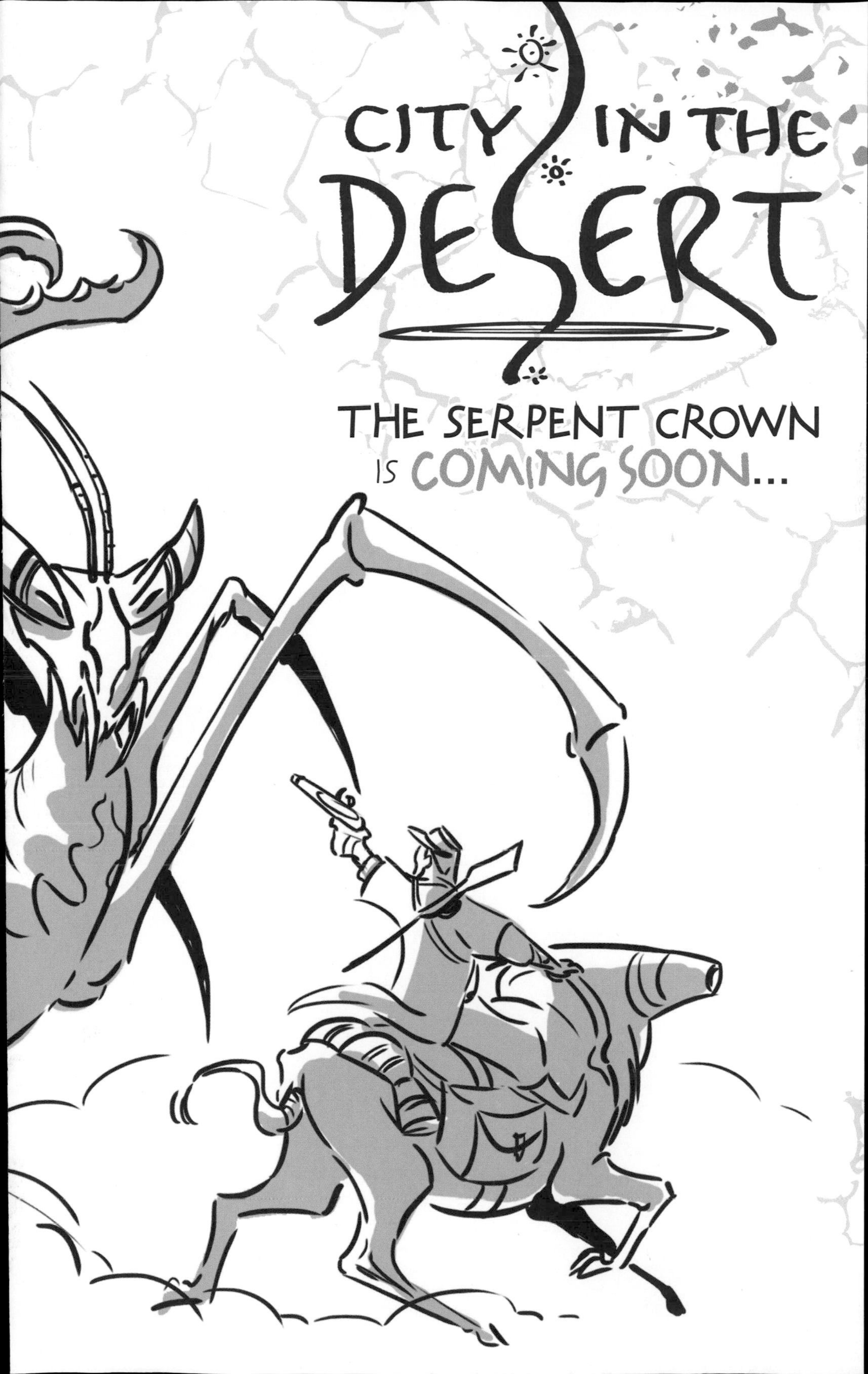
CITY IN THE DESERT
THE SERPENT CROWN
IS COMING SOON...

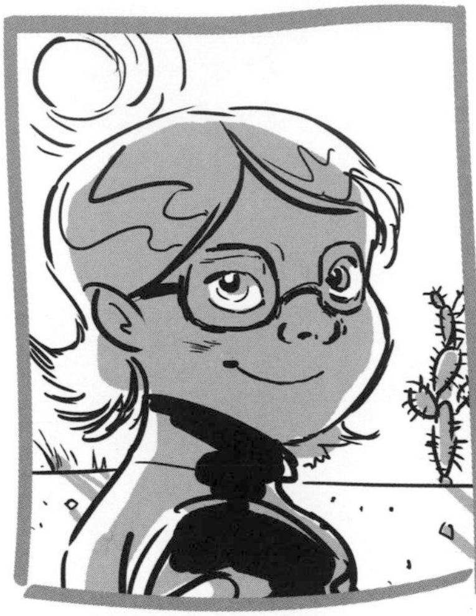

MORO ROGERS

MORO LIVES IN EL SEGUNDO WITH HER HUSBAND, JASON, AND GOZER THE CAT. *CITY IN THE DESERT* IS HER FIRST GRAPHIC NOVEL.

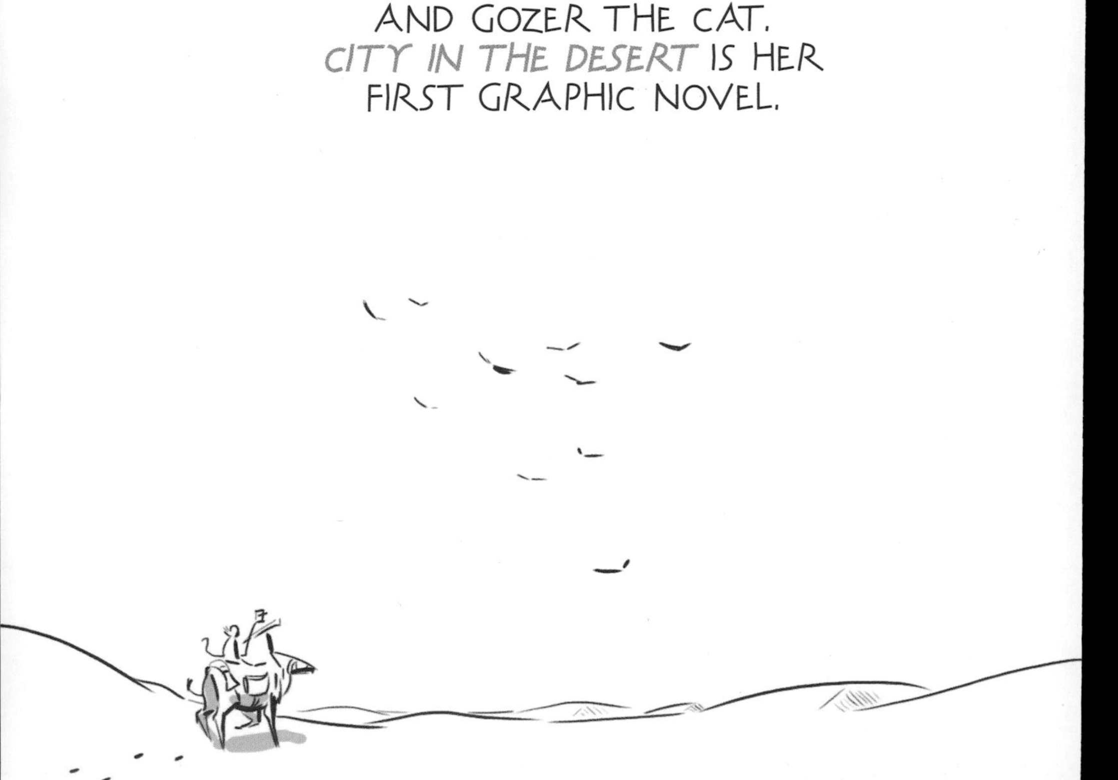